Classic Vintage

CRAWLERS & DOZERS

Volume 2

By Roger V. Amato & Donald J. Heimburger

Acknowledgments
Tom Berry, archivist, Historical Construction Equipment Association (HCEA); Caterpillar, Inc.; Circus World Museum, Baraboo, Wisconsin; Fred Dahlinger; Doug Frey; Buck Guyther, Mario Torres, Tom Trenka, Dave Werner, Vernon Simpson, Jere Wissler and Gary Hirschlieb, Michael Androvich, HCEA; Gary Hansen; Dale Hardy, LeTourneau, Inc., Longview, Texas; Jeff Huff, Vintage Tracks Museum; Mark S. Kuhar, Pit & Quarry magazine; The Lumbermen's Museum, Patten, Maine; David Maginnis; Jim Mitchell, John Deere Construction Equipment Co.; Bruce Nelson; Eric C. Orlemann, ECO Communications; Jim Owensby; Russ Porter; David Wright, The Wright Museum, Laconia, New Hampshire; Richard Yaremko; and Landis Zimmerman, Ephrata, Pennsylvania.

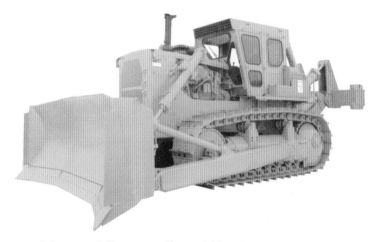

Library of Congress Control Number 2009906290

ISBN: 978-0-911581-63-8
First Edition
Printed in Korea

Editor: Donald J. Heimburger; book design, Rachel L. Boger

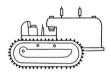

Front cover credits: Roger Amato, Russ Porter
Back cover credits: Roger Amato, John Deere Construction Equipment Co., Eric C. Orlemann

Heimburger House Publishing Company
7236 West Madison Street
Forest Park, Illinois 60130
United States of America
www.heimburgerhouse.com

TABLE OF CONTENTS

In Volume I we traced the development of the crawler tractor and bulldozer and covered the machines of Allis-Chalmers, Case and Caterpillar to 1949. This second volume covers Caterpillar from 1950 through the 1970s, Cleveland Tractor, Deere, Eimco, Euclid and Terex, International Harvester, other lesser-known crawler manufacturers, wheel dozers, blade makers, other attachments for crawlers, and non-construction uses of crawlers, along with sections on the uses of crawlers in the circus and by railroads. The objective of these books is to discuss the major manufacturers and describe in as much detail as possible the features of each model (engine type and horsepower, weight and unique characteristics); trace the evolution of the bulldozer and describe the different makes and models of blades and other attachments; and show crawler tractors and wheel dozers in a variety of uses, in addition to bulldozing, including as many action shots as possible.

Caterpillar D-6B dozer

MAJOR MANUFACTURERS

The period 1950-1979 witnessed Caterpillar's golden years of growth, profitability and new product development. During this time dozers and loaders evolved from tractors with attachments to integrally-built machines, and the company became the undisputed leader in the crawler and wheel dozer markets. Caterpillar's dozer line expanded from eight-tracked models in 1950 to 17 tracked dozers and eight-wheel dozer models by 1979. The late 1970s saw Caterpillar revamp its crawler line with the introduction of elevated sprocket undercarriages.

Cleveland Tractor (Cletrac) was one of the earliest crawler makers, starting in 1916; it grew to one of the top four producers by the mid-1930s. One of Cletrac's major innovations was controlled differential steering, by which power was applied differentially through planetary gears to make turns, instead of the steering clutches used by other manufacturers. Oliver acquired Cletrac in 1944 and continued offering dozers and loaders until 1965.

John Deere began building crawlers in 1948 after its purchase of the Lindeman Power Equipment Co. which made track conversions for Deere's wheel tractors. Deere concentrated on small farm and construction crawler tractors until the mid-1970s when it introduced the mid-sized Model 750 and Model 850 dozers. Deere has since grown to one of the top crawler manufacturers, and now offers dozer models weighing up to 39 tons and with 324 hp.

Cletrac Model BG dozer

Eimco was primarily a manufacturer of loaders and other equipment for underground mines, but in 1950 it began offering a loader attachment for crawler tractors. The company expanded its surface equipment to an innovative line of rear-engine dozers and loaders until 1969 when it became a part of Envirotech. Euclid was another old line manufacturer of construction and mining machinery, but never made crawlers until it was acquired by General Motors in 1954. GM immediately launched the mighty twin-engine TC-12 and remained in the crawler business through its change to Terex in 1968, and into the early 1980s.

International Harvester dominated the agricultural machinery business in the first several decades of the 20th century and began making crawler tractors in the late 1920s. By the mid-1950s, IH was produc-

John Deere Model 40C dozer

Euclid Model TC-12 dozer

International T-9 tractor

Yuba 25-40 tractor

ing a full line of "Big Red" earthmoving equipment including dozers and loaders. The construction equipment line was purchased by Dresser in 1982, and it became part of Komatsu in the late 1990s. Virtually the same crawler line is still made in Poland under the Dressta label.

SMALLER MANUFACTURERS

Other short-lived manufacturers described include Lombard, Bates, Electric Wheel, Leader, Mead-Morrison, Yuba and about 50 other companies. Wheel dozers offered by crawler tractor makers such as Allis-Chalmers, Caterpillar, Euclid and IH are included in those manufacturers' chapters; the other wheel dozer brands like LeTourneau and Michigan are discussed in a separate chapter. The last sections discuss blade makers including LeTourneau, Baker, Bucyrus-Erie, Heil and Gar Wood, other attachments such as scrapers, graders, rollers, sideboom cranes and winches, and non-construction uses of crawlers including agriculture, logging, mining, railroading, and in circuses.

LIFE OF A DOZER UPDATED

In Volume I, we presented results of a 1999 survey of crawler dozers by *Construction Equipment* magazine. A new survey was made by the magazine in December 2003. It reported that the number of dozers in active service in the U.S. increased by 5% since 1999 to 145,520; since 1995, the number has increased by 16%. The number of firms that own or lease a dozer increased 13% from 1999 to 43,582, and the number of building contractors operating dozers jumped by 45%.

The average age of a crawler dozer is now 8.6 years, up slightly from 8.5 in 1999 and 8.3 in 1995, indicating the machines are kept in use a little longer. This is supported by the 8% decrease in number of dozers purchased new from 1999 (87,430) to 2003 (80,259). Annual use decreased from 1,175 hours in 1999 to 1,110 hours in 2003. On average, dozers are traded in after 9.9 years and downgraded to secondary functions at 11.1 years. They are typically scrapped at 19.2 years, a little sooner (19.6) than in 1999.

Crawler dozers with less than 100 hp make up the largest percentage (43%), an increase of 7% from 1999. Dozers with horsepower between 100 and 149 represent 27% of the fleet, and those with 150 hp or more make up 30%. Currently, 87% of dozers are owned, 7% are rented and 6% leased. The number of leased dozers grew by 5% from 1999. Firms doing highway and other heavy construction bought the most new dozers, and those firms with more than $25.1 million in heavy equipment are the largest buyers.

The number of crawler loaders in service dropped from 35,000 in 1995 to 24,427 in 2003, a 30% decline. This is mainly due to increased uses of hydraulic excavators and wheeled backhoe-loaders. Of the crawler loaders currently in use, 39% have bucket capacities larger than 2 yards, 33% have capacities of 1.5 to 2.0 yards, and 28% have buckets smaller than 1.5 yards. Crawler loaders are used an average 1,025 hours per year – 85 hours less than a dozer, and down from 1,057 hours in 1995. On average, a crawler loader is used in its primary purpose for 13 years. It is then used in secondary functions for another 5.9 years, and scrapped after nearly 19 years.

Super Dozers –
The World's Most Powerful Crawler Tractors

Since inventing the first engine, man has continually sought to improve its performance and power. No sooner had the first engine successfully powered a tractor, the manufacturer (and its competitors) were busy trying to improve it, usually by increasing power. Technological advances such as steam, gasoline, diesel and turbochargers were introduced and changed the system, followed by periods of improvements within the system. One of the major limitations to powering mobile machinery is its ability to move efficiently and do work. Placing a larger engine didn't always make it do more work, but rather increased weight and lessened its ability to be operated easily. Crawler tracks provided much better weight distribution and superior traction than wheels, but there was always the tradeoff between traction and the speed of wheels.

The first commercially successful crawler was the steam-powered Lombard, introduced in 1900. Lombard rated the engine at 100 hp at a recommended operating boiler pressure of 200 p.s.i. Holt built the first gasoline-powered crawler tractor in 1906, which it rated at 40 belt and 25 drawbar hp. Tractor size and power increased rapidly; by 1911 Holt's Model 60 with 60 belt hp was in production and the next year Best began building its CLB 75 with 75 belt hp. In 1915, Holt introduced its Model 120, a 28,000-lb. crawler with 120 belt and 70 drawbar hp, and Best began offering a 90 belt hp tractor, the CLB 90, in 1917.

All of these behemoths used tiller wheels and were designed for pulling plows and other agricultural implements. They lacked the agility to push a blade and back up, especially in narrow confines. When bulldozer blades began to be offered commercially in the 1920s, most were attached to smaller or mid-sized tractors without tiller wheels such as the Holt 5- and 10-Ton, Best Thirty and Sixty and the Monarch 35. The Best (and after 1925, Caterpillar) Sixty emerged as the most powerful tractor of the early 1920s. It was tested at the Nebraska Tractor Testing Lab in 1921 at 56 bhp and in 1924 at 72 bhp. The gas-powered Monarch 75 took the lead in 1925 at 78 bhp, followed in 1927 by Cletrac's Model 100, also gas-powered, at 120 bhp. Unfortunately, the 100 sold only a few units and production ended in 1930. The next most powerful tractor was the Allis-Chalmers LO with a light oil-fueled motor, offered in 1931 at 91.6 bhp. Also in 1931, Caterpillar introduced the first diesel-powered crawler (Diesel Sixty) with 77 bhp, followed by the Diesel Seventy Five in 1933, rated at 93bhp.

The first diesel to break the 100 hp mark was the Cletrac diesel Model 80D in late 1933 with its 103 bhp rating; after 1933, all of the most powerful dozers were diesel-fueled. It took four years for Cletrac's record to be topped with the introduction of the Caterpillar D-8 (1H) at 115 bhp in 1938. As expected, Caterpillar has held the power lead nine times through the 1970s, followed by Allis-Chalmers at six, Euclid with three and Cletrac with two. The A-C HD-41, introduced in 1970, with 524 fwhp, had the longest standing record at seven years, when the Caterpillar D-10 easily took the title with its 700 fwhp.

In 1981, two "one-of-a-kind" super dozers were built: one by Komatsu with 1000 fwhp; the other was a shop-built dozer using mostly Caterpillar parts assembled by Italian contractor Umberto ACCO with 1,300 ghp. Caterpillar launched its D-11R dozer in 1987, rated at 850 fwhp; it is now called the D-11T, still with 850 fwhp but weight has increased to 230,100 lbs. The current record holder is the Komatsu D575A-2SD Super Dozer, introduced in 1995. It produces 1,150 fwhp and weighs 168 tons (157 tons when first offered).

The table at right lists the most powerful commercially-built crawler tractors between 1900 and 2000. Some models only represent the largest crawler available from its manufacturer at the time.

Super dozers
Super dozers Euclid TC-12 and Allis-Chalmers HD-41 are seen side by side at an Historical Construction Equipment show. The HD-41 took over the title as world's largest dozer from the TC-12 in 1970.

Year	Model	Horsepower	Fuel	Weight
1900	Lombard Log Hauler	100 bhp	steam-powered	38,000
1906	Holt 40	40 bhp	gasoline	16,000
1911	Holt 60	60 bhp	gasoline	23,500
1912	Best CLB 75	75 bhp	gasoline	24,800
1915	Holt 120	120 bhp	gasoline	28,000
1917	Best CLB 90	90 bhp	gasoline	26,500
1920	Best Sixty	60 bhp	gasoline	21,000
1924	Best Sixty	72 bhp	gasoline	25,860
1925	Monarch 75	78 bhp	gasoline	23,000
1927	Cletrac 100	120 bhp	gasoline	28,089
1931	Allis-Chalmers LO	91.6 bhp	gas-oil	24,950
1933	Cat Diesel Seventy-Five	93 bhp	diesel	30,050
1933	Cletrac 80D	103 bhp	diesel	24,000
1935	Caterpillar RD-8	98 bhp	diesel	32,000
1938	Caterpillar D-8 (1H)	115 bhp	diesel	33,400
1940	Allis-Chalmers HD-14	132 fwhp	diesel	28,750
1946	Caterpillar D-8 (2U)	144 fwhp	diesel	43,800
1947	Allis-Chalmers HD-19	163 fwhp	diesel	40,000
1947	International TD-24	180 fwhp	diesel	36,275
1951	Allis-Chalmers HD-20	175 fwhp	diesel	41,800
1954	Caterpillar D-8 (14A)	191 fwhp	diesel	46,600
1954	Allis-Chalmers HD-21	204 fwhp	diesel	44,725
1954	Caterpillar D-9D	286 fwhp	diesel	56,250
1955	Euclid TC-12	365 fwhp	(twin diesel engines)	58,100
1955	International TD-24 (241)	202 fwhp	diesel	43,250
1956	Caterpillar D-9D	320 fwhp	diesel	59,580
1956	Euclid TC-12-1	413 fwhp	(twin diesel engines)	62,500
1958	Euclid TC-12-2	431 fwhp	(twin diesel engines)	71,250
1959	Caterpillar D-9E	335 fwhp	diesel	70,400
1961	Caterpillar D-9G	385 fwhp	diesel	77,300
1962	International TD-30	320 ehp	diesel	61,000
1963	Allis-Chalmers HD-21A/P	320 fwhp	diesel	57,100
1967	Euclid/Terex 82-80DA	476 fwhp	(twin diesel engines)	73,000
1970	Allis-Chalmers HD-41	524 fwhp	diesel	147,500
1974	Caterpillar D-9H	410 fwhp	diesel	91,000
1977	Caterpillar D-10	700 fwhp	diesel	190,300
1985	Dresser TD-40	460 ehp	diesel	134,000
1987	Caterpillar D-11R	850 fwhp	diesel	214,800
1995	Komatsu D575A-2SD	1,150 fwhp	diesel	314,000

ABBREVIATIONS USED

ACMOC - Antique Caterpillar Machinery Owners Club

HCEA - Historical Construction Equipment Association

Hp - Horsepower is defined as the force required to lift 16.5 tons (33,000 pounds) at the rate of one foot per minute. It is equal to an expenditure of 746 watts or 33,000 foot-pounds of energy per minute.

These are the most common horsepower terms:
bhp - Belt hp is the power measured by a dynamometer from a belt connected to the power take-off. Similar to PTO hp and Engine hp.
dbhp - Drawbar hp is the pull (in lbs.) multiplied by the speed (mph) divided by a constant. Dbhp is less than belt and PTO hp due to losses in the drive train, rolling resistance, and slippage, and it is sometimes expressed as a percent of PTO hp. It is a measure of the complete machine rather than the engine itself.
ehp - Engine hp is the actual hp as measured by a dynamometer in contrast to theoretical hp calculated from a formula. Most construction equipment engines are rated by ehp. Same as Belt hp and Brake hp.
fwhp - Flywheel hp or Net hp is the power calculated at the flywheel under SAE standard ambient temperature and barometric conditions (85 0 F / 290 C and 29.38 in. Hg / 995 mbar) using 35 API gravity fuel oil at 600 F/ 15.60 C with all accessories connected including the fan, fuel pump, oil pump, muffler, air pump, hydraulic pump and generator.
ghp - Gross hp is the output of an engine measured without accessories or attachments connected. Same as Maximum hp.
pto hp - Power take-off hp is the energy output measured at the pto connection from the engine or transmission, usually at the rear of the tractor. PTO hp is mostly used in reference to agricultural or logging equipment.
dbp - Drawbar pull is a measure of the pulling power of a tractor, in pounds. It is sometimes expressed as a percent of the tractor weight.
OHV - overhead valve engine
PCU - power control unit yd - Yard refers to a cubic yard of dirt or rock; weight ranges from 2,400 lbs for dry dirt to 3,000 lbs or more for rock.

8

CHAPTER ONE

CATERPILLAR TRACTOR COMPANY
1950 to 1979

CATERPILLAR

A Defining Decade

The 1950s were a defining decade for Caterpillar in terms of technological advancement, product development and growth. The company severed its agricultural roots and concentrated almost entirely on heavy construction. A great emphasis was placed on new product development, including towed and motorized scrapers, push-dozers, loaders and hydraulic rippers. Among the important technological advances were turbocharged engines, oil-cooled or wet master and steering clutches, torque converters, powershift transmissions, integrally-built dozers and crawler loaders, and replacement of cable control by hydraulics.

D-4
A pair of D-4 (7U) tractors pull sleds of Christmas trees in this December 1950 photo. The D-4 (7U) was offered from 1947 to 1959. *Don Heimburger*

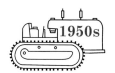
1950s

A new line of diesel engines, the "300" series, replaced the first generation "1000" series developed in the 1930s and an Engine Division was established. Caterpillar purchased the Trackson Co. in 1951, an allied manufacturer of loader and pipelayer attachments for its crawler tractors, helping to further diversify its product line. The company emerged as the undisputed leader in construction equipment sales during the 1950s, and it also became a multinational corporation with the opening of factories in Australia, Brazil and the United Kingdom.

Caterpillar continued its five-model tractor line from the 1940s: D-2, D-4, D-6, D-7 and D-8. The D-2 (4U and 5U series) with its 41-fwhp D311 engine was upgraded in 1954 to 48 fwhp. The D-2 was dropped from the product line in 1957. The D-4 (6U) and (7U) series tractors were produced through 1959; both were powered by a D315 engine rated at 55 fwhp. Straight and angle-dozer blades were offered for each model along with hydraulic controls; cable operation remained an option for the D-6, D-7 and D-8 tractors.

The D318 engine powered the D-6 (8U) and (9U) series dozers; it was initially rated at 80 fwhp, then upgraded in 1954 to 93 fwhp. Both series were available through 1959. The D-7 (3T) with its D8800 engine was offered until 1955, when it became the D-7C (17A) with a D339 engine and 128 fwhp. A turbocharger was added in 1959, bringing it up to 140 fwhp, and the model was changed to D-7D (17A). The D-8 (2U) was built until 1953, when the (13A) continued with the same D13000 engine to 1955.

The D-8 (13A) was replaced in 1955 by the D-8 (14A) and (15A) dozers with a D342 engine rated at 191 fwhp. The D-9D, launched in 1954 with great fanfare, was Caterpillar's first new crawler tractor since the 1930s. With its D353 engine rated at 286 fwhp, the D-9D claimed title as the world's most powerful single-engine crawler. Two transmissions were offered: gear drive for the (18A) and a torque converter for the (19A). The D-9D was upgraded with a turbocharged D353TA engine with 320 fwhp in 1956.

The company began its long involvement with wheel dozers in 1951 when it offered a cable-operated blade attachment for the DW-10 tractor. The following year it introduced a larger blade for the DW-20 tractor with 225 fwhp. In 1956, Caterpillar launched the 668 wheel dozer, a DW-20 with all-wheel drive and a turbocharged 300-fwhp engine. None of these first generation machines sold well, and they were taken off the market in 1958. On a more positive note, Caterpillar introduced its No. 6 shovel in 1952, the first integrated crawler loader built by one firm. The popularity of the No. 6 shovel ushered in the 933-955-977 series crawler loaders in 1955 which led the company to become the top manufacturer of crawler loaders.

Early 1950s dozer line

Caterpillar entered the 1950s with the same five crawler models offered during the previous decade: D-2, D-4, D-6, D-7 and D-8. The D-2, D-4 and D-6 were available in two track gauges, while the D-7 and D-8 each had one, creating eight different series of crawlers. The D-2 could be ordered with 40-in. (4U series) or 50-in. (5U) gauge, the D-4 with 44-in. (6U) or 60-in. (7U), and the D-6 with 60-in. (8U) or 74-in. (9U) gauge. The D-7 (3T) came with 74-in. gauge and the D-8 (2U) with 78-in. gauge. The machines shown here are Caterpillar's first in-

D-6 with No. 6A angleblade dozer

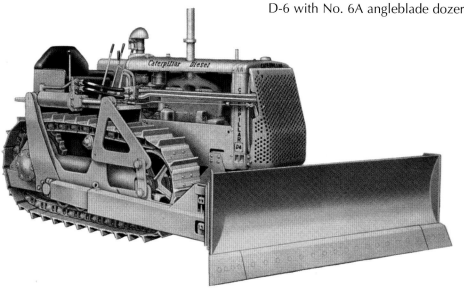

D-4 with No. 4A angleblade dozer

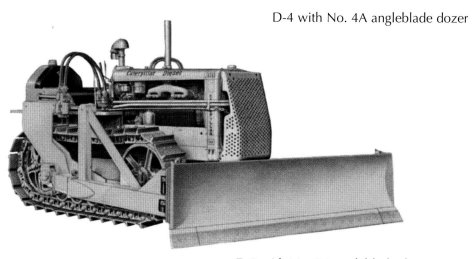

D-2 with No. 2A angleblade dozer

D-8 with No. 8A cable-operated angle-blade dozer

D-7 with No. 7A cable-operated angle-blade dozer

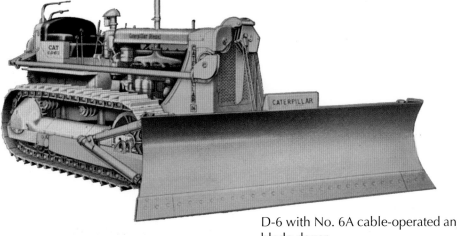

D-6 with No. 6A cable-operated angle-blade dozer

tegrally-built dozers with the tractor, blade and lifting mechanism designed and assembled together. Caterpillar now concentrated on construction machines, leaving its agricultural roots behind.

The Interstate Highway Decade

Construction of the Interstate Highway System drove most of the development of construction equipment during the 1960s. In terms of new products, it was the most prolific decade for Caterpillar with a greatly expanded motor scraper line, wheel loaders, dump trucks, new graders and crawler loaders, and integrally-built wheel dozers and compactors. New manufacturing plants were built in France and Belgium, and a joint venture was established with Mitsubishi Industries to build and market Caterpillar's machines in Japan.

The company entered the 1960s with a five-model dozer line: D-4C, D-6B, D-7D (17A), D-8H and D-9E. A sixth model was added in 1966, the D-5. Caterpillar also began offering Special Application or SA models for agricultural work and Low Ground Pressure (LGP) models with extra wide and extended tracks.

The D-4C had a D330 engine with 65 fwhp. It was replaced by the D-4D in 1967 with the same engine and horsepower. The D-5 was initially powered by a D315 engine with 93 fwhp; in 1967 it was given a D333 with the same horsepower. The D-6B, launched in 1959, also used the D333 as did the D-6C, which appeared in 1967 with 125 fwhp.

The D-7E, introduced in 1961, had a D339T engine with 160 fwhp to 1966, after which it was rated at 180 fwhp. The D-8H first appeared in 1958 and continued through the 1960s. It had a D342 engine with 225 fwhp, later increased to 270 fwhp.

The D-9E, producing 320 fwhp from its D353TA engine, was replaced by the D-9G in 1961 with 385 fwhp from the same engine. Two other configurations were offered for the D-9G: the two in-line mated D-9Gs or DD-9G dozer and the two side-by-side dozers or SxS D-9G, both with 770 fwhp. These were largely the result of ideas and development work done by Caterpillar dealer Peterson Tractor Co. of northern California.

After poor results with wheel dozers in the 1950s, Caterpillar completely redesigned the machine and introduced its first integrally-built wheel dozers in 1963. These were the rear-engine, 300-fwhp 824 and 360-fwhp 834 models. The 800-series wheel dozers were good performers, and the line has survived to the present day. The company also sold the front-engine 830M wheel dozers to the U.S. Army during most of the 1960s. The crawler loader line expanded from the three models of the late 1950s to six models ranging from 1 1/4-yard to 5-yard capacities: 933G, 941, 951, 955H, 977H and 983. Introduced in 1969, the 5-yard 983 was the largest crawler loader in the world for a number of years. It had a D343 engine with 275 fwhp.

Decade of Refinement and Advancement

During the 1970s, Caterpillar refined the large product line it had established in the 1960s and launched its innovative elevated sprocket design. Each of the six dozer models from the 1960s went through at least one upgrade and two new models were added, a "smallest" and "largest." The 62-fwhp D-3 was introduced in 1973, and the 700-fwhp D-10 appeared in 1977, the first of the elevated sprocket dozers and a major departure in the design of bulldozers. Another new product of the 1970s was the Model 225 hydraulic excavator, the first of a long line of these machines. Other innovations of the 1970s included sealed and lubricated tracks (1973) and a new line of engines, the "3000" series.

In addition to the D-3 and D-10 dozers, upgrades to existing models took place. The D-4D with 65 fwhp, which was offered to 1977, became the D-4E with 75 fwhp. The D-5 also continued to 1977 with a 3306 engine rated at 105 fwhp; it was replaced in 1977 by the D-5B with the same engine and power. The D-6C lasted to 1977 with 140 fwhp; it then became the D-6D with a 3306 engine with the same power rating. The D-7F, introduced in 1969 with 180 fwhp, continued to 1975 when it was replaced by the D-7G rated at 200 fwhp from a 3306 engine.

After a long run of the D-8H (since 1959) with 270 fwhp from a naturally aspirated D342 engine, the D-8K was launched in 1974 with 300 fwhp from its D342T turbocharged engine. That same year, the D-9G was replaced by the D-9H with power increased to 410 fwhp from the same D353TA engine. Likewise, the multi-tractor rigs were upgraded to the DD-9H and SxS D-9H, both with combined fwhp of 820.

The crawler loader line was also upgraded and expanded during the 1970s. The 1-yard 931 with 62 fwhp was added in 1973, while the 941 became the 941B with 1.5-yard capacity and 80 fwhp. The 951B was upgraded to the 951C at 1.75 yards and 95 fwhp and the 955K changed to the 955L with a 2-yard bucket and 130 fwhp. The 977K became the 977L with 2.5- to 3.25-yard capacity and 190 fwhp and the 983 was upgraded to the 983B with 275 fwhp and 4.5- or 5-yard buckets.

The wheel dozer line gained the 814 (170 fwhp) in 1970 but lost the 834 in 1974 (it was reoffered as the 834B again in 1982). The 300-hp 824B was available throughout the 1970s. Caterpillar's last major change of the 1970s was in paint color. New Federal regulations for paints with high lead content drove the company to change from Hi-way Yellow which had been used since 1931 to Caterpillar Yellow, a drab brownish yellow in 1979. Unfortunately, the new paint weathered poorly, and Caterpillar switched back in the 1990s.

D-2 (4U)
The D-2 (4U) tractor has a 40-inch track gauge and weighs 6,700 to 7,400 lbs. Introduced in 1947, it remained in production through 1957. It is powered by a D311 engine with 41 fwhp; in 1952, horsepower was increased to 48 at the flywheel.

D-2 (5U)
The 5U is identical to the 4U except for its 50-inch track gauge. Due to its wider tracks, it is a little heavier at 6,900 to 7,600 lbs. This is a 1955 D-2 (5U) with a hydraulic toolbar with dozer blade and ripper at the ACMOC Show in Chillicothe, Illinois that has been re-fitted with narrow street-pad tracks. It is owned by Fred Stitt of Kansas.

POWER FARMING

WITH "CATERPILLAR" DIESEL FARM TRACTORS.

THERE'S NO STRAINING TO STAY IN THE SEAT WHEN THE TRACTOR RIDES LEVEL LIKE THAT IS THERE, PETE?

In many areas good f...
complete system of dif...
Crawler tractors with...
easily handle this tou...
traction even in sticky...

D-2
Power Farming booklet shows various attachments and uses of the D2 tractor. *Collection of Don Heimburger*

tracks cover the
or inefficient slip-
less ground pres-
n walking. Other
of the track-type

Heavy-duty offset disk harrows are often used in field work for the entire preparation of the seedbed — one time over. "Caterpillar" track-type Tractors provide plenty of power for socking the disks in deep for a better job.

Cultivator tools on the tool bar are often used in seed-bed preparation for certain crops, for loosening and breaking the soil prior to planting.

D-2 (5U) Orchard

A 1957 D-2 (5U) "orchard" model was on display at the 2000 ACMOC Show in Chillicothe, Illinois.

D-4 (6U)

The D-4 (6U) was offered from 1947 through 1959. Its D315 engine was rated at 55 bhp to 1954, 60 bhp to 1956, and 63 bhp to 1959. Weight ranges from 10,200 lbs to 10,500 lbs, and the tractor has a 44-in. track gauge.

D-4 Orchard

A view of a D-4 "orchard" tractor built in 1954. The "orchard" version has a lower profile with under-engine exhaust, tail seat, and fuel tank behind the engine.

D-4 (7U)

The (7U) is the 60-inch track gauge model. Like the D-4 (6U), the (7U) was built from 1947 through 1959, and has the same 55 bhp engine to 1954. Power increased to 60 bhp in 1955, and 63 bhp from 1956 to 1959. Weight of the 7U is a ton or more greater than the 6U at between 12,900 lbs. and 13,300 lbs. The D-4 (7U) tractor shown is a 1952 model with a Caterpillar No. 40 hydraulic pull-scraper. The machines were brought to the 2000 ACMOC Show held in Chillicothe, Illinois.

D-6 (8U)

The 8U and 9U series dozers were made from 1947 to 1959, and they turned out to be very popular machines with nearly 40,000 units sold. The 8U series came with a 60-in. track gauge, but nearly everything else was the same as the 74 in. gauge D-6 (9U) tractor. This is a 1954 (8U) model with a Caterpillar No. 6 hydraulic blade.

D-6 (9U)

The 74-inch gauge 9U series is powered by a D318 engine with 80 bhp; in 1954 it was upgraded to 93 bhp. The weight of the 9U ranges from 22,500 lbs. to 23,800 lbs. with a blade attached. This dozer belongs to contractor David Werner of Egg Harbor, New Jersey. *David Werner*

15

D-7 (3T)

RIGHT. The 3T series proved to be a very popular model, with more than 28,000 units built during its lifespan, 1944 to 1955. In 1954, bhp was increased from 93 to 108.

D7 (3T)

BELOW. This D-7 (3T) moves dirt with its No.7S cable-operated blade at the 2002 HCEA Show in Albany, Minnesota. The blade measures 10 ft. 3 1/2 in. wide and weighs 4,840 lbs.

D-7 (17A)

LEFT. The 17A or D-7C replaced the 3T series in 1955 and continued to be offered through 1962. The D339 engine replaced the D8800 which increased horsepower to 128 bhp. In 1959, a turbocharger was added to the engine, increasing horsepower to 140 fwhp, and the tractor became the D-7D (17A). Weight of the 17A ranges from 36,100 lbs. to 36,600 lbs., and it has a drawbar pull of 28,700 lbs. *Richard Yaremko*

D-8 (2U)

LEFT AND ABOVE. The first post-war D-8 was the 2U series, built from 1945 to 1953. During that period, more than 23,500 units were made. Like its predecessors, the 1H and 8R series tractors, it has a D13000 engine rated at 132 bhp to 1948, when horsepower was increased to 144 bhp; then 160 bhp in the early 1950s.

CONVERTS WORKPOWER INTO PULL!

FREE TRACK OSCILLATION FOR FULL TRACTION

"Caterpillar's" equalizer spring construction plays a most important part in giving the D8 Tractor its ability to travel over rough country without undue twist or strain and to maintain full traction under adverse conditions. The heavy leaf spring supports the front end of the tractor, the ends of the spring resting in brackets on each track roller frame. The spring is free to rock under the engine's supporting member. Thus as either track oscillates up or down, the spring tilts in the "saddle" without tilting or straining the engine or transmission. The equalizer spring supports only the weight of the front end of the tractor — it has no additional burden of keeping the track roller frames in alignment. Two auxiliary leaf springs hold the main spring in position.

RUGGED STRENGTH TO DO THE JOB!

The massive, rugged construction of the D8 track assembly is shown here. Broad, long tracks that grip the ground and support the tractor. Sturdy diagonal braces, widely spaced, for permanent track alignment. Heavy equalizer spring that permits free track oscillation.

Shown, too, is the heavy drawbar, pulling from a point well forward and under the tractor to give a maximum of stability. It is guided by a heavy guide bar attached to the rear of the transmission case designed with ample strength to take the vertical thrust of drawn equipment. The heavy, wide-swinging forged steel drawbar is attached to forged steel brackets by oversize steel bolts. A hardened steel plate, fitting under the drawbar where it rests on the guide bar practically eliminates all wear on the drawbar at this point.

Five practical speeds forward and three reverse adapt the D8 Tractor to the needs of every job. From a low of 1.7 M.P.H. with a tested drawbar pull of 28,700 pounds for the heaviest pulls, loading scrapers, etc., to a high of 4.8 M.P.H. and a pull of 9,500 pounds for rapid travel when hauling — all are at the instant command of the operator and are selected by a gear shift lever and a forward and reverse lever.

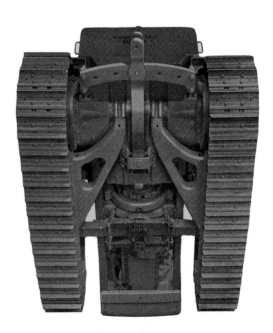

D-8 (13A)

RIGHT. The 13A series replaced the 2U in 1953 but was produced for only three years. It has the same D13000 engine which was upgraded to 185 fwhp and weighs 39,000 lbs.

D-8 (2U) Push Cat

LEFT. In the early days of motor scraper development, contractors were constantly looking for better ways of push-loading the machines. Horsepower for crawler tractors generally lagged behind that of the larger scrapers, sometimes requiring two or more push-tractors to work in tandem. This was particularly true in the mountainous parts of the West, where elevations above 5,000 feet caused lower engine efficiencies. To solve this problem, the McCoy Co., Caterpillar's equipment dealer in Colorado, modified D-8 2U and 13A series dozers for high altitude pusher service. McCoy replaced the D13000 engines in the D-8s with D337s, the same engines used in Caterpillar's DW-20 and DW-21 scrapers. The D337s were supercharged with Roots blowers and had oversized radiators and torque converter transmissions. These engines put out 225 fwhp, compared with 160 fwhp for the D-8 (2U) and 186 fwhp for the D-8 (13A). The modified Push-Cats were known as "McCoy Specials" such as this D-8 (2U)-20116 built in 1953. McCoy became the Wagner Equipment Co. in 1976.

D-8 (14A)

Caterpillar redesigned the D-8 in 1955, replacing the engine with a D342 rated at 191 fwhp, and for the first time it offered the option of either direct drive or torque converter transmissions. The 14A is the direct drive model; the 15A had the torque converter. Both series were offered through 1958, weighing between 43,500 lbs. and 49,300 lbs. This D-8 (14A) dozer belongs to contractor Louis McMaster and is being operated at the HCEA National Show in Brownsville, Pennsylvania.

D-8 (14A) and (15A)

A cutaway drawing of the D-8 shows its D342 engine, transmission, final drive and undercarriage. *Caterpillar, Inc.*

Here's why the D8 is a good investment

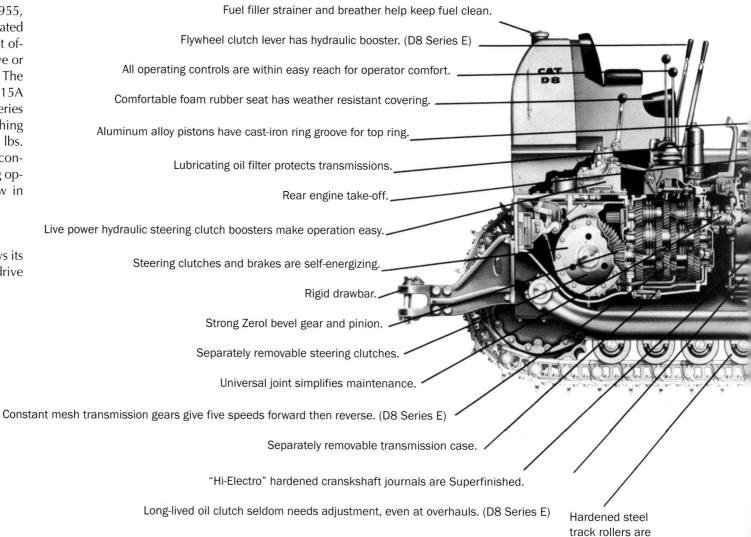

Fuel filler strainer and breather help keep fuel clean.

Flywheel clutch lever has hydraulic booster. (D8 Series E)

All operating controls are within easy reach for operator comfort.

Comfortable foam rubber seat has weather resistant covering.

Aluminum alloy pistons have cast-iron ring groove for top ring.

Lubricating oil filter protects transmissions.

Rear engine take-off.

Live power hydraulic steering clutch boosters make operation easy.

Steering clutches and brakes are self-energizing.

Rigid drawbar.

Strong Zerol bevel gear and pinion.

Separately removable steering clutches.

Universal joint simplifies maintenance.

Constant mesh transmission gears give five speeds forward then reverse. (D8 Series E)

Separately removable transmission case.

"Hi-Electro" hardened cranskshaft journals are Superfinished.

Long-lived oil clutch seldom needs adjustment, even at overhauls. (D8 Series E)

Hardened steel track rollers are sealed to keep oil in, dirt out.

Guide sleeves lengthen valve stem life are replaceable.

Replaceable valve guides insure smooth operation.

Alloy steel valves, valve rotators and replaceable, hardened valve seats for long wear.

Swirl-type precleaner reduces frequency of air cleaner and maintenance.

Valve rocker arm mechanism is pressure lubricated.

Generous cooling area keeps engine cooled properly.

Seated cooling system prevents loss of coolant and formation of scale.

D-8H
The D-8H replaced the D-8 (14A) and (15A) machines in 1958. Although a number of changes were made over the years, the tractor remained in production through 1974. *Pit & Quarry*

Positive acting water regulators control air temperature.

Oil cooler gives increased oil life.

Rugged, high capacity Caterpillar-built Diesel Engine.

Heavy-duty guard protects radiator from possible damage.

Easily replaceable filters protect fuel injection equipment.

Fast acting vertical-type governor gives quick response to load changes.

Caterpillar-built fuel system includes interchangeable injection pumps--capsule-type injection valves.

Replaceable wet-type cylinder liners are precision honed.

Dual-position disc-type idlers give increased tractor versatility.

All track parts are heat-treated for long life-- "water quenched" track shoes.

Drilled connecting rods carry oil for piston cooling.

Triple-section oil pump insures positive lubrication.

7-roller track frames fabricated of high-strength steel.

Durable, aluminum alloy bearings gives superior service.

Heavy-duty equalizer spring distributes weight evenly.

The Caterpillar D-9

Although Caterpillar introduced the D-9 in 1954, production did not start until 1955. It was the company's first new crawler tractor model since the 1930s. With its 286 fwhp D353T power plant, the D-9 easily took the title of most powerful single-engine crawler tractor. It kept the title until 1970 when Allis-Chalmers' HD-41 appeared. The first D-9, also known as the D-9D, was offered in two versions: the 18A with direct drive and the 19A with torque converter transmission.

D-8H

The D-8H was given four different series numbers: 35A, with torque converter; 36A, with direct drive; 46A, with power shift; and 68A, for power shift models built in the United Kingdom. The 46A model, also introduced in 1958, marked the first power shift transmission on a Caterpillar tractor. All D-8H's are powered by a D342T turbocharged engine that initially produced 225 fwhp. In 1959 it was increased to 235 fwhp. Weight of the machine ranges from 53,655 lbs. to 57,200 lbs. This machine was operated by the Williams Construction Co. in Dorsey, Maryland in 1995.

D-9 (19A)

The big dozer shown with an enclosed cab is a 19A series from 1955 with a torque converter. It was operating at the 2001 HCEA National Show held in Canandaigua, New York.

D-9 (18A)

The D-9 (18A) tractor weighs 56,200 lbs.; with a blade, its weight increased to more than 30 tons. In 1956, Caterpillar increased power of the D-9 to 320 fwhp. This direct drive D-9 (18A) was built in 1957 and belongs to New Jersey contractor David Werner. Werner still uses the machine along with other vintage Caterpillar dozers in his grading business. *David Werner*

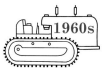

D-4C

LEFT. The D-4C (39A) and (40A) tractors were introduced in late 1959 as replacements for the D-4 (6U) and (7U). A new engine, the D330 rated at 65 fwhp, replaced the D315 and weight was increased to about 14,000 lbs. The (39A) has a 44-in. track gauge; the (40A) has a 60-in. gauge. *Collection of Eric C. Orlemann*

D-4D

BELOW. The D-4D replaced the D-4C in 1967, and it remained in production through 1977. Like the D-4C, it had a D330 engine rated at 65 fwhp to 1972. Unlike the D-4C, it came with only a 60-in. track gauge. The weight range of the D-4D was increased from the C by more than a ton to between 15,300 and 18,000 lbs.

TOOL BAR   TOOL BAR BULLDOZER

Special Application Tractors

Caterpillar reaffirmed its agricultural roots in the mid-1960s when it unveiled the Special Application or SA series of crawler tractors. The machines were designed for pulling farm implements and featured low ground pressure tracks with optional shoe widths, extended exhaust and air cleaner stacks, and an optional hydraulically-operated, reversible tool bar for pulling and pushing implements. Starting with the D-4D SA, D-5 SA, and D-6B SA in 1966, the line evolved into the highly successful Challenger tractor line. The D-4D SA (68 dbhp), D-5 SA (90 dbhp), and D-6C SA (125 dbhp) shown represent the early 1970s Special Applications lineup. *Caterpillar, Inc., Vernon Simpson collection*

TOP. D-5 SA
MIDDLE. D-6C SA
BOTTOM. D-4D SA

The D5 Tractor model brings modern, big-tractor features and operating conveniences to the medium-size tractor class. Features include:

WIDE VERSATILITY

▶ Full power shift with 3 speeds forward, 3 speeds reverse, or choice of two direct drive transmissions, 5 or 6 speeds forward.

▶ 93 flywheel horsepower Cat Diesel Engine with adjustment-free Cat fuel system and 24½% torque rise for superior lugging ability.

▶ Console-mounted steering clutch and governor controls and clean, open operator's compartment.

▶ Long-life undercarriage, with Sealed Track, Lifetime-Lubricated rollers and bolt-on sprocket rim segments.

D-5
Interestingly, Caterpillar's first D-5 tractor was offered only in 1939. Known as the 9M series, only 46 were built, and it did not appear again in the product line until 1966 with the introduction of the D-5 (37J). The 37J was initially powered by a D315 engine with 93 fwhp. In 1969, the D315 was replaced by the D333 and horsepower increased to 105 fwhp. The D-5 was available in either 60-inch or 74-inch track gauge and weight ranges from 18,200 to 25,000 lbs. Production of the D-5 continued to 1977 with the 3306 engine and 105 fwhp; the D-5B continued from 1977 to 1985 with the same engine and power rating. It was also available in low ground pressure (LGP) and special application (SA) versions. *Caterpillar, Inc., Vernon Simpson collection*

D-6B

TOP. The D-6B was offered between 1959 and 1967. All D-6Bs came with direct drive transmissions. The tractor is powered by a D333 engine with 93 fwhp. The D-6B was built with 74-in. gauge tracks and weighs between 23,000 and 24,300 lbs. This dozer is a 44A series built in 1962 and belongs to contractor Mark Olsen of Manassas, Virginia.

D-6C

BOTTOM. The D-6B was replaced by the D-6C in 1967, and it remained in production through 1976. Several 6-cylinder engines were used in the D-6C: D333, D333T (turbocharged), 3306 and 3306T. Horsepower ranges from 125 to 140 fwhp. Other improvements on the D-6C include optional powershift transmission, oil-cooled steering clutches and brakes, hydraulically-actuated steering clutches, double-reduction final drives, console-mounted controls and an equalizer bar suspension system. *Caterpillar, Inc., Vernon Simpson collection*

D-6D

LEFT AND LOWER LEFT. The D-6D was built from 1977 to 1995. Powered by a 3306T engine, the dozer is rated at 140 fwhp and weighs between 30,900 and 38,300 lbs. *Caterpillar, Inc., Vernon Simpson collection*

D-7E

BELOW. Introduced in 1961, the D-7E was manufactured through 1969. It was available with either direct or powershift transmissions. All versions of the D-7E have the D339T engine, which was initially rated at 160 fwhp but increased in 1966 to 180 fwhp. The dozer weighs between 41,400 and 44,000 lbs. This 1966 D-7E with hydraulic dozer works on a small earth dam in Seward, Nebraska.

D-7E (48A)

This D-7E (48A) dozer with a cable-operated blade resides at the Sanders Quarry in Warrenton, Virginia. The 48A series is the powershift version of the D7E; the direct drive version is the 47A series.

D-7E (75E) Military

In 1961, Caterpillar received a large order for D-7E dozers from the U.S. Army. The machines had powershift transmissions, winches and D339T engines rated at 160 fwhp. This former Army D-7E (75E) with Jersey spreader was working near Arcola, Virginia.

29

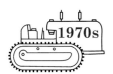

1970s

Mid-1970s Dozer Line *Caterpillar, Inc., Vernon Simpson collection*

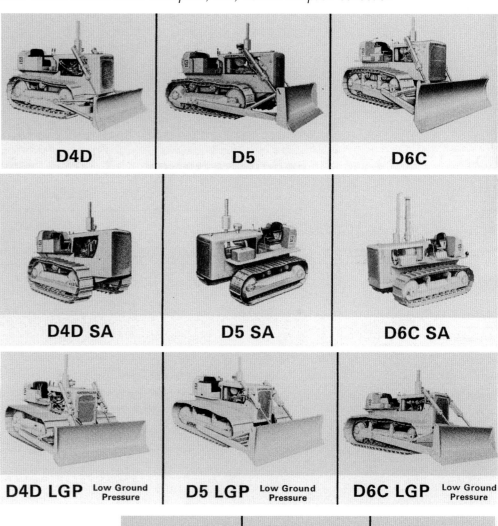

D4D	D5	D6C
D4D SA	D5 SA	D6C SA
D4D LGP (Low Ground Pressure)	D5 LGP (Low Ground Pressure)	D6C LGP (Low Ground Pressure)

| D7F | D8H | D9G |

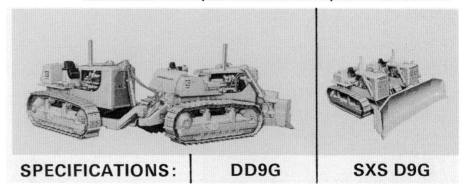

| SPECIFICATIONS: | DD9G | SXS D9G |

D-7F

TOP. In 1969, the D-7E was replaced by the D-7F, and it was sold through 1975. Like its predecessor, the F was available with either direct drive or powershift transmissions. It was powered by D339T and 3306T engines, both of which produced 180 fwhp. The D-7F weighs between 41,400 and 44,300 lbs.

D-7G

BOTTOM. The D-7G was the last of the standard, non-elevated sprocket machines of the D-7 series. It was offered from 1975 to 1986 in both direct drive and power shift versions. It is powered by a 200-fwhp model 3306T turbocharged diesel and weighs 44,000 to 52,100 lbs.

D-8K

Caterpillar replaced the D-8H with the K in 1974. The D-8K was available through 1982; one series was direct drive (76V) and two were powershift drive (66V and 77V). The D-8K weighed between 68,700 and 69,300 lbs. and was powered by a D342T turbocharged diesel rated at 300 fwhp. More than 26,000 units were sold.

D-8H

The power of the D-8H was increased in 1966 from 225 to 270 fwhp and weight increased from 57,700 lbs. to 60,500 lbs. Caterpillar advertised that the D-8H's track rollers, track carrier rollers and idlers came with metal-to-metal sealing surfaces which were lubricated at the factory and required no further greasing until the undercarriage was rebuilt. This dozer is a series 68A at the R.C. Peoples, Inc. yard in Bear, Delaware.

D-4E

The D-4E was launched in late 1977 and remained in production to 1991. Power ranged from 75 to 80 fwhp and weight from 19,874 to 22,240 lbs.

D-3

After dropping the D-2 in 1957, Caterpillar had no tractor for farming and small construction jobs. Deere, Case, Allis-Chalmers and International Harvester all offered such machines and most models sold well. Cat decided to re-enter the market in 1973 with the D-3 dozer. The machine was only built in Japan to take advantage of lower manufacturing costs. It came with a 3204 engine rated at 62 fwhp and weighs 13,600 to 14,000 lbs. The D-3B replaced the D-3 in 1979 with 65 fwhp from the 3204 DI engine.

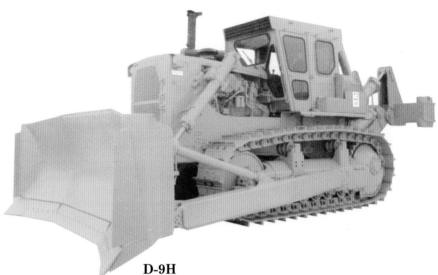

D-9H
Shown with optional ROPS Modular Cab, lights and hydraulic control, 9U bulldozer and multishank ripper. *Caterpillar, Inc., Vernon Simpson collection*

D-9G
TOP LEFT. Caterpillar began building the D-9G (66A) in 1961, and it stayed in production through 1974. It was the first Cat dozer available only with a powershift transmission. The big crawler came with a D353TA turbocharged-aftercooled engine rated at 385 fwhp. Weight of the machine ranged from 73,300 to 95,100 lbs., depending on attachments.

D-9H
MIDDLE AND LOWER LEFT. In 1974, the D-9G was replaced by the D-9H. Power from the same engine was boosted to 410 fwhp and weight increased by more than three tons to 79,500 lbs. (93,600 lbs. with blade, ROPS and all fluid tanks full). *Caterpillar, Inc., Vernon Simpson collection*

CATERPILLAR'S QUAD-TRACK DOZERS

The idea of combining two engines to create a more powerful earthmoving machine goes back at least as far as 1940, when R.G. LeTourneau, Inc. joined two Cummins diesels for its model A-5 and A-6 Tournapull scrapers. Howard Peterson, founder of Peterson Tractor & Equipment Co., the Caterpillar dealer for the San Francisco Bay area, had worked for LeTourneau, along with his younger brother Robert "Buster" Peterson. During his tenure with LeTourneau, Buster was involved in the development and testing of the A-5 and A-6 scrapers and gained an appreciation of running two motors in tandem. In 1943, Buster joined his brother at Peterson Tractor and developed a long line of innovative earthmoving products. One of these was the joining of a pair of Caterpillar D-8 tractors into one unit, which was tested around 1950. The primary need for such a machine was push-loading larger scrapers that were coming on the market like the 30- and 40-yard models offered by LeTourneau after World War II and the 18-yard, twin-engine model introduced by Euclid in 1948. The bigger scrapers often required two push-dozers to work in tandem, but that necessitated two operators and extra time to keep realigning the machines. It was no coincidence that the first new product to be developed by Euclid after the GM merger was a twin-engine dozer, the TC-12. At the time, Euclid was a leader in the large scraper market.

One of the first successful attempts at joining two crawler tractors was for a joint-venture contract with Morrison-Knudsen and Peter Kiewit companies using a pair of Allis-Chalmers HD-19s with a 22-ft. wide blade. The dozers worked successfully together and were used in several large earthmoving projects in the Western U.S. After field testing several Caterpillar D-8 pairs, Peterson obtained a patent on the design in 1954, the same year the D-9 dozer appeared. Peterson turned next to connecting a pair of tractors in tandem using a ball and socket hitch. He adapted this concept to the D-9, the most powerful single-engine crawler on the market. Several D-9 tandem units were built and sold by Peterson, but the

*Dual D9H Tractor shown with optimal ROPS canopy and track roller guards.

DD-9H "Quad-9H"
Vernon Simpson collection

DD-9H
The DD-9H replaced the DD-9G in 1975. Combined power of the two tractors increased to 820 fwhp. *David Maginnis*

availability of the powershift transmission on Caterpillar's largest dozers in 1959 made operation of the units much easier. The D-9G, introduced in 1961, came with powershift and a 385 fwhp D353TA engine and Peterson combined these machines. In 1963, Buster Peterson demonstrated his first set of twin D-9G push-dozers, which he named the "Quad-Trac."

At this point, Caterpillar Tractor Co. became interested in the concept and joined with Peterson Tractor to further improve the design. The result was the introduction by Caterpillar of the DD-9G or Quad-9G in 1965. The unit produced a combined 770 fwhp, weighed 176,900 lbs., and was available through 1974. It was replaced in 1975 by the DD-9H dozer. Using the same engine, the power of the DD-9H was increased to 820 fwhp and its weight to 178,800 lbs.

Quad-9 sales were good at first, with many of the larger contractors such as Morrison-Knudsen, Western Contracting and Peter Kiewit purchasing numerous units; however, by 1978 sales slowed to the point that it was dropped from the product line. As a testament to the design and quality of the Quad-9 dozers, some units were still in operation during the 1990s.

*Side-by-Side D9H Tractor shown with optional ROPS canopy.

SxS D9H
Vernon Simpson collection

SxS D-9G
Along with the "Quad-9" or DD-9 concept, Peterson Tractor Co. also fathered the idea of joining two Caterpillar tractors side by side to push one large blade. The first such design was a pair of D-8s joined together with one set of tracks which was patented by Peterson in 1954. From this arrangement, Peterson went on to develop D-9s joined in a side-by-side arrangement but with two sets of tracks. Caterpillar bought the patent from Peterson and launched an SxS D-9G dozer in 1969, featuring two D-9G tractors lashed together behind a 24-ft. wide blade. The tractors were designated 29N and 30N series. The combined power of the unit is 770 fwhp and it weighs 182,000 lbs. Applications included large earthmoving projects such as earthen dams and surface mine reclamation.
Eric C. Orlemann

SxS D-9H
The SxS D-9G was replaced by the "H" in 1975 which was produced through 1977 as the 99V/12U series. Combined power from its pair of D353TA engines was increased to 820 fwhp and weight to 183,900 lbs. Like the SxS D-9G, the "H" was equipped with a 24 ft. by 7 ft. 2 in. blade, had a 19-ft. track gauge and 27 in. track shoes. As with the SxS D-9G, the "H" had three connections with ball and socket joints: (1) a 16 in. tubular connected the rear of the tractors, (2) a diagonal brace connected the inside track roller frames, and (3) an inside-mounted "C" frame with horizontally-mounted steel balls held the dozer blade. *Eric C. Orlemann*

WHEEL DOZERS

Caterpillar entered the wheel dozer market in 1951 by offering a cable-controlled blade attachment for its 115-hp DW-10 tractor. Called the 10S blade, it was developed in response to wheel dozer models launched by R.G. LeTourneau, Inc. and LaPlant-Choate Manufacturing Co. in the late 1940s.

In 1952, Caterpillar introduced the 20S blade for its larger DW-20 tractor, rated at 225 fwhp. Although the DW series tractors were popular for scraper power, few of the units were sold with blades. The problem with Caterpillar's wheel dozers was their front-wheel steering. The outside-mounted push arms of the dozer limited the degree to which the front wheels could be turned, resulting in a very wide turning radius. Front-wheel steering also made it difficult to push full loads in anything but a straight line.

In spite of slow sales of these attachments, the company continued its wheel dozer development program, offering an improved version of the DW-20/20S in 1956, the model 668/668S. Power was increased to 300 fwhp, and it featured four-wheel drive and hydraulic or cable-operated blades. As with some of the other wheel dozer models, the 668 had been designed as a multi-purpose military industrial tractor, a prime mover for pulling trailers and artillery, an airplane tug and as a dozer or snowplow. The Armed Services did much to promote wheel dozer development during the 1950s and 60s, by both its in-house research and testing and by the promise of large contracts for machines that could meet rigid specifications. The concept of a dozer that could be driven over paved roads at moderately high speeds was of great interest to military engineers at the time.

In 1962, Caterpillar won a contract with the U.S. Army to produce a four-wheel drive, articulated wheel dozer. This was the 830M, a 26-ton front-engine tractor with 335 fwhp, a hydraulic blade, and a cable control unit for scraper operation. A more powerful version, the 830MB, was ordered in 1966 with 357 fwhp. Both models used the D343 engine.

In 1963, Caterpillar introduced its first two integrally-built wheel dozer models for civilian sales. These were the 824 with 275 fwhp and the 834 with 360 fwhp.

Both had D343 engines in the rear, articulated steering, and all-wheel drive.

A smaller model, the 814 with 170 fwhp, joined the line in 1970, along with a line of compactor dozers, models 815, 825 and 835. The three-model wheel dozer line was expanded in the 1990s with the addition of the 844 with 620 fwhp and the 854 with 800 fwhp. The 844 and 854 were based on wheel dozers previously produced by Tiger Engineering Pty. of Australia. Caterpillar's current wheel dozer line still has five models: 814F, 824H, 834H, 844H and 854G with engines ranging from 240 to 800 fwhp.

Although not true Caterpillar products, the DW-6 skid-steered wheel tractors from the Clewiston Motor Co. deserve mention. Clewiston, the Caterpillar dealer for south Florida, converted D-6 crawlers to wheel tractors in the early 1950s and continued into the 1960s. Although most were built for pulling wagon trains of sugar cane and other agricultural products, some were equipped with blades or push-blocks from Balderson, Inc., an attachment supplier affiliated with Caterpillar.

DW-10S and DW-20S
The No.10S blade was first introduced in 1951 for the 115 fwhp DW-10 and the No.20S blade appeared for the DW-20 tractor in 1952. The DW-20 initially had 225 fwhp; a later version was increased to 300 fwhp. The No. 20S blade measures 12 ft. 7 5/8 in. wide, and the total weight of the machine is 45,500 lbs. *Eric C. Orlemann collection*

DW-6

The DW-6 is actually a D-6 crawler that was converted to a wheel tractor by the Clewiston Motor Co., the south Florida Caterpillar dealer. Clewiston became the Kelly Tractor Co. in 1963. A number of these skid-steer tractors were built during the 1950s and 1960s primarily for pulling wagon trains of sugar cane. However, this DW-6B received a Balderson hydraulic blade. Balderson Inc., the Caterpillar-affiliated blade manufacturer, offered hydraulic blades for the DW-6 tractors. The DW-6B is a 44A series from 1961 with 115 fwhp.

668

In spite of soft sales, Caterpillar didn't give up on the idea of a wheel dozer. In 1956, it offered the 668 as an upgraded version of the DW-20. The 668 was available with a 12 ft. 10 in.-wide No.668S blade with either cable or hydraulic lifting, and it was marketed for use in handling coal or other lightweight materials. Like the DW-20 Series E, it came with a D337 engine rated at 300 fwhp. However, unlike the DW-20, it had four-wheel drive. The 668 was also used as a tractor unit with the Caterpillar No. 456 scraper and by the military as a utility tractor and airplane tug. Mechanical problems developed in the drive trains, and the tractor was taken off the market only a year after its debut, making it one of the shortest-lived Caterpillar tractors. *Historical Construction Equipment Association*

814

The 814 was launched in 1970, seven years after its bigger brothers, the 824 and the 834. The dozer is powered by a D333 engine with 170 fwhp and weighs 40,100 lbs. This machine has an inside-mounted blade; an outside mount was also available with hydraulic cylinders to change the blade tilt angle. *Pit & Quarry*

824
Caterpillar introduced both the 824 and 834 wheel dozers in 1963. The 824 is powered by a D343 engine with 275 fwhp. It came with a 3-speed powershift transmission and could move as fast as 21 mph. Here a model 824 cleans up shot rock in a quarry. *Pit & Quarry*

834
A cabless 834 with its 360-fwhp D343 engine push-loads a Caterpillar 641 motor scraper. *Pit & Quarry*

834

A model 834 spreads fill with its 14 ft. 8 in. blade on an earthen dam project. The 834 weighed 76,000 lbs. and boasted 360 fwhp, just 15 hp less than the D-9G crawler of the same era. *Caterpillar, Inc., Vernon Simpson collection*

824B

The 824B is powered by a D343 engine with 300 fwhp and has a weight of 61,500 lbs. This 824B is on a Peter Kiewit Co. job at the Anchorage International Airport, Alaska.

815 Compactor-Dozer

The Compactor Dozer is a first cousin to the wheel dozer, with steel compaction wheels replacing the rubber tires. The 815 Compactor was basically the same machine as the 814 wheel dozer. Caterpillar also offered the larger Model 825 and 835 Compactor dozers. Although widely accepted by highway contractors, Caterpillar had a difficult time convincing the Army Corps of Engineers, TVA and other dam builders that it could compact soils as well as traditional sheepsfoot rollers.

825B Compactor-Dozer

The 825B was introduced in 1970 along with sisters 815 and 835. It weighs 63,000 lbs. and its 6-cylinder D343 engine is rated at 300 fwhp. This 825B was working on a Lane Construction Corp. road project on I-495 in Springfield, Virginia.

830MB

In the mid-1960's, Caterpillar upgraded the 830M to the more powerful "B" series. The same D343 engine now had 357 flywheel hp and 448 gross hp. Weight of the tractor and dozer went up to 52,890 lbs. This former military dozer-scraper unit, or at least its operator, has the perfect job– reshaping the beach before the summer crowds arrive in Avalon, New Jersey.

830M

In 1962, Caterpillar won a contract with the U.S. Army to build a four-wheel drive articulated wheel dozer. The machine was similar to the Caterpillar 824 and 834 wheel dozers, but the D343 engine was placed in the front of the 830M. The engine is rated at 420 gross and 335 flywheel hp. The tractor weighs 52,000 lbs. with blade and winch attachments. Specifications in the contract called for a tractor that could pull an 18 cu. yd. scraper and travel in a convoy at a constant speed of 25 mph. *Caterpillar, Inc.*

TRACK LOADERS

The concept of the loader attachment for crawler tractors began during the 1920s, closely following the development of the mechanically-operated bulldozer blade. Most of the early loaders could be adapted to any crawler tractor make depending, of course, on the size of the bucket and power of the tractor.

One of the earliest loader attachments was built by the Killefer Co. of Los Angeles, California, who successully mated a small scraper bowl to the front of a Holt tractor in 1926. The bowl was raised by a winch mounted on the front of the machine.

By 1928, the Trackson Co. and Drott Manufacturing Co., both from Milwaukee, Wisconsin, also offered loader attachments with ¹/₃ yard buckets. The Trackson loader was cable operated, much like the Killefer design, while Drott's was a combination cable and hydraulic system.

During the early 1930s, Trackson introduced a ¹/₂ yard High Shovel attachment and in 1937, became an affiliated supplier to Caterpillar. By the early 1940s, it developed a four-model line of T-series cable-operated loaders called Traxcavators: the ¹/₂ yard T-2 for the D-2 tractor; the T-4 (1 yard) for the D-4; T-6 (2 yards) for the D-6; and the 2¹/₂ yard T-7 for the D-7. In 1950, Trackson introduced the HT-4 Traxcavator, a 1.25 yard all-hydraulic loader for the D-4 (7U) tractor.

Largely due to the success of this machine, Caterpillar purchased the Trackson Co. in 1951. Two years later, the company replaced the HT-4 with its No. 6 Shovel, the first integrally-built track loader. Based largely on the D-6 (9U) tractor, it was rated at 66 fwhp and had a capacity of 2 yards. The No. 6 was replaced in 1955 with a three-model line of Traxcavators: 933 with a 1-yard bucket, the 1¹/₂ yard 955, and the 2¹/₄ yard 977. The Traxcavator line went through a number of upgrades through the 1960s and in 1969, a fourth model the 983, was added. With its 275 fwhp and 5-yard bucket, it was the largest crawler loader available for several years. The 933 was dropped in the late 1960s, and the 941 and 951 loaders were added. A smaller model joined the loader line in 1973, the 931, with 62 fwhp and a 1-yard bucket.

During the early 1980s, Caterpillar redesigned its track loaders and launched a four-model line of rear-engine machines. These were the 943, 953, 963 and 973 models along with the front-engine 931B; these loaders ranged in capacity from 1 to 3 3/4 yards. The 931B and 943 were replaced by hydrostatically-controlled 933C, 953C, 963C and 973C with 90 to 242 fwhp and 1.5 to 4.2 yard capacities.

Trackson Model T-2 Traxcavator
Trackson offered its "Traxcavator" front loader attachments for crawler tractors in the late 1930s, and by the mid-40s had a four-machine lineup for Caterpillar tractors: the Model T-2 (1/2 yard) for the D-2; Model T-4 (1 yard) for the D-4; Model T-6 (2 yards) for the D-6; and Model T-7 (2½ yards) for the D-7. The Traxcavator pictured is a 1947 model on a Cat D-2 (4U) tractor at Lapeer, Michigan.

Trackson T-6 Traxcavator
The machine shown is a 1948 Traxcavator with a 2 yard bucket on a D-6 tractor at the 1999 HCEA National Show in Brownsville, Pennsylvania. The D-6 of this era came with a D318 engine that develops 80 fwhp.

Trackson T-7 Traxcavator
With its 2½-yard bucket, the T-7 Traxcavator was the largest of the cable-operated loaders available from Trackson. This T-7 is on a 1948 D-7 (3T) tractor that was operated at the 2002 HCEA Show in Albany, Minnesota.

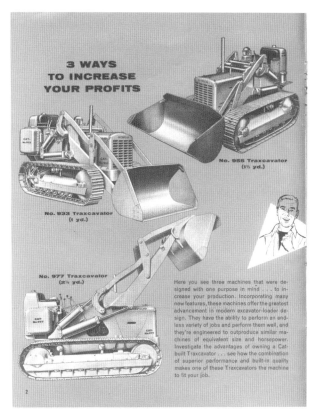

**Late 1950s
Traxcavator line**
933, 955 and 977 track
loaders. Caterpillar, Inc.
From brochure "Your
Guide to Caterpillar Earthmoving Equipment" *Ver-
non Simpson collection*

Caterpillar HT-4 Traxcavator
The HT-4 came with the standard 55-hp D315 engine used in the D-4
(7U). The HT-4 loader attachment was first offered by the Trackson Co. in
1950; Caterpillar purchased Trackson in 1951 and offered the HT-4 under
its own name until 1955. This picture, taken in 1953, shows a Caterpillar
HT-4 on a D-4 (7U) tractor with a 1.25 yard bucket. *Pit & Quarry*

Caterpillar No. 6 Shovel
The No. 6 Shovel (Series 10A) appeared in 1953 and was the first integrated front loader built by Caterpillar. The loader has an 8-foot-
wide bucket with a capacity of 2
yards. The bucket has an automat-
ic tip-back angle of 35° and a
dumping angle of 50°. The loader
is powered by a D318 engine, initially rated at 66 fwhp; it was later
increased to 100 hp. *Gary Hansen*

933

In 1955, Caterpillar announced a new line of Traxcavator crawler loaders to replace the No. 6. These were designated as Models 933, 955 and 977. The 933 has a 1 yard bucket and a 50-hp engine; the 955 has a 1½ yard capacity, and the 977 can handle up to 2¼ yards.

955

The 1½ yard 955 is equipped with a 70-hp D315 engine and weighs 21,500 lbs. Maximum dumping height of the bucket is 10 feet 8 inches. The first model was actually the 955C series 12A, introduced in 1955; in 1958 it became the 955E, and the manufacturing site switched from Peoria to Aurora, Illinois. The 955 here was built in 1958 and was brought by owner Alan Smith to the 2000 ACMOC Show in Chillicothe, Illinois.

977

The first 977 rolled off the assembly line in 1956. It was actually a 977D series 20A powered by a Cat D-318 engine with 128 hp. The 977E was launched in 1958 followed by the 977H (Series 53A) in 1960. The capacity of the H series was increased to 2½ yards, and it was powered by the larger D333 engine.

955 Dozer-Loader

BELOW. Caterpillar offered a combination 1½ yard bucket and 955A angledozer blade for the 955 during the late 1950s. *Historical Construction Equipment Association*

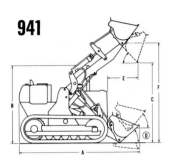   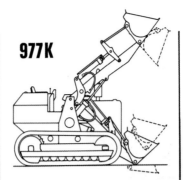 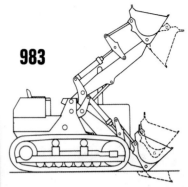

Late 1960s-early 1970s crawler loader line
Caterpillar offered five crawler loader models from 1969 through the 1970s: models 941 (1½ yards), 951B (1½ to 1¾ yards), 955K (1¾ to 2 yards), 977K (2½ to 3 yards) and 983 (4½ to 5 cubic-yards). Flywheel horsepower ranged from 70 to 275. *Caterpillar, Inc., Doug Frey collection*

983
ABOVE. In 1969, Caterpillar introduced its largest tracked loader, the 4 ½-to-5 cu-bicyard Model 983. Powered by a D343 turbocharged engine rated at 275 fwhp, the loader was offered until 1978. The 983B with the same bucket capacity and horsepower was built from 1978 to 1982. The 66,200-lb. loader exerts more than 48,000 lbs. of breakout force on the bucket teeth. Optional buckets include a 4½ yard general purpose, 4½ yard slag, 5 yard loose material, and a 5 yard rock buck-et. *David Werner*

931
BELOW. Caterpillar's smallest crawler loader, the 1 yard 931 loader was launched in 1973 along with the D-3 dozer. The two machines shared many of the same components including the 62 fwhp 3204 engine. As with the D-3, all 931s were built in Japan.

CHAPTER TWO

CLEVELAND TRACTOR COMPANY & THE OLIVER CORPORATION

Founded by Rollin H. White, Cleveland Tractor grew to become one of the top crawler tractor manufacturers during the 1930s and 1940s. White, son of the inventor of the White Sewing Machine, developed an early interest in automobiles in the late 1800s and began building steam-powered cars in 1900. By 1906, he was experimenting with steam-powered trucks, and along with two of his brothers, formed the White Motor Co. White Motor would become a major truck and bus manufacturer and was the largest employer in Cleveland for many years.

Always trying to make a better machine, White left the truck business in 1914 and the next year began building

Model 30A
A Cletrac Model 30A orchard tractor from 1928 resides at the Vintage Tracks Museum, East Bloomfield, New York. The Model 30A was powered by a Wisconsin "H" six-cylinder gasoline engine capable of 45 bhp and 38 dbhp.

51

Cletrac Tractors and Differential Steering

Steering in any full track-laying machine is controlled by varying the speed of the track on one side of the machine in relation to the speed of the track on the opposite side. Two methods of steering and controlling track speed are (1) clutch-type steering, in which the speed of each track is varied by disconnecting, braking, and reconnecting the power to the track located on the side of the machine to which it is desired to turn; and (2) controlled differential steering and braking. Steering by controlling the action of the differential was designed and developed by Cletrac and covered by a U.S. patent granted to Rollin White in 1920. It is a system of actuating the differential through planetary gear control. This method of steering allows power to be engaged to both tracks at all times.

Cletrac's steering system was controlled by two levers. Pulling on either lever operated a band which contracted around and stopped the corresponding steering drum. This actuated the planetary gears and caused the tractor to turn. When the tractor moved straight ahead, the right and left steering drum were free to turn with the entire differential assembly as a unit. A pinion in front of the steering drums drove a bevel gear, turning the entire differential unit and transmitting equal power and speed to each track. When steering, pressure on either steering lever stopped the associated steering drum, which actuated the planetary gears on that end of the steering assembly. Through the gears thus set in motion, the differential action was controlled. This changed the ratio of speed of the drive shafts – one is slowed, the other goes faster. The difference between a controlled and an ordinary differential is that the speed and action of each track is under positive mechanical control at all times.

STRAIGHT AHEAD

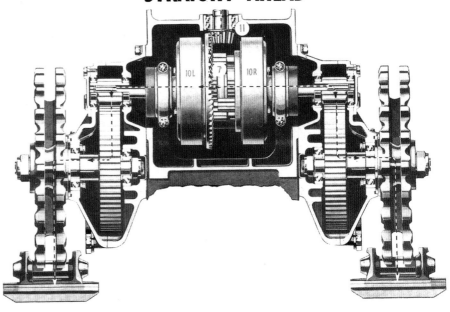

TURNING

crawler tractors in a small shop in East Cleveland, Ohio. Initially called the Cleveland Motor Plow Co., White changed the name to Cleveland Tractor Co. in 1917. The first tractor, called the Model R, weighed just over a ton and was powered by a 10-dbhp Buda engine. Rollin White developed the Model R jointly with his brother Clarence, who managed a pineapple plantation in Hawaii at the time and understood the need for a small cultivating tractor that could operate in wet climates. The Model R was specifically designed for use on small- and medium-sized farms, and it was Rollin White's idea to build an easily affordable crawler and become the Henry Ford of the tractor business. His tractor used a unique system for control known as "differential steering" (see sidebar) in which planetary gears maintain power to each track while the machine is turning, unlike the other crawlers on the market that required clutching and braking to turn. Every crawler made by Cleveland Tractor and its successor, the Oliver Corp., used the differential steering system.

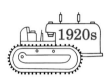

Cleveland Tractor Co. factory
A technician tests the fan and radiator of a Cletrac engine.

Sales of Cleveland tractors increased from 1,000 units in 1917 to more than 10,000 in 1920, and the company expanded its product line to the Model H in 1917, Model W in 1919 and Model F in 1920. Horsepower of the three crawlers ranged from 16 to 20 bhp. Along with its increased popularity came its shortened name–Cletrac. Initially, Cletrac tried using motors from a number of manufacturers such as Weidley, Wisconsin, Buda, Cummins (only in the Model FDLC) and Continental (only in Model AG-6), and the company even built some of its own engines. However, by the mid-1930's, Cletrac settled mainly on Hercules engines, and it stayed with Hercules to the end. The company was one of the earlier manufacturers to offer diesel power with the introduction of its Model 80D in 1933; the engine for the 80D was also a Hercules.

By 1930, Cletrac had expanded its line to six models using a numerical designation that approximated the drawbar horsepower of the tractor. These included Models W, 20K, 30B, 40, 80-60 and 100. During its period of production, the Model 100 was the most powerful tractor available and one of the first to surpass the 100 hp mark (see "super dozers"). In its earliest years, Cletrac designed and marketed its tractors primarily for agriculture, but as public works and military projects expanded in the 1930s and 1940s, Cletrac machines were frequently seen on construction jobs, and large numbers were purchased by the Armed Services.

The new markets also moved Cletrac to a close association with The Heil Company, a builder of dozer blades, scrapers and other tractor attachments. Cletrac was the first crawler tractor manufacturer to apply streamlined styling to its machines in the mid-1930's; competitors quickly picked up on this trend, and by the late 1930's, nearly all had restyled their tractors. Along with the restyling, Cletrac went from the numerical model designation to a letter system based on size and fuel type. In 1940, Cletrac offered 12 crawler tractor models, most of which were available with either gas or diesel engines. During World War II, Cletrac built several unique crawler tractors for special military uses (see Model MG-2 later in this chapter).

Cleveland Tractor Co. was bought by the Oliver Corporation in 1944, and in the early 1950's, redesigned its entire crawler tractor line. The new models were given the OC prefix, for Oliver-Crawler, and ranged from the OC-3 at 26 bhp to the OC-18 at 161 bhp. A line of crawler loaders was also added beginning in 1957 with bucket sizes

Model H
The Model H was introduced in 1917, replacing the Model R. The H was the second tractor model produced by Cletrac. It enjoyed brisk sales, with nearly 13,000 units built through 1919, when the W took its place. The H is powered by a Weidley four-cylinder gas engine rated at 20 bhp and 12 dbhp. This 1918 Model H is owned by Cletrac collector Landis Zimmerman.

53

Model W

ABOVE. The Model W enjoyed a long life in the Cletrac product line, lasting from 1919 to 1932. It was also one of Cletrac's all-time best sellers with nearly 20,000 units sold. It used both Cletrac and Weidley four-cylinder engines rated at 20 bhp and 12 dbhp, although this dozer now uses an engine from a Ford Model A automobile. This Model W is a 1921 version with a blade of unknown origin. It was being operated at the Easy Diggin' Show in Mt. Hope, New Jersey.

Model W

BELOW. As with Models R, H, and F, the W had a 2-speed transmission (one forward and one reverse) giving it a speed range of one to four MPH. Its weight was 3,418 lbs., resulting in a ground pressure of 4.5 lbs. per square inch with its 38-in. track gauge. The W sold for $1,495.00 FOB Cleveland. *James Owensby collection*

Model F

Cletrac only offered the Model F for three years (1920-1922) but still sold 3,000 units. Intended as a cultivating tractor for truck farms, vineyards, orchards and Christmas tree farms, the machine weighed only 2,000 lbs. Three versions of the F were offered: 24-in. gauge, 36-in. gauge and a high-clearance 36-in. gauge. The Model F had an elevated sprocket and has been cited as an inspiration for Caterpillar's current undercarriage design for its larger dozers. Note there are no idler sprocket wheels in its undercarriage; the tracks attached to a roller chain moved along slots in the side frames. Power comes from a Cletrac 4-cylinder, vertical L-head engine with 16 bhp and 9 dbhp. The tractor can pull 1,780 lbs. or 89% of its weight. It sold for $850 FOB Cleveland, Ohio. *James Owensby collection*

Model 20K
Cletrac introduced the Model 20K in 1925 and it remained in production through 1932. The 20K is powered by a four-cylinder gas engine built by Cletrac who rated it at 27 bhp and 20 dbhp. Weight of the machine is 4,838 lbs.

Model 40-30
Cletrac offered the 40-30 only in 1931, replacing it with the Model 35 in 1932. The 40-30, powered by a Hercules WXT six-cylinder engine was rated by a Nebraska Test at 45.64 bhp and 40.66 dbhp and weighed about 5 tons. *Richard Yaremko*

from 5/8 to 2¼ yards. The company began utilizing attachments from Ware Machine Tool and A.C. Anderson and even purchased the Be-Ge Manufacturing Co. to add construction-oriented implements to its product line, but it was never able to carve a significant niche in the construction equipment business.

As sales and profits declined during the late 1950's, Oliver was acquired by the White Motor Co. in 1960, the same company established by Rollin White. In 1962, the crawler manufacturing facilities were moved from Cleveland to the Oliver factory in Charles City, Iowa. Only two crawler models were built at the Charles City plant: the OC-4 and OC-9 in dozer and loader versions. Unfortunately, White Motor could not save the crawler business, and the last Oliver-Cletrac tractor rolled out of the factory in 1965.

Model 100
With a six-cylinder Wisconsin ET engine developing 120 bhp and 100 dbhp, the Model 100 was the largest Cletrac up to that time and one of, if not the most powerful, tractor of its day. The 100 was replaced by the Model 80-60 in 1930 and the 80 in 1932. Although offered for four years (1927-1930), only 108 units of the Model 100 were sold. Perhaps the machine wasn't marketed properly or maybe the public wasn't ready, especially after the Great Depression began in 1929. Timing is everything.

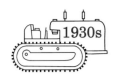

Early 1930s tractor lineup
Timber Times, Phil Schnell and Steven Gatke collection

Model 15

Model 25

Model 35

Model 80

Model 55

Model 15

Cletrac introduced the Model 15 in 1931 as a replacement for the Model W. The Model 15 was offered for only three years, 1931 through 1933, and just over 1,000 units were sold. It weighed 5,800 lbs. and was the first tractor to have a one-piece forged track shoe. Its Hercules gasoline engine was rated at 26 bhp, and it delivered 22 dbhp. This 1931 tractor was displayed at the 2003 HCEA Show in Albany, Minnesota.

Model 35

ABOVE AND UPPER RIGHT. Cletrac offered the Model 35 from 1932 through 1936 as a replacement for the Model 40-30 tractor. It competed against the Caterpillar Forty and RD6, A-C Model K, and I-H Model T-40 and TD-40 tractors. Power for the Model 35 is supplied by a Hercules 6-cylinder, 383 cu.in. gas engine rated at 49.43 bhp and 44 dbhp. The tractor without attachments weighs 10,400 lbs. *James Owensby collection*

Model 20C

The Model 20C, first offered in 1933, replaced the Model 15. It retained the same Hercules OOC four-cylinder gas engine, although horsepower was increased to 29 bhp and 24.6 at the drawbar. The weight of the tractor was an even 3 tons.

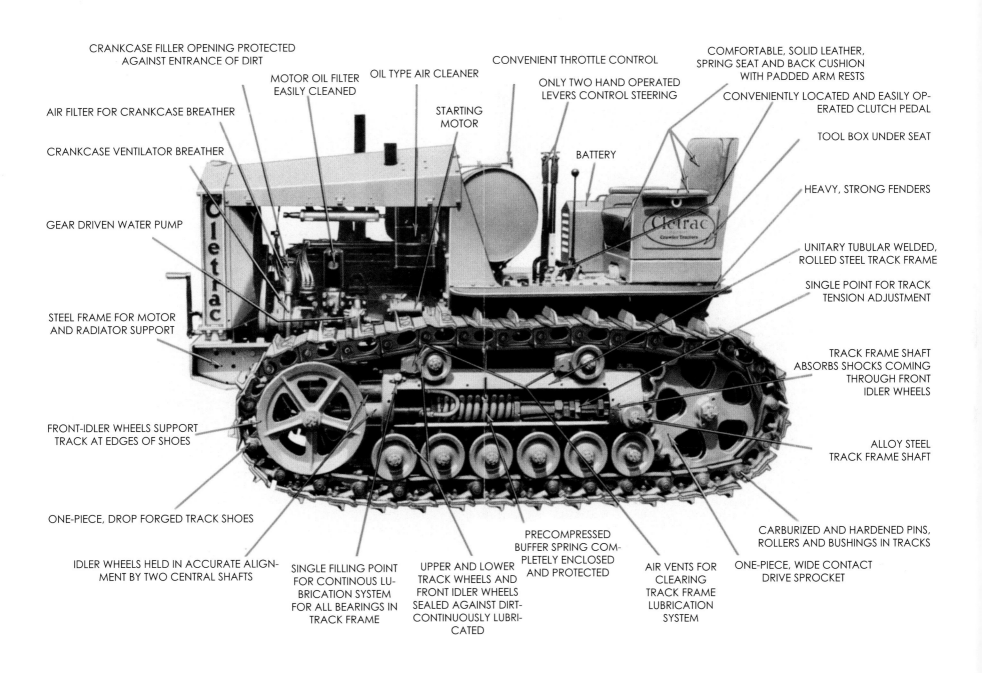

CRANKCASE FILLER OPENING PROTECTED
AGAINST ENTRANCE OF DIRT

MOTOR OIL FILTER
EASILY CLEANED

OIL TYPE AIR CLEANER

CONVENIENT THROTTLE CONTROL

COMFORTABLE, SOLID LEATHER,
SPRING SEAT AND BACK CUSHION
WITH PADDED ARM RESTS

AIR FILTER FOR CRANKCASE BREATHER

STARTING
MOTOR

ONLY TWO HAND OPERATED
LEVERS CONTROL STEERING

CONVENIENTLY LOCATED AND EASILY OP-
ERATED CLUTCH PEDAL

CRANKCASE VENTILATOR BREATHER

BATTERY

TOOL BOX UNDER SEAT

GEAR DRIVEN WATER PUMP

HEAVY, STRONG FENDERS

UNITARY TUBULAR WELDED,
ROLLED STEEL TRACK FRAME

STEEL FRAME FOR MOTOR
AND RADIATOR SUPPORT

SINGLE POINT FOR TRACK
TENSION ADJUSTMENT

TRACK FRAME SHAFT
ABSORBS SHOCKS COMING
THROUGH FRONT
IDLER WHEELS

FRONT-IDLER WHEELS SUPPORT
TRACK AT EDGES OF SHOES

ALLOY STEEL
TRACK FRAME SHAFT

ONE-PIECE, DROP FORGED TRACK SHOES

CARBURIZED AND HARDENED PINS,
ROLLERS AND BUSHINGS IN TRACKS

IDLER WHEELS HELD IN ACCURATE ALIGN-
MENT BY TWO CENTRAL SHAFTS

SINGLE FILLING POINT
FOR CONTINOUS LU-
BRICATION SYSTEM
FOR ALL BEARINGS IN
TRACK FRAME

UPPER AND LOWER
TRACK WHEELS AND
FRONT IDLER WHEELS
SEALED AGAINST DIRT-
CONTINUOUSLY LUBRI-
CATED

PRECOMPRESSED
BUFFER SPRING COM-
PLETELY ENCLOSED
AND PROTECTED

AIR VENTS FOR
CLEARING
TRACK FRAME
LUBRICATION
SYSTEM

ONE-PIECE, WIDE CONTACT
DRIVE SPROCKET

Model 35
"Cletrac Crawler Tractors-Features of Construction" *Timber Times, Phil Schnell and Steven Gatke collection*

Model E-31

The E-31, also called Model EN, was available from 1934 to 1939. Like the Model 15 and 20C, it is equipped with the Hercules OOC four-cylinder engine rated at 30.5 bhp and 22.11 dbhp.

Model E-38

This is the pre-streamlined version of the E-38 which was offered from 1934 to 1936. Power is from a Hercules OOC engine rated at 30.5 bhp and 22.11 dbhp. The Model E series was designed for cultivating work. Cletrac offered five track configurations for use in a variety of row widths depending on the type of crop: the E-31, E-38, E-62, E-68 and E-76 versions, with the number representing the track gauge in inches.

Model E-38

LEFT. In 1936, Cletrac redesigned the grill, engine housing and operator area of its tractors. The boxy look of the 1920s and early 1930s was replaced by more rounded styling, giving the tractor a streamlined appearance in keeping with the Art Deco look that had become very popular. The streamlined version of the E-38 was sold from 1936 to 1938. It kept the same Hercules gas engine as its unstyled sister.

Model E-68
Also powered by the 30.5 bhp Hercules OOC engine, the E-68 is the second widest track width offered for the E series. The E-68 was produced from 1934 to 1941. This is a 1937 "styled" model in the James Owensby collection.

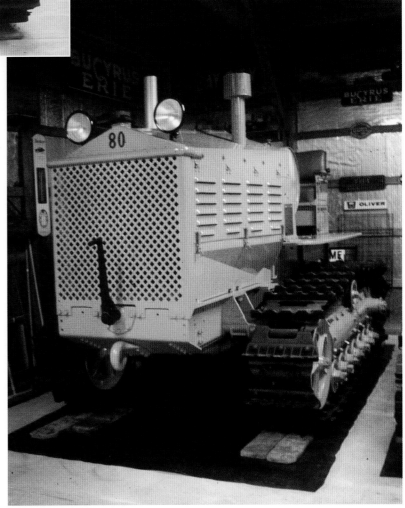

Model 80
Cletrac only offered the Model 80 in 1932. It was a replacement for the 80-60, and it took over as the largest machine in the Cletrac catalog. The 80 had a Wisconsin DT-4 six-cylinder gas engine rated at 90.23 bhp and 83.53 dbhp. In 1933 it was replaced by Models 80G and 80D. The 80G has a Hercules HXE six-cylinder gas engine with 103 bhp and 86.4 dbhp; the 80D has a Hercules DHX diesel, advertised at 103 bhp and 92.3 dbhp. Both machines were built through 1936. The tank at the rear of the engine housing holds 80 gallons of gasoline, which the tractor burns at the rate of 10 gallons an hour. The tractor shown is a 1933 Model 80G, serial number 598. *James Owensby collection*

Model 80D

Introduced in 1933, the 80D was Cletrac's first diesel-powered tractor. Its engine was a Hercules DHXB engine rated at 103 bhp. The machine shown is a Blue Ox Logging Special with bumper, radiator guard, and belly pan pulling logs with a Carco logging arch in Oregon. *John Henderson Collection, courtesy of Oso Publishing Co.*

Model 80G

A 1934 Model 80G is at the 2000 HCEA National Show in Seward, Nebraska. The tractor's serial number is 630, and it was used for many years as a utility tractor at the Nebraska Tractor Testing Lab at the University of Nebraska in Lincoln. Ironically, the 80G was never tested by the Nebraska Lab. It weighs 23,000 lbs.

Swamp Special

Swamp Special Cletracs are equipped with wide tracks that are used where the surface conditions demand a larger ground contact than that of the standard models.

Industrial Special

The Industrial Special is built for work and equipment requiring a tractor with greater length and width than standard.

Logging Special

The Logging Special is equipped with spark arrester, radiator guard, lower track wheel guards, crankcase guard, front bumper and front pull hook.

Special Models

Starting in the early 1930s, a number of models were offered for special tasks such as logging, working in wet soils, etc. *Timber Times, Phil Schnell and Steven Gatke collection*

Hillside Special

When working on sides of hills, or for use with special equipment it is sometimes necessary to use a tractor with a greater distance than standard between tracks. The Hillside Special Cletracs are built for this work.

1940s

Model HG

The HG continued the small tractor lineage from the Models F and 15. The smaller models sold well to row-crop farms, tree farms and other agricultural uses where maneuverability was important. The HG series was introduced in 1939, and it was available through 1951. Four models were built with track widths of 31, 42, 60 and 68 inches. Weights of the tractor range from 3,025 to 3,820 lbs., depending on track configuration. The HG was initially powered by Hercules four-cylinder gasoline engines that Cletrac rated at 20.58 bhp and 14.78 dbhp. A 1939 Nebraska Tractor Test gave it slightly less, 19.36 bhp and 14.01 dbhp. By the late 1940s, power was increased to 26.36 bhp and 21.85 dbhp.

Orchard Special

The Cletrac Orchard Special has a low seat permitting the tractor to be driven under low branches of the trees.

Factory Special

The Factory Special Cletrac is used in factories and similar places. Eight hundred square inches of track surface is pulling at all times. This tractor is equipped with rubber tracks, and front and rear bumpers.

HG-42
This HG-42 is a 1945 model on display at the 2000 ACMOC Show held in Chillicothe, Illinois. *Don Heimburger*

1940s Tractor Lineup
Models AG, BG, BD, CG, DG, and DD. Not shown are the E, FG and FD tractors. *Doug Frey*

CLETRAC MODEL AG

Maximum Drawbar Horsepower Corrected to Sea Level................	44.6
N. A. C. C. Rating........	43.3
Maximum Drawbar Pounds Pull Corrected to Sea Level	
1st Gear.............	9600
2nd Gear...........	5550
3rd Gear............	3250
Approximate Weight— Equipped with Standard Grousers.............	11500
Maximum Belt Horsepower Corrected to Sea Level..	56

CLETRAC MODEL CG

Maximum Drawbar Horsepower Corrected to Sea Level................	44.6
N. A. C. C. Rating........	43.3
Maximum Drawbar Pounds Pull Corrected to Sea Level	
1st Gear.............	9600
2nd Gear...........	5550
3rd Gear............	3250
Approximate Weight— Equipped with Standard Grousers.............	11500
Maximum Belt Horsepower Corrected to Sea Level..	56

CLETRAC MODEL DG

Maximum Drawbar Horsepower Corrected to Sea Level................	60
N. A. C. C. Rating......	51.4
Maximum Drawbar Pounds Pull Corrected to Sea Level	
1st Gear...........	10800
2nd Gear..........	7850
3rd Gear...........	4660
Approximate Weight— Equipped with Standard Grousers..........	12000
Maximum Belt Horsepower Corrected to Sea Level	69

CLETRAC MODEL BG

Maximum Drawbar Horsepower Corrected to Sea Level................	35
N. A. C. C. Rating......	33.75
Maximum Drawbar Pounds Pull Corrected to Sea Level	
1st Gear............	7400
2nd Gear..........	5000
3rd Gear...........	3580
Approximate Weight— Equipped with Standard Grousers.............	8350
Maximum Belt Horsepower Corrected to Sea Level.	44

CLETRAC MODEL DD—DIESEL

Maximum Drawbar Horsepower Corrected to Sea Level................	61.18
Maximum Drawbar Pounds Pull Corrected to Sea Level	
1st Gear.............	11770
2nd Gear..........	8600
3rd Gear...........	5238
Approximate Weight— Equipped with Standard Grousers.............	12700
Maximum Belt Horsepower Corrected to Sea Level.	67.71

CLETRAC MODEL BD—DIESEL

Maximum Drawbar Horsepower Corrected to Sea Level...............	35
Maximum Drawbar Pounds Pull Corrected to Sea Level	
1st Gear............	7770
2nd Gear..........	5000
3rd Gear...........	3580
Approximate Weight— Equipped with Standard Grousers........	8800
Maximum Belt Horsepower Corrected to Sea Level	46

HG-68
In 1950, horsepower of the HG was increased to 26 bhp and 22 dbhp from a larger engine. The HG-68 with its 68-in. track gauge was the widest HG offered and weighs 3,513 lbs.

Model AG
LEFT. The A models were the second smallest after the HGs in the Cletrac "letter series" line. The AG was produced from 1936 to 1942 and is powered by a four-cylinder 226-cu. in. Hercules OOC gas engine that develops 34.2 bhp and 27 dbhp. Weight of the Model AG is 6,800 lbs. The AG-6 was first offered in 1944 and remained in the catalog through 1957. It has a Continental six-cylinder gas engine rated at 38.8 bhp and 30.6 dbhp. The AG-6 weighs 7,411 lbs. The machine shown is a 1941 AGH with a 50-in. track gauge and a Gar Wood hydraulic angling blade.

Model AD
The Model AD was produced between 1937 and 1959, indicating it was a very popular model. It was offered with a four-cylinder Hercules diesel engine with an output of 38 bhp and providing 30.5 dbhp. The Model AD weighs 8,012 lbs. This 1948 AD with a dozer blade was photographed at the Ageless Iron Show in Ankeny, Iowa in 1997.

Model CG
Cletrac released the CG in 1936. Those produced during the first year were unstyled like this 1936 Model CG. In 1937 it received the streamlined look with rounded grill, hood with fuel tank, and seat. The CG was tested at 51.13 bhp and weighed 11,500 lbs.

Model BGSH
A Model BGSH or "Hillside" version of the BGS was offered with wider tracks (20-in., 18-in., or 16-in.) for hilly farms or for grading in steep terrain. This BGS with a Heil blade was built in 1946.

Model BD
The diesel-powered version of the B models was the BD. The BD was produced from 1936 to 1956 and competed well specification-wise with the Caterpillar D-4, A-C HD-5 and IH TD-9 tractors. The BD has a Hercules DJXC six-cylinder engine rated at 48.09 bhp and 38.05 dbhp. The tractor weighs 9,749 lbs. This is a 1947 Model BD owned by collector Harold Radant of Manitowoc, Wisconsin.

Models BG and BGS

TOP RIGHT. Cletrac offered the Model BG from 1937 to 1944 and continued the line with the Model BGS from 1944 to 1955. Both models came with the Hercules JXD six-cylinder gasoline engine rated at 50 bhp and 38 dbhp. Weight of the BGS ranges from 8,600 to 9,100 lbs. This is a 1941 BG with a Maine hydraulic bulldozer blade. *Edgar Browning*

Model DD

ABOVE. The "DD" models were some of Cletrac's most popular products, remaining in the product line from 1936 to 1958. The DD was initially offered with a four-speed transmission; in 1939, it was changed to six speeds. Model DD has a Hercules six-cylinder DRXB diesel with 67.71 bhp and 61.19 dbhp. This is a 1946 Model DD dozer with a Heil hydraulic blade. With the blade attached, the DD weighs 13,708 lbs. The DD in the photo is being operated by Bob Kelley at the HCEA National Show in Brownsville, Pennsylvania in 1999.

MG-2

With the advent of long-range bombers during World War II came a need for heavy-duty servicing vehicles or tugs, as they are now called. Cleveland Tractor was awarded a contract to build a series of crawler tractors that were specially adapted for moving large aircraft and trailers in all kinds of weather and ground materials. Military equipment engineers particularly liked the idea of Cletrac's differential steering system for smoother operation, and it was used in a number of other military tracked vehicles.

Three models were manufactured during the War: the MG-1, between 1941 and 1944; MG-2, during 1942 and 43; and the MG-3, during 1942 only. All three models were equipped with aircraft drawbars, winches, electric generators and an air compressor. The undercarriages have rubber tracks with elevated sprockets and idler wheels like those on tanks for higher speeds. Because of their special application, GI's nicknamed the tractors "Bomber Nurses." The "nurse" shown is an MG-2 built in 1943. The Model MG-2 has a six-cylinder, 404-cu.in. WXLC-3 Hercules gas engine listed at 150 bhp, one of the most powerful tractor engines offered at the time. The total weight of the machine is 13,800 lbs., including more than a ton of auxiliary equipment. The tractor is exhibited at the Wright Museum in Laconia, New Hampshire. The museum features World War II equipment and memorabilia from the 1940s.

Model DG

The "D" tractors also were available (1936 to 1956) with a gas-powered engine, thus the "G" designation. Like the Model DD, the DG initially had a four-speed gearbox which was upgraded to six forward speeds in 1939. The DG's engine is a Hercules RXC with six cylinders listed at 69 bhp and 61.2 dbhp. Weight of the tractor is 12,917 lbs. The DG tractor shown is a 1947 model belonging to antique equipment collector Dave Geis of Seward, Nebraska.

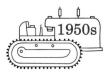

FD

RIGHT. A Model FD tractor pulls a Heil hydraulic scraper on a portion of the Pennsylvania Turnpike in 1939. *Heil Environmental*

FDE

ABOVE. The Model FD was upgraded to the FDE in 1945 and it remained in production to 1952. Power was increased to 130 bhp and 110 dbhp. The FDE weighs 30,025 lbs. without blade, and nearly 40,000 lbs. with this Heil cable-operated Trailbuilder blade. This dozer is owned by Ed McElhone.

FD and FG

RIGHT. Cletrac began its "F" series tractor line in 1936, offering both gasoline and diesel-powered versions. Between 1936 and 1938, both came with four-speed transmissions (three speeds forward, one reverse). From 1938 to 1944, the "F" tractors had six speeds (four forward, two reverse). The gasoline version is the FG, the diesel is the FD. The FG has a Hercules six-cylinder engine with 110 bhp and 94 dbhp and weighs 26,750 lbs. The FD is powered by a Hercules six-cylinder diesel rated at 107.5 bhp and weighs 25,800 lbs. This Model FD resides in the Heidrick Ag Museum.

HG

RIGHT. Oliver-Cletrac continued building the HG tractor through 1951 when it was replaced by the OC-3. This HG with 42-in. track gauge is a 1950 model with a hydraulic blade. It was brought to the Shenandoah Valley Steam & Gas Show in Berryville, Virginia.

OC-3

In 1951, Oliver redesigned its tractor line, and the OC-3 was its first new product. The OC-3 replaced the HG series as the smallest Oliver crawler, and it remained in production through 1957. It is powered by a four-cylinder Hercules gas engine with 21.85 dbhp, 26.36 bhp, and weighs 3,820 lbs. This is a 1953 OC-3 tractor at the Vintage Tracks Museum in East Bloomfield, New York.

OLIVER OC-4 Crawler Tractor
BULLDOZER SPECIFICATIONS

OLIVER TRACTOR	OC-4
General Dimensions	
Track Gauge	42"
Maximum width track shoe	12"
Over-all length (tractor and dozer)	111"
Over-all width (tractor and dozer)	60"
Blade length	60"
Blade height	26"
Performance	
Maximum blade lift above ground line	26"
Maximum blade drop below ground line	13"
Weight	
Tractor	4,005 lb.
Dozer	832 lb.

OC-4

The OC-4 series, launched in 1956, overlapped (for one year) and then superceded the OC-3. The OC-4 with a four-cylinder gas engine (26.36 bhp) was offered from 1956 to 1958. The OC-4 (3D) was introduced in 1957 and remained in the lineup through 1965. It had a three-cylinder diesel engine listed at 30.45 bhp. The OC-4 (3G) was produced between 1958 and 1965. It is powered by a three-cylinder gas engine with 30.2 bhp. This bulldozer is an OC-4 (serial no. 3TG-914) from 1957 and is being operated at the Vintage Tracks Museum in East Bloomfield, New York.

OC-6

The OC-6 was offered from 1953 through 1960. It was available with either a gasoline engine (OC-6G) delivering 45 bhp or a diesel (OC-6D) with 43 bhp. This tractor is a 1953 gasoline-powered model at the 2000 Rough and Tumble Show in Kinzer, Pennsylvania owned by Harry Wilson.

OC-6
The OC-6G weighs 5,605 lbs.; the OC-6D weighs 5,750 lbs.

OC-12

Oliver offered two versions of the OC-12: the gasoline-powered OC-12G and the diesel OC-12D. Both had Hercules six-cylinder engines with horsepower in the 60 bhp and 53 dbhp range and both machines weigh a little over 5 tons. Both the OC-12G and OC-12D were available between 1954 and 1960. This OC-12 tractor belongs to Cletrac collector Luke Rizzuto.

OC-12

A number of blades and other attachments were available for the OC-12. These included straight and angling blades from Heil (shown), Ateco, BeGe, and A.C. Anderson, loader buckets were from Ware Machine Works, rippers from Ateco and Hyteco, and winches from CARCO. *Doug Frey*

OCX-12D

This bulldozer is an experimental model built in 1959 with a Hercules DD-298 six-cylinder diesel engine rated at 80 fwhp. Weight of the dozer is 14,900 lbs. The OCX-12D is owned by Landis Zimmerman, who operated it at the 2001 HCEA National Show in Canandaigua, New York. Although it was a successful design, it was never placed into production.

Specifications of the Hydraulic Bulldozer for the OLIVER Model OC-12 Crawler Tractor

OLIVER TRACTOR	OC-12
Blade Model	HB-12W

General Dimensions
Track Gauge	60″
Maximum width track shoe	18″
Over-all length (tractor and blade)	146 1/2″
Blade length	95 1/2″
Blade height	35 1/2″
Faceplate thickness	1/4″

Cutting Edges
Center Section
Length	60″
Height	6″
Thickness	5/8″

End Bits
Length	17 3/4″
Height	8″
Thickness	7/8″

Hydraulic System
Pump-gallons per minute under 800 psi at 1,800 rpm	24
Bore of hydraulic cylinder	4″
Stroke of hydraulic cylinder	28 1/8″
Normal hydraulic operating pressure	800 psi
Maximum hydraulic operating pressure	1,000 psi

Performance
Maximum blade lift (power)	37 1/2″
Maximum blade drop	13″
Speed of blade lift per second at 100% efficiency at 1000 rpm	10.4″
Blade end lift adjustment	11 1/2″

Weight
Tractor	10,432 lb.
Dozer	2,868 lb.

OC-12

In 1959, an advanced feature was offered for the OC-12 called the Spot-Turn steering system. Spot-Turn was a clutched steering unit that allowed the operator to make pivot turns. Like all Cletrac steering units, Spot-Turn was a "wet" system, meaning it was bathed in oil. Other crawler tractor makers did not offer wet clutching systems until many years later. *Landis Zimmerman*

OLIVER OC-15 Crawler Tractor HYDRAULIC ANGLEBLADE

OLIVER TRACTOR	OC-15
Blade Model	**HT-15**

Tractor Equipment Specifications

Over-all length (blade straight)	14' 5 3/8"
Over-all length (blade angled)	16' 11 3/8"
Maximum track shoe width	20"
Total weight (tractor and angleblade with 5 LTW and 16" grousers)	19,440 lb.
Height	67"
Width (blade straight)	12' 2"
Width (blade angled)	11' 1/2"

Blade Information

Length	12' 2"
Height (less spill board)	34 1/2"
Height (with spill board)	40 3/4"
Maximum blade angle	25°
Maximum lift above ground (blade straight)	32"
Maximum drop below ground (blade straight)	14"
Maximum tilting adjustment (RH or LH)	11"
Center cutting edge (reversible)	3/4" x 8" x 105"
End bits (reversible)	1" x 8" x 22 1/4"
Weight, shipping (approx.)	4,598 lb.

Blade - 1/4" alloy steel moldboard with box section reinforcements

Hydraulic System

Cylinders	2 required, double acting
Bore	4"
Stroke	28 1/8"

Pump - Capacity @ 1,500 rpm @ 1,000 psi Coupling

Valve - Single valve with raise, lower, hold and float positions, open center by-pass

Capacity - Hydraulic system   9 gal. (approx.)

OC-15

The OC-15 appeared in 1956 and was offered to 1961. Available only with diesel power, it has a Hercules DRXC six-cylinder diesel engine rated at 104.6 bhp and 94.17 dbhp. Weight ranges from 17,335 to 19,440 lbs. depending on attachments. *Doug Frey*

OLIVER Model OC-18 Crawler Tractor
Engine-Frame-Mounted-Bulldozer

Tractor Model No.	**OC-18**
Blade Model No.	**THB-18**

Tractor and Blade Dimensions

Over-all length (blade straight)	17' 11"
Maximum track shoe width	26"
Total weight (22" grousers)	
POWER-TURN	41,241 lb.
Reg. Conv.	40,441 lb.
Height	7' 1 9/16"
Width (blade straight)	10' 10"

Blade Dimensions

Height (less spillboard)	49"
Height (with spillboard)	57"
Length	10' 10"
Shipping weight - dozer only	7,942 lb.
32 gals. oil	232 lb.
Center cutting edge	1" x 10" x 90 7/8"
End Bits	1" x 10" x 19 1/2"

Performance

Maximum lift above ground	47 3/4"
Maximum drop below ground	14 1/4"
Blade travel over all	62"
Maximum tilting adjustment	14 1/2"
Blade lift time	4 sec.
Blade lower time	4.2 sec.
Blade float lower time (max. raise to ground)	5.6 sec

OC-18

Oliver introduced the OC-18 in 1952 as a replacement for the FDE, and it remained in their product line to 1960. The largest crawler tractor built by either Oliver or Cletrac, the OC-18 weighs 33,300 lbs. without attachments. It is powered by a six-cylinder Hercules DFXE, an 895 cubic-inch diesel engine that Oliver rated at 161 ghp and 133 dbhp. An OC-18 was rated by the Nebraska Tractor Testing Lab at 128 dbhp, but the lab did not test its bhp. *Pit & Quarry*

OC-9

In 1959, Oliver redesigned its crawler line with a modern look with squarer engine housing and headlights set inside the grill. The new dozer received a Trans-O-Matic powershift transmission and a more powerful Hercules diesel engine rated at 62 ghp. Weight of the bare tractor was 9,725 lbs. The OC-9 was built in Cleveland, Ohio from 1959 to 1961; in 1962, Oliver crawler production was moved to Charles City, Iowa and the OC-4 and OC-9, both upgraded to Series B models, were the only two crawler models available. Oliver ended its crawler tractor production in 1965. *Landis Zim-merman*

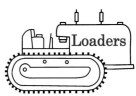

BGSH with Drott Bullclam

Drott was another supplier of loader buckets and lifting arms for crawler tractors. The Bullclam on this 1948 Model BGSH tractor was the forerunner to Drott's 4-in-1 buckets offered during the 1950s and 60s. The loader is owned by David Burnham.

OC-46

LEFT. The OC-46 debuted in 1957 and was offered through 1965, one of the last crawler machines built by Oliver. Based on the OC-4G and OC-4D, it was available with either a Hercules three-cylinder diesel rated at 30.45 bhp or a three-cylinder gas engine with 30.2 bhp. The OC-46 comes with a 5/8-yd. bucket and weighs between 8,080 and 8,110 lbs. Most of the Oliver loader buckets were built by the Ware Machine Works of Ware, Massachusetts. The machine in the photo is a 1960 diesel model that was used for many years at Boys Town outside of Omaha, Nebraska. It was displayed at the 2000 HCEA National Show in Seward, Nebraska.

OC-156
At 2¼ yards bucket capacity, the OC-156 was the largest crawler loader offered by Oliver. Launched in 1956, it was sold through 1961. The OC-156 was powered by a Hercules six-cylinder diesel rated at 104.6 bhp, and it weighed 28,200 lbs. *Landis Zimmerman*

OC-126
Introduced in 1954, the 126 is the loader version of the OC-12 tractor. As with the OC-12, it was available through 1960 with a Hercules six-cylinder gas engine rated at 60.3 bhp or a Hercules six-cylinder diesel with 59 bhp. It has a 1½ yard bucket and the gas version weighs 15,306 lbs. while the diesel weighs 15,651 lbs. The OC-126 has a dumping height of 10 feet 3.5 in. *Landis Zimmerman*

OC-46

With the relocation of the Oliver crawler factory from Cleveland to Charles City, Iowa came a newly-designed series of loaders: the Series B OC-46 and OC-96. As with previous versions, buckets for the OC-46 Series B were made by Ware and those for the OC-96 Series B were made by Heil. Both loaders had shuttle-shifting or travel reversers that allowed rapid shifting from forward to reverse, an important feature for a loader. *Landis Zimmerman*

OC-96

The 1¹/₈ yard capacity OC-96 was produced from 1959 to 1961. The weight of the crawler loader is 14,575 lbs. The OC-96 has an eight-foot dumping height and a beakout force rating of 9,200 lbs. It was replaced in 1962 with the Series B with a more powerful Hercules 4-cylinder diesel engine rated at 62 ghp. From 1959 to 1965, a Trans-O-Matic powershift transmission with two forward and two reverse speeds was standard on all OC-9 and OC-96 crawlers. *Landis Zimmerman*

CHAPTER THREE

DEERE & COMPANY

Deere & Company began as a tiny blacksmith shop started by John Deere in 1836 in the community of Grand Detour, Illinois. The following year, Deere developed the first self-scouring steel plow in his shop, which along with the harvester and thresher revolutionized farming. Deere also started the practice of building plows before he had orders, then taking them on the road to sell, rather than waiting for individual orders. As brisk sales followed, Deere opened a plow factory in Moline 12 years later. In 1868, the business was incorporated under the name of Deere & Company, the name of the company today. It is also one of the few firms in the construction and agricultural equipment businesses that has escaped mergers and buyouts. In 1918, Deere purchased the Waterloo Gasoline Traction Engine Co. of Waterloo, Iowa and began a legendary line of wheel and crawler tractors.

Deere in the Woods
A Model 1010 with a No. 624 blade pulls logs out of a forest while a sister machine loads the logs on a truck. *John Deere Construction Equipment Co./Jeff Huff*

The John Deere crawler tractor line is traced to the late 1920s, when the Lindeman Power Equipment Co. of Yakima, Washington started experimenting with converting Deere wheel tractors to crawler tractors. Until its association with Lindeman, Deere was largely an agricultural equipment company, having made only a few forays into construction and logging through its wagons, graders and specialized wheel tractors. The Lindeman conversions were mainly designed for orchard applications; the Yakima Valley is renowned for its prolific apple and cherry orchards. In the mid-1930s, Lindeman made similar modifications to Deere GPO and BO orchard tractors. The Model BO-L (orchard-Lindeman) sold very well, prompting Deere to buy Lindeman Power Equipment Co., including the Yakima factory in 1947. Deere believed there was a market for small and medium size crawlers, not only for orchards and farming, but in construction, logging and other industrial applications. It proved to be a wise decision for the company.

Deere redesigned the Model BO-L and produced its new Model MC in late 1948. The next year, Deere offered the Model 1000 tool carrier attachment for the MC, which included a blade and a hitch for special attachments. Crawler tractor assembly was moved to the company's Dubuque, Iowa facility in 1954, where it remains today. Dubuque Works now stretches over a mile in length and covers nearly 1,500 acres. In 1952 the MC was replaced by the Model 40C, which in turn was replaced by the Model 420C in 1955 and the 430C in 1958. Deere established a Construction Equipment Division in 1956 and offered 50 different attachments for crawler tractors. The Model 440C,

introduced in 1958, was available with either a Deere gasoline (440IC) or GM diesel engine (440ICD) and was the first Deere crawler to be painted Industrial Yellow.

The company introduced the first hydraulic direction reverser for its new Model 1010 and 2010 crawlers in 1960. The 1010 and 2010 were also the first Deere crawlers to have optional Deere-built diesel engines. In 1965, the 1010 and 2020 were replaced by the JD350 and JD450 models. Both models were available with either gas or diesel engines and with either dozer or loader attachments.

The bicentennial year 1976 saw the introduction of the JD750 dozer and JD755 loader with dual-path hydrostatic drive, a first in the industry. Both machines were rated at 110 ehp, the first Deere crawlers over the 100 hp mark. The JD850 dozer and JD855 loader, both with 145 ehp and hydrostatic drive, debuted in 1978 and remained the largest crawlers offered by the company until 2001.

In 1999, Deere offered the "H-Series" line of crawlers including the 450H, 550H and 650H tractors, while continuing its 455G, 555G, 655C and 755C crawler loaders. The two formerly largest dozers, the 750C and 850C, introduced in 1995, are also still in production as J-Series machines. However, two larger dozers have been added to the line: the 39-ton 1050C with 324 nhp in 2001 and the 26-ton 950J with 247 nhp in 2003. Both are powered by Liebherr diesel engines.

In 2003, Deere offered two crawler loaders: the 655C Series II and 755C Series II, both rear-engine machines, while the 455G and 555G loaders were dropped.

An undated aerial view of the Deere tractor factory in Waterloo, Iowa. *Don Heimburger*

Lindeman Power Equipment Co.

Founder Jesse G. Lindeman was born in 1900 on a farm in Cass County, Iowa. After serving in the U.S. Army's Air Service during WWI, he settled in the fertile Yakima Valley of Washington in 1920. Jesse and brothers Harry and Ross worked for a farm implement company, which went bankrupt in 1923. The enterprising brothers bought the remains of the firm and in 1924 were awarded a Holt Tractor dealership. However, in the following year after the Best-Holt merger, the newly-formed Caterpillar Tractor Co. rescinded their franchise in favor of a longer-established Best Tractor dealer in the area.

Undaunted, the brothers became the John Deere dealer for the Yakima area under the name Lindeman Power Equipment Co. late in 1925. Fourth brother Joseph joined the company that year. The Lindemans produced a long line of implements specially designed for the burgeoning fruit growing industry in the area. These included roto-tillers, orchard disc harrows, orchard sprayers, land-slopers, two-way plows, hydraulic hitches, tool carriers and special equipment for harvesting and hauling fruit.

The Lindemans also started modifying John Deere wheel tractors to make them better suited for orchard work. Wheel tractors lacked the low clearances, maneuverability to weave around tree trunks and the traction to climb the steep orchard hills. They began with a Model D tractor, to which they added a set of tracks from a Best crawler. Next they converted a Model GPO, the first

Deere tractor specifically designed for orchard tasks. Both conversions were marginally successful; however, when Deere launched its Model B line in 1935, the Lindemans had the perfect tractor for crawler conversions. After testing a number of machines, they started assembly line production in March 1939.

Under an agreement, Deere shipped the engines and transmissions to Yakima where they received a Lindeman undercarriage. At peak production after WWII, the company employed more than 400 people. Most of the assembly line conversions were on Model BO tractors; however, a few BRs and at least one BI also got Lindeman crawlers. The price of a Lindeman BO-L crawler was $1,315 with an additional $17.50 for a PTO. A total of 1,732 Lindeman conversions were made until January 15, 1947, when Deere purchased Lindeman for $1,250,000 and took over production.

In 1954, Jesse and Joseph Lindeman established Northwest Equipment Co. and continued making agricultural and industrial tractor attachments. Joseph died in 1982 and Jesse sold the company. A smaller firm, Lindex Co., Inc. was started in 1985 under Jesse's direction. It made power takeoff units and three-point hitches for crawler tractors. Jesse Lindeman passed away in 1992 at age 92.

John Deere BO tractor
The (BO) orchard version of the Model B wheel tractor was offered from 1935 through 1952. Although Lindeman modified a few other models, the BO was the tractor of choice for its track conversions with 1,625 converted.

Lindeman Model BO-L
Here is a rear view of the Lindeman BO-L tractor with steel tail seat. With the track frame only 9 in. off the ground, no exhaust stack or air intake above the hood, and low tail seat, the machine was well adapted for the low clearances of orchard work.

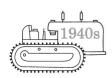

John Deere-Lindeman BO-L

The Model BO-L (Lindeman track conversion on a Deere BO tractor) was produced from 1939 to 1947. The tractor shown is a 1947 machine, one of the last BO-L models produced. Deere acquired Lindeman in 1947 and replaced the BO-L with the Model MC in late 1948. Since this tractor was built after the Lindeman acquisition, it should be called a Deere Model BO-C (BO tractor with crawlers). The BO uses a Deere 2-cylinder gas engine which was tested at the University of Nebraska at 18.53 bhp and 14.03 dbhp.

MC

Offered from late 1948 (the first Model MC rolled out of the factory on December 28, 1948) to 1952, the MC was the first crawler tractor designed and built by Deere. The "M" stood for the two-cylinder, 100.5-cu. in engine adapted from the Deere Model M farm tractor; the "C" identified it as a crawler tractor. The tractor weighs 3,875 lbs. without attachments and has a 2-cylinder gas engine rated at 20.45 bhp and 18.15 dbhp.

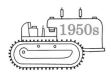

40C

The Model 40C replaced the MC in the summer of 1952, and it was in production through 1955. The horsepower of the 40C increased to 24.9 bhp and 22.4 dbhp. Weight of the 40C is an even 2 tons. The 40C proved to be a popular tractor, with more than 17,000 units sold.

420C

The Model 420C took the place of the 40C in 1956, and it was offered through 1958. The tractor is powered by a 113-cu. in Deere gasoline engine rated at 29.21 bhp, 27.08 dbhp; distillate and LP gas engines were also offered.

420C

The 420C weighs between 4,150 and 4,700 lbs. depending on track width. It was offered with standard 12 in. or optional 10 in. and 14 in. tracks, or 12 in. snow tracks with four or five track rollers. *Jeff Huff*

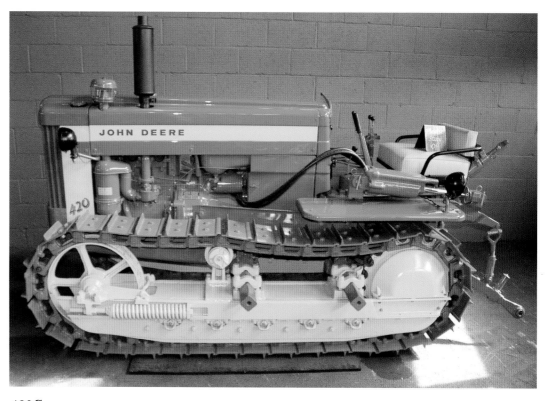

420C

This 420C 27-drawbar horsepower crawler was built in 1957, and is one of 5,336 built. It weighs just over two tons, and when not on display at the John Deere Pavilion in Moline, Illinois, it is kept at owner Barry Stelford's home in Urbana, Illinois.

430C

RIGHT. Deere introduced the Model 430C in 1958, and it was sold through 1960. It uses the same 2-cylinder Deere gas engine as the 420C with 29.21 bhp and 27.08 dbhp and has the same weight (4,150-4,700 lbs.). *John Deere Construction Equipment Co.*

440IC

BELOW. The 440IC was offered from 1958 to 1960 with two versions available: the 440IC with a Deere gasoline engine rated at 29.72 bhp and 24.12 dbhp, and the 440ICD with a GM 2-53 diesel rated at 32.88 bhp and 26.15 dbhp. The letter I indicates an industrial machine, C stands for crawler and D for diesel power. The weight of the 440IC is 5,850 lbs.; weight of the 440ICD is 6,220 lbs. These were the first Deere crawlers to be painted Industrial Yellow.

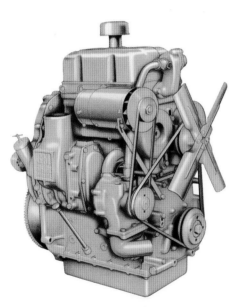

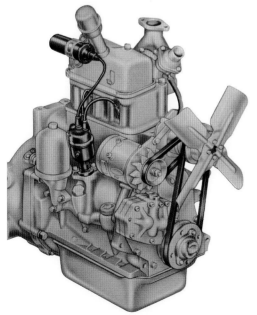

602 BULLDOZER

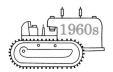

350

RIGHT. Deere dropped the "C" or crawler designation from its model numbers in the early 1960s. The Model 350 was introduced in 1965, and it continued through 1970 when it was replaced by the 350B. The 350 was available with either 3-cylinder Deere gas or diesel engines; both produce 42 ehp and 30 dbhp. The weight of the Model 350 is 9,300 lbs.

450

BELOW. Like the Model 350, the 450 was introduced in 1965, and it was also available with either gas or diesel power. The gas engine is a four-cylinder as is the Deere diesel. Both are rated at 57 ehp and 44 dbhp. The Model 450 weighs between 10,590 and 12,578 lbs. *John Deere Construction Equipment Co.*

350C

The Model 350C appeared in 1975 and was produced through 1986. It weighs 10,099 lbs. and is powered by a Deere 3-cylinder diesel engine with 42 ehp. This machine is a wide-track version, photographed in the snow in Maryland. Deere's first wide-track crawler was introduced in 1966 on the Model 350.

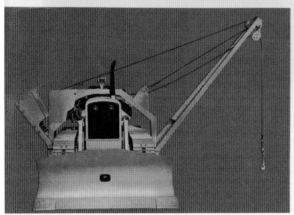

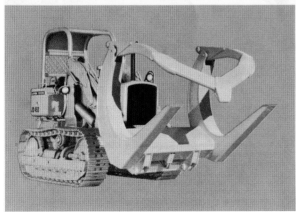
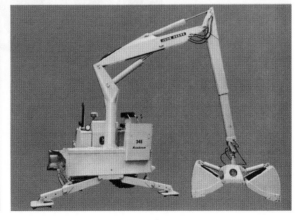

450 Attachments
A wide variety of attachments were available for the Model 450 including (from upper left) ripper, brush rake and operator protection, cable layer, backhoe, clamshell, log loader, and side boom. *John Deere Construction Equipment Co.*

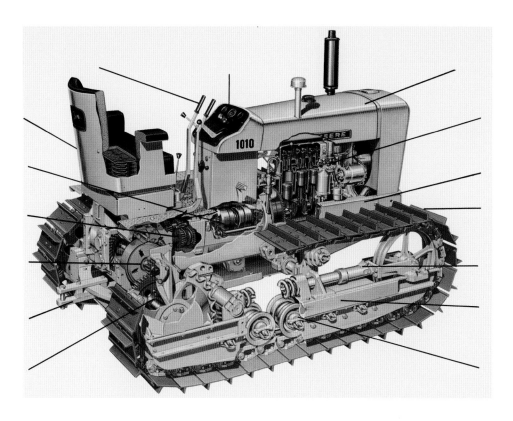

1010 Logging Special

ABOVE. A Model 1010 with winch, inside-mounted blade and operator's protection was available for loggers.

LEFT. An operator's view of the controls and gauges of a 1010 dozer. *John Deere Construction Equipment Co.*

1010C

ABOVE LEFT. The Model 1010C appeared in 1960 and remained in the product line through 1965. It was available with either a Deere 4-cylinder diesel engine or 4-cylinder gasoline engine; both are rated at 41.5 ehp. The diesel version weighs 6,850 lbs; the gasoline version weighs 6,748 lbs. *John Deere Construction Equipment Co.*

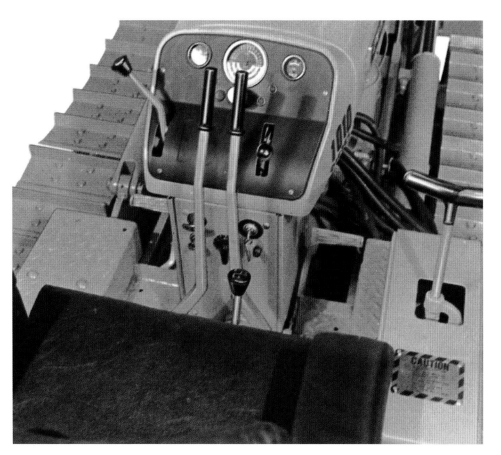

2010C

Like its sister 1010C Model, the 2010C was offered from 1960 through 1965. And like the 1010C, two versions were offered: a diesel-powered model with a four-cylinder engine (52 ehp) and weight of 8,864 lbs., and a 4-cylinder gasoline-powered model, also with 52 ehp and weight of 8,762 lbs. The 2010C also came with a choice of either a four-range forward hydraulic transmission with Hi-Lo reverse or a four-range constant-mesh manual transmission. This Model 2010C works with a No. 624 outside-mounted blade. *Pit & Quarry*

Other Applications for the 2010C
The Model 2010C could be rigged for log loading, excavation with front-end loader and backhoe attachments, logging, cable laying and pipeline work. *John Deere Construction Equipment Co.*

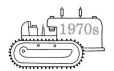

750
The 750 was offered from 1976 to 1986. Power is provided by a Deere 6-414T diesel engine rated at 110 ehp; it was the first Deere crawler to exceed 100 hp.

550
Deere introduced the Model 550 in 1976 with a 72 ehp Deere 4-276T turbocharged engine. The 550B appeared in 1985 with 78 ehp from the same engine. The 550B weighs 15,536 lbs.

750B

RIGHT. Introduced in 1985, the 750B was rated at 120 ehp from its 6-414T 6-cylinder turbocharged diesel engine, 10 hp more than the Model 750.

850

BELOW. Launched in 1978, the Model 850 was Deere's largest dozer for 23 years, when it was upstaged by the 1050C in 2001. The 850 is powered by a Deere 6-619T 6-cylinder diesel rated at 145 ehp and weighing 36,124 lbs. The 850 was available with a standard model 6545 blade measuring 10 ft. 3 in. wide or a Model 5640 angledozer blade measuring 12 ft. 8 in. wide that can be hydraulically angled up to 250 degrees to the left or right and hydraulically tilted. *John Deere Construction Equipment Co.*

Operator's view of the 850
John Deere Construction Equipment Co.

420C

Offered between 1956 and 1958, the 420C is powered by a 2-cylinder gas engine with 29 bhp and 27 dbhp. The 4,700 lb. loader has the longer 5-roller tracks for lower ground pressure and stability. The bucket is a Model 90 with 1/3 yard capacity. The 420C front loader shown is a 1957 model.

2010C

The 2010C crawler was available with a 1 yard heavy duty bucket, as shown here, a 1 1/2 yard light material bucket or log loader. *John Deere Construction Equipment Co.*

Models 440IC and 440ICD loaders
The 7/8 yard Model 440IC loader was available from 1958 through 1960 with a Deere gasoline engine or an optional GM 2-53 diesel. The diesel was rated at 32.9 bhp and the gasoline at 29.7 bhp. *John Deere Construction Equipment Co.*

1010C

ABOVE. The 1010C loader in action. *John Deere Construction Equipment Co.*

1010C

BELOW. In addition to the ³⁄₄ yard heavy duty bucket and 1¹⁄₄ yard light material bucket, a number of other attachments were available for the 1010C including hydraulic ripper, pulpwood loader, timber loader, fork-lift, dozer blade and loader-dozer combination. As with the 1010C dozer, the loader was offered from 1960 to 1965 with Deere gasoline or diesel engines rated at 41.5 ehp. *John Deere Construction Equipment Co.*

LOWER RIGHT. A 1010C loader with backhoe digs a utility trench.

ATTACHMENTS

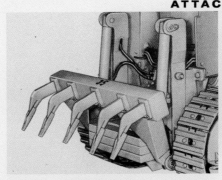

35 Hydraulic Ripper: Working width: 44 in.; Penetration: 10-3/4 in. max. Positive down pressure. Shanks: Uses 1 to 5 (3 are standard equipment), adjustable for depth. Replaceable tips. Three counterweights.

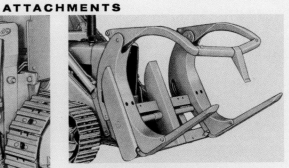

Pulpwood Loader: Choice of widths (center to center of forks) 47-5/16 in. (Model 850-C) or 29-3/16 in. (Model 850-D). Fork length: 41-3/4 in. Upper grapple: dual-cylinder operation. Continuous-radius masts. Lift, at ground—7100 lb.; Lift at 10 ft.—3800 lb.

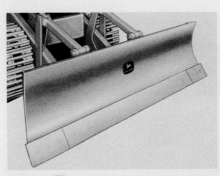

805 Bulldozer Blade: Box-welded, 23-inch-high mold-board. Reversible 3-piece cutting edge, 72 in. wide. Penetration: 10 in. max. Tilt: manual, 14 in. right, 7 in. left. Hydraulic pitch adjustment. Depth-gauge shoes are available.

806 Bulldozer (not shown): For use in conjunction with loader. Can be removed or remounted in minutes. Box-section boom and blade. Reversible 3-piece cutting edge, 90 in. wide. Lift: 42-1/2 in. Cut: 17 in. max. Angling: 25 degrees right or left.

850-A Basic Fork Lift: Width: adjusts 18-3/4 to 48 in. center to center of forks. Fork length: 41-3/4 in. Pivot shaft: 2-9/16 in. dia. steel rod.

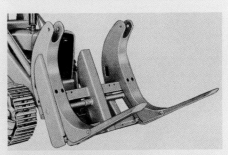

850-B Timber Loader: Fork settings: 47-5/16 or 29-3/16 in. center to center. Forks: 41-3/4 in. long; box construction; heat-treated cast-steel tips. Continuous-radius masts.

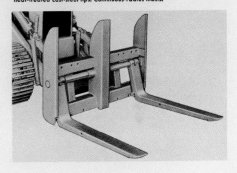

3-21-2

95

350

ABOVE. Introduced in 1965, the Model 350 was available with a ³/₄ yard standard bucket and a No. 93 backhoe. Two other optional buckets were a 1¹/₄ yard light material and Drott 4-in-1 with ³/₄ yard capacity. The 350 was available with either Deere gasoline or diesel engines; both were rated at 42 ehp.

450

RIGHT. The Model 450 loader was available with several bucket options: a 1¹/₈ yard digging bucket, a 1³/₄ yard light material bucket and a 1¹/₈ yard Drott 4-in-1 bucket that served as a clamshell, loader, scraper and dozer. *John Deere Construction Equipment Co.*

455E

The 450 series of loaders evolved to the 450B in 1970 with 65 ehp, and the 450C in 1974, also with 65 ehp. In the early 1980s, the loaders became the 455 series while the dozers remained as 450s. A Model 455E loader awaits its next assignment in Warrenton, Virginia.

455D

Available in the early 1980s, the 455D was rated at 67 ehp from a Deere 4-cylinder turbocharged diesel engine. With its standard 1¼ yard bucket, the loader weighs 17,150 lbs.

Backhoe attachment
The easily-attached backhoe unit for the 455G loader makes it a very versatile machine, particularly for new home construction.

555 loader-backhoe
The 555 produces 78 ehp from its Deere 4-276T turbocharged engine and weighs 18,800 lbs. with its 9300 backhoe. The machine was photographed at a used equipment dealer's yard in Montvale, Virginia. The bucket capacity is 1³/₈ yards.

755

The 2 yard 755 loader was initially offered with 110 ehp from its 6-414T engine, but power was increased in the mid 1980s to 120 ehp. This Model 755B was photographed at Herndon, Virginia and weighs 35,000 lbs. By contrast, the current Model 755C Series II loader has a bucket capacity of 3.14 yards, 177 nhp and a weight of 46,300 lbs.

855

The Model 855 has a 2¾ yard bucket and is powered by a Deere 6-619T engine rated at 145 ghp. *Richard Yaremko*

CHAPTER FOUR

EIMCO CORPORATION

The name Eimco evolved from the Eastern Iron and Metals Co., a Utah-based manufacturer of mining machinery and ore processing equipment. The company was established in 1884 by Nathan Rosenblatt, an emigrant from the Brest-Litvosk area of southwestern Russia. Rosenblatt learned iron casting in Russia and found there was a need for cast iron tools and equipment in the mining camps of the Western U.S.

Initially, Rosenblatt took covered wagons full of tools and reconditioned equipment to sell at the mining camps. As his business grew, he opened a shop in Salt Lake City, Utah and in 1913 acquired the American Foundry & Machinery Co., a

Model 104B "Rocker Shovel"

This 104B overshot loader is on display at the World Museum of Mining in Butte, Montana. The World Museum is a fitting place for the machine, since it was developed from an underground mine loader and in close association with Anaconda Mining Co., the operator of most of the copper mines in and around Butte. The overshot loader is mounted on a Caterpillar D-4 (7U) tractor with a 55 fwhp D-315 engine.

local foundry. The foundry enabled Eastern Iron and Metals to become a manufacturer of new equipment and tools. The "Eastern" part of the name referred to Salt Lake City being in eastern Utah and east of most of the region's mining activity in the late 19th century.

In 1916, Rosenblatt opened Utah's first open-hearth steel mill but still specialized in making mining machinery. His son Joseph took over the reins of the company in the late 1920s and steered it through a long period of diversification and growth. By 1930, the name had been shortened to Eimco, which is still in use.

Also in 1930, Eimco joined with Anaconda Mining Co. to develop an automated "shoveler" to remove rock and ore from new drifts, a task that had been done by manual labor since the dawn of the iron age. The machine created used a small bucket with air-driven rocker arms to pick up material and dump it into an ore car behind. This was the first commercially successful mechanical mine loader. The prototype was called the Eimco-Findlay Shovel and was tested in 1931 at Anaconda's North Lilly Mine in Eureka, Utah.

Two years later, Eimco marketed its Model 11 Rocker-Shovel, a 1/4 yard underground loader mounted on railroad wheels. The unit, powered by an Ingersoll-Rand compressed air motor, was a huge success. Models 12 (1/4 yard) and 20 (1/3 yard) appeared in 1936, and the Model 40 with a 1/2 yard bucket was introduced in 1938; all moved on narrow gauge railroad wheels. During WWII, large numbers of Eimco underground loaders were used in Malta, Gibraltar, and other sites in Europe and the Pacific to carve out bomb shelters for command posts and storage cavities for munitions and supplies.

In 1950, Eimco introduced its first above-ground, crawler-mounted loader, the Model 104 Rocker-Shovel. The overshot

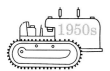

Model 104 "Rocker-Shovel"
The Eimco overshot loader fills a Koehring Dumptor quarry truck in 1951. The machine shown has a two-yard bucket for loading sand and gravel. Eimco advertised that the Model 104 could load up to 6 yards per minute. *Pit & Quarry*

loader was mounted on a Caterpillar D-4 tractor with several bucket sizes available from 1¼ to 2 yards. Success of the Model 104 led to development of other crawler-mounted machines. In 1954, the company offered its Model 105 series which could be ordered with bulldozer, front-end loader or overshot loader attachments. Rather than using Caterpillar tractors, Eimco designed and built its own undercarriages with Cummins and GM diesel power.

Always maintaining close ties to the mining industry, the company tried to incorporate special needs such as the ability to work in unusually hard rock, in tight quarters, and in areas with poor visibility. Unique features of the dozer/loader were its single-cast mainframe, rear-mounted engine and independently-powered tracks. Dozer attachments were expanded to angledozers, push plates, U-blades and ripping and land-clearing blades; a number of different bucket types were also offered for the loaders.

Special models were offered for heavy duty work such as in steel mills and for smelter material handling. By the early 1960s, Eimco offered three series of crawlers ranging from 100 to 218 hp: the 103, 106 and 165. Like the Model 105 series, they were available with dozer, front loader, log stacker or Rocker-Shovel attachments. Bucket sizes ranged from 1½ to 3 yards. Model numbers for the 103/105/106 tractors were increased by 20 for the front loaders (123/125/126), by 30 for the heavy duty steel mill loaders, and 40 for the log loaders.

The last crawler model from Eimco was the 165, which was available from 1961 until about 1969. It was powered by GM 6V-53 or Cummins V6R-180 engines rated at 175 fwhp.

Model 103
Eimco introduced the Model 103 in 1959. With its rear-mounted engine, it continued the design from the Model 105 of 1954. Initially, the 103 was powered by a 100-fwhp Cummins 4-cylinder diesel engine; it was later offered with a GM 4-71 diesel or a Cummins 6-cylinder engine with 159 fwhp. *Pit & Quarry*

During the mid-1950s, Joseph Rosenblatt realized that Eimco would need significantly more capital to stay in the crawler tractor business and decided to sell the company to the Ogden Corp. in 1957. Rosenblatt remained as head of the new Eimco Division until 1963. Evirotech of Menlo Park, California took over the Eimco Division in 1969 and stopped manufacturing crawler tractors that year, concentrating on underground mining machiery.

In 1982, Eimco's Mining Equipment Division was acquired by Baker International of Houston, Texas, which became part of Tampella OY of Finland in 1989. The Swedish mining and construction group, Sandvik AB, purchased the Eimco Mining Equipment Division in 1997. Its Western Region office is still located in Salt Lake City. As part of this deal, the rights to the Rocker-Shovel loader line were acquired by Trident S.A. of South Africa. Trident continues to offer this line of underground mining equipment including a crawler-mounted version with a ¾ yard bucket.

EIMCO 103 DOZER — STRAIGHT BLADE

CABLE CONTROL — SINGLE DRUM

100 H.P. DIESEL ENGINE

33,600 LBS. MAXIMUM DRAWBAR PULL

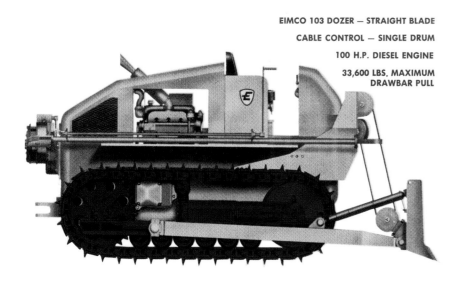

Model 105
ABOVE. Introduced in 1954, the Model 105 was available with either hydraulic or cable-operated straight or angle-dozer blades. *Roger Amato*

Model 103 dozer with cable-operated blade
The weight of the dozer with cable control is 22,400 lbs. Blade dimensions are 8 ft. 3 in. wide and 38 in. high. *Roger Amato*

Model 103 dozer with hydraulic blade
LOWER LEFT. Blade dimensions are the same as the Model 103 with a cable-controlled blade. The weight of the dozer is slightly more at 22,900 lbs. *Roger Amato*

EIMCO 103 DOZER

STRAIGHT BLADE HYDRAULIC CONTROL

100 H.P. DIESEL ENGINE

33,600 LBS. MAXIMUM DRAWBAR PULL

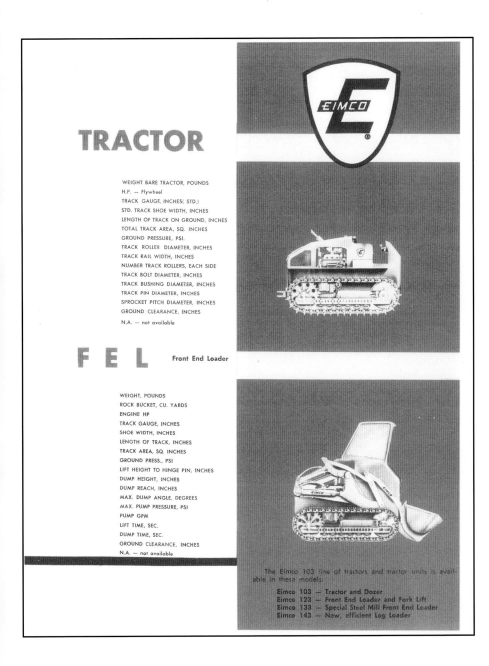

TRACTOR

WEIGHT BARE TRACTOR, POUNDS
H.P. — Flywheel
TRACK GAUGE, INCHES(STD.)
STD. TRACK SHOE WIDTH, INCHES
LENGTH OF TRACK ON GROUND, INCHES
TOTAL TRACK AREA, SQ. INCHES
GROUND PRESSURE, PSI.
TRACK ROLLER DIAMETER, INCHES
TRACK RAIL WIDTH, INCHES
NUMBER TRACK ROLLERS, EACH SIDE
TRACK BOLT DIAMETER, INCHES
TRACK BUSHING DIAMETER, INCHES
TRACK PIN DIAMETER, INCHES
SPROCKET PITCH DIAMETER, INCHES
GROUND CLEARANCE, INCHES

N.A. — not available

F E L   Front End Loader

WEIGHT, POUNDS
ROCK BUCKET, CU. YARDS
ENGINE HP
TRACK GAUGE, INCHES
SHOE WIDTH, INCHES
LENGTH OF TRACK, INCHES
TRACK AREA, SQ. INCHES
GROUND PRESS., PSI
LIFT HEIGHT TO HINGE PIN, INCHES
DUMP HEIGHT, INCHES
DUMP REACH, INCHES
MAX. DUMP ANGLE, DEGREES
MAX. PUMP PRESSURE, PSI
PUMP GPM
LIFT TIME, SEC.
DUMP TIME, SEC.
GROUND CLEARANCE, INCHES

N.A. — not available

The Eimco 103 line of tractors and tractor units is available in these models:

Eimco 103 — Tractor and Dozer
Eimco 123 — Front End Loader and Fork Lift
Eimco 133 — Special Steel Mill Front End Loader
Eimco 143 — New, efficient Log Loader

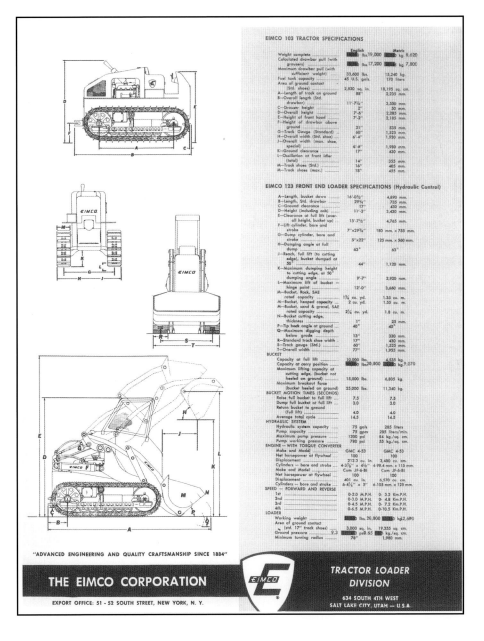

103

Specifications for the Model 103 tractor and front end loader.
James Owensby

Model 105 dozer
With a hydraulic angledozer attached, the Model 105 weighs 34,000 lbs. *Vernon Simpson*

Model 105
Eimco had the Model 105 tested at the Nebraska Tractor Test Lab in 1958. The tractor produced 72.29 dbhp and pulled 27,141 lbs., or 90.6% of its 29,955-lb. weight. No belt hp was reported. The 105 was the only Eimco model that was independently tested. *Vernon Simpson*

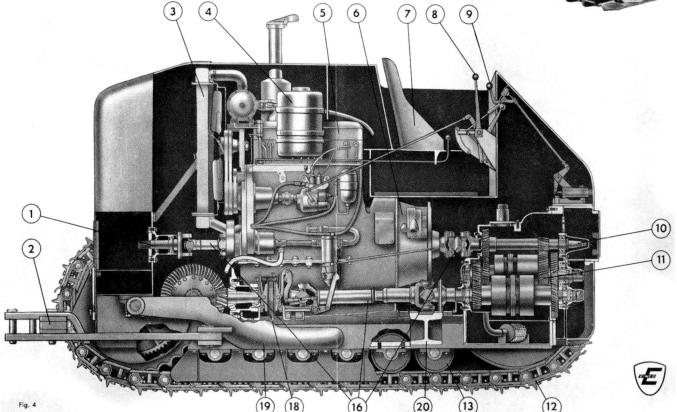

1. Rear power take-off
2. Drawbar
3. Radiator
4. Air cleaners
5. Power unit
6. Torque converter
7. Seat
8. Auxiliary equipment controls
9. Tractor controls and instruments
10. Front power take-off
11. Main transmission
12. Track
13. Track rollers
16. Universal joints
18. Brakes
19. Diagonal brace
20. Equalizer bar

Model 105
A cutaway drawing of the Model 105 tractor. *Vernon Simpson*

EIMCO'S UNIQUE TRANSMISSION

A bird's-eye view cutaway of the Model 105 shows the torque converter transmission and drive trains that allow independent full power to each track. This enabled reversal of one track and forward motion on the other at the same time for pivotal turning and was one of the earliest offerings of this feature. The transmission also allowed shifting from one speed to another while in motion and under full load. The machine could also be instantly reversed at any speed. The Eimco transmission combined features of the torque converter, constant mesh gearing (every gear stays in constant mesh), and hydraulically-actuated friction clutches. It had a sealed oil bath and pressured lubrication to all parts.

The shaft arrangement of the transmission is shown in the accompanying drawing. The gears and power input shaft from the engine and torque converter are on the right. This shaft turns constantly while the engine is running. The individual drive shafts to each of the final drives are powered on demand from the transmission. These shafts can be reversed individually so that either track can be driven forward or in reverse for spin turns. Since all gears are on parallel shafts, no planetary gears are needed, thus eliminating high-wear parts. *Vernon Simpson*

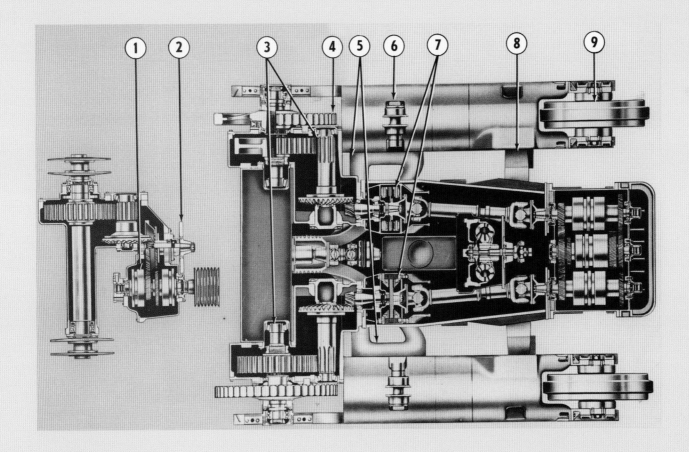

Model 105

Front and side drawings of the 1½ yard Model 105 Rocker-Shovel. *Vernon Simpson*

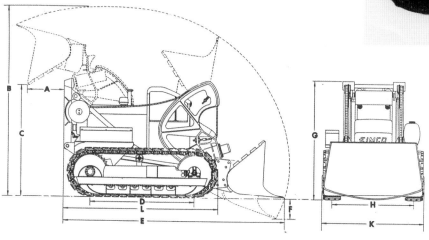

SPECIFICATIONS

PATENTED AND PATENTS PENDING

Model 105

A Model 105 with Rocker-Shovel attachment. *Historical Construction Equipment Association*

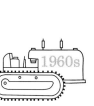

Model 106

The Model 106 is powered by a GM 6V-71 diesel with 205 fwhp. It was available from 1959 to 1962, when replaced by the 106B with 218 fwhp and the 106C in 1964. *Historical Construction Equipment Association*

NOW . . .

. . . even stronger

one-piece arms . . .

. . . with Eimco's unitized "Stress Flow construction on every Eimco Front End Loader

LOOK WHAT THE EIMCO 165 WILL DO FOR YOU . . .

Model 165

The Model 165 Tractor Dozer was offered from 1962 through 1969 and was the last crawler model built by the company. The 165 was upgraded to the 165B in 1963 and to the 165C in 1964, all with the same power rating. Power is supplied by either a GM 6V-53 or Cummins V6R-180 engine; both are rated at 175 fwhp. The weight of the tractor ranges from 31,000 lbs. for the early version to 38,300 lbs. for the last version, the 165C. *Roger Amato*

Model 126 Loader

ABOVE. Based on the Model 106 tractor, the 3 yard 126 loader was also powered by a GM 6V-71 engine with a rating of 205 fwhp. The Model 126 weighs 58,800 lbs. *Historical Construction Equipment Association*

Model 123 Loader

RIGHT. The 123 loader was based on the 103 tractor. The Model 123 has a 2½ yard bucket and a GM 4-53 engine with 100 bhp. The loader went through several upgrades, primarily with engines. The 123B produced 150 fwhp, and the 123C produced 159 fwhp.

CHAPTER FIVE

EUCLID ROAD MACHINERY COMPANY, EUCLID & TEREX DIVISIONS OF GENERAL MOTORS CORPORATION & TEREX CORPORATION

Euclid was established as the Euclid Crane and Hoist Co. in 1909. As the name advertised, the firm initally manufactured lifting equipment; the Euclid part of the name came from the Cleveland, Ohio suburb where the company's shop was situated. George Armington, founder of Euclid and his five sons, steered the firm for more than 50 years.

TC-12-2
This 1958 Model TC-12-2 moves dirt with a Gar Wood cable blade at the 2008 HCEA Show in Brownsville, Pennsylvania. The horsepower for the TC-12-2 is listed at 431 ghp and 402 fwhp from its pair of GM 6-71 engines.

One of the sons, Arthur Armington, was placed in charge of developing a line of earthmoving equipment, and he managed this unit until his death in 1937. Arthur experimented with various types of earthmoving equipment such as pulled scrapers and dump-wagons in the early 1920s and organized a Road Machinery Division in 1926. Rapid sales in the division, including a line of hydraulically-operated bulldozer blades, led to the establishment of the Euclid Road Machinery Co. in 1931.

Euclid unveiled its first rubber-tired tractor with a 7-cu.-yd. bottom dump trailer in 1934. From this machine, Euclid grew to become the leading off-road dump truck and dump trailer maker for the next 30 years. It also challenged LeTourneau and the other early motor scraper builders with its own single-engine model in 1938 and a twin-engine version in 1948.

Even though Arthur Armington was interested in crawler tractors and had built a few experimental models, Euclid Road Machinery stayed out of the crawler business, preferring to concentrate on rubber tired tractors, off-road trucks, scrapers and belt loaders. The company felt that developing a crawler line would be a drain of its capital and would detract from its other products. However, the Armingtons could see that Euclid's main competitors — Caterpillar, Allis-Chalmers and International Harvester — had crawler tractors and were rapidly expanding their construction equipment lines to be a one-stop shop for supplying nearly every product that an earthmoving contractor needed.

To remain in the business, the Armingtons realized that Euclid would have to become a part of a company with deeper pockets, so they approached the company with the deepest pockets of all in the early 1950s, General Motors. General Motors liked the deal and acquired Euclid in 1953, making it an operating division. GM was already interested in getting into the construction equipment business, and many of Euclid's machines used GM diesel engines, so the Euclid acquisition proved to be a perfect match.

Ironically, the first new product after the takeover was a crawler, the twin-engine TC-12 bulldozer in 1955. With 388 ghp and a weight of 32 tons, it was by far the largest crawler tractor in the world, and it was watched closely by Caterpillar and the other crawler makers. A single-engine dozer roughly half the size of the TC-12 was launched in 1958. Called the C-6, it was the forerunner of a line of dozers that was sold through the 1980s. In 1963, the Euclid Division bought the rights to Gar Wood's line of dozer blades and allied equipment. Gar Wood had been the principal supplier of attachments for Euclid crawlers.

Euclid experimented with wheel dozers between 1949 and the early 1970s, but none were made in large quantities. However, much of this work formed the basis for the Euclid (and later Terex) wheel loaders which first appeared in 1957.

The Euclid Division of GM was split due to an antitrust suit in 1968. The off-road dump truck line was sold to White Motor Co., while the earthmoving part of Euclid became GM's Terex Division. Terex crawlers were designated by an "82" followed by the model number, a practice started by Euclid in 1966. Thus, the C-6 became the Model 82-30, the TC-12 became the 82-80, along with several other new models.

In 1980, the Terex Division was purchased by the IHB Group of Germany, which declared bankruptcy in 1983. Terex became part of the Northwest Engineering Company in 1986, and the company stopped building crawler tractors the same year. It is now an independent corporation and has expanded greatly by acquiring other equipment makers; however, it still has not re-entered the crawler tractor business.

TC-12
The earliest production version of the TC-12 had combined power of 388 ghp and 365 fwhp and featured an automobile-like grill, somewhat similar to the Corvette grills of the mid-1950s. *Vernon Simpson*

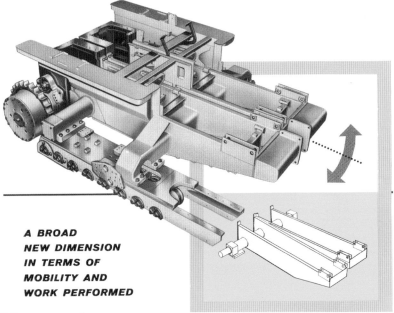

TC-12 main frame
The two sides of the tractor are mounted on separate frames which allows limited oscillation on a 7" diameter cross shaft (dead axle). This dual construction permits separation of the two halves for easier transporting. *Vernon Simpson*

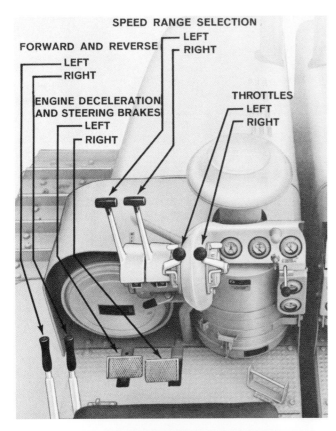

SPEED RANGE SELECTION
— LEFT
— RIGHT

FORWARD AND REVERSE
— LEFT
— RIGHT

ENGINE DECELERATION AND STEERING BRAKES
— LEFT
— RIGHT

THROTTLES
— LEFT
— RIGHT

TC-12 controls

The TC-12 can be steered in several ways: (1) a gradual change in direction is made by adjusting the speed of one engine, (2) a conventional turn is made by putting one transmission in neutral and applying the brake and (3) the tractor can be spun around its center axis by running one crawler forward and the other in reverse. *Vernon Simpson*

TC-12

BOTTOM & MIDDLE LEFT. A prototype TC-12 is being tested by GM-Euclid in 1954. *Pit & Quarry*

TC-12

BOTTOM RIGHT. A rear view of one of the earliest TC-12 dozers. *Pit & Quarry*

EUCLID TC-12

Shortly after acquiring Euclid, General Motors' management decided the time was right to enter the crawler tractor market. However, to do so successfully, they knew they would have to make a big splash. As both construction projects and equipment were growing steadily larger, GM began work on what would become the world's largest bulldozer. Rather than a machine with one large engine, designers and engineers focused on a twin-engine crawler.

This was not an entirely new concept; R.G. LeTourneau had successfully built motor scrapers in the late 1930s and 1940s with two side-by-side engines, and Caterpillar dealer Peterson Tractor Co. tested twin engines on a D-8 dozer as early as 1950. Also, the Army's Engineering Research and Development Laboratory had experimented with double engine bulldozers and crawler tractors in the early 1950s.

After testing several prototypes extensively in 1954-55, the TC-12 debuted later in 1955. It was powered by two GM 6-71 engines with combined gross horsepower of 388 and 365 fwhp. Each motor drives one track through a propeller shaft and a unit assembly that includes a Torquematic transmission with three forward and three reverse speeds, a steering brake and a planetary final drive. The transmission has no clutches, and shifting is done under full power. The weight of the tractor is about 53,000 lbs., or 64,000 lbs. with a blade attached. The dimensions of the machine are 16 ft. long, 11 ft. 4 in. wide, and it was available with either a 13.5-ft. standard blade or a 17-ft. angledozer blade. Rear-mounted radiators were another unique feature of the TC-12 (and later Euclid dozers). Rear-mounted radiators were more efficient at cooling and less prone to damage from rock, dirt and dust.

TC-12

Euclid Division engineers continued fine-tuning the TC-12 and replaced it with the TC-12-1 in 1956. The horsepower was increased to 436 gross and 413 flywheel and weight with blade was increased to 67,000 lbs. In 1958, the Model TC-12-2 was issued with total weight increased to 71,250 lbs. This turned out to be the most popular version, with 512 units sold. This is a view of the rear-mounted radiators on a TC-12-2 push dozer on display at the 2002 HCEA Show in Albany, Minnesota.

TC-12

A Gar Wood push block is mounted on this TC-12-2. Push-loading large scrapers was a duty for which the TC-12 was specifically designed.

C-6

Shortly after Euclid unveiled the TC-12, the division developed a single engine crawler. Called the C-6, it is in effect half of a TC-12. It is powered by a GM 6-71 engine with 218 gross hp (207 fwhp and 194 drawbar hp) and weighs 34,000 lbs. with blade attached. Between 1955 and 1957, the Euclid Division built and tested 30 pre-production machines. Commercial production of the C-6 began in 1958; an improved Model C-6-2 appeared in 1959 with nine more horsepower and four tons of additional weight. This machine with a cable-operated blade was photographed in a field near Dubuque, Iowa on the Illinois side of the Mississippi River. *Don Heimburger*

C-6-3

In 1959, Euclid made a number of changes to the C-6 and added a series number after the "6" to identify the newer models, from the C-6-2 to the C-6-5. The changes resulted in increased power (227 gross hp and 42,000 lbs. for the C-6-2 to 240 ghp and 43,100 lbs. for the C-6-5). This machine is a Model C-6 Series 3, built in 1962 with a hydraulically-operated blade. It was in operation at the 1998 HCEA National Show in Lapeer, Michigan.

C-6

A wide variety of blades and other attachments were offered for the C-6 tractor. *Vernon Simpson*

ANGLE BLADE SHOWING WELD-ON PUSH PLATE

FULL "U" BLADE WITH AUXILIARY DIRT SHIELD

STRAIGHT BLADE FOR GENERAL PURPOSES

COAL DOZING BLADE OVER 17' WIDE

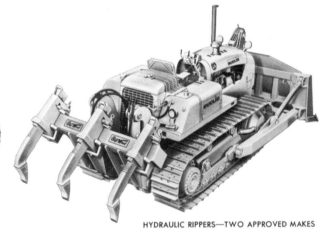

HYDRAULIC RIPPERS—TWO APPROVED MAKES

HYDRAULIC RIPPERS

FRONT MOUNTED PUSH BLOCK ON "C" FRAME

REAR MOUNTED SOLID PUSH BLOCK

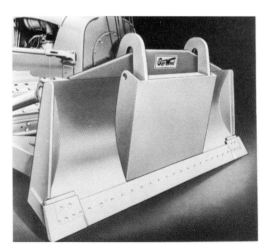

DETACHABLE PUSH PLATE MOUNTED ON BLADE

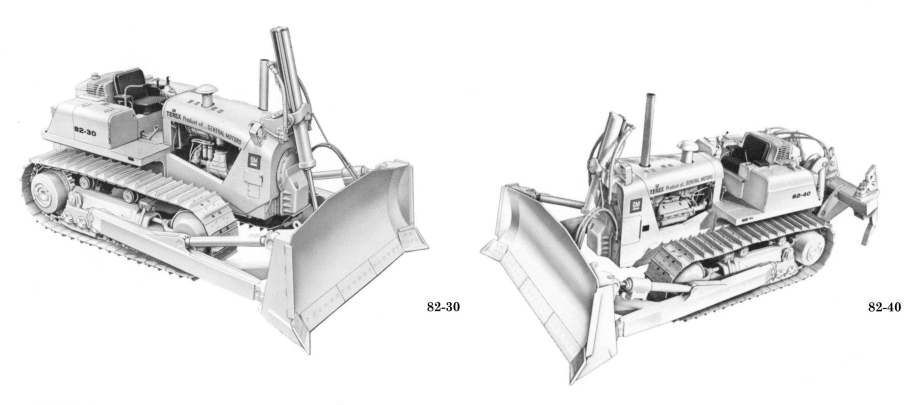

82-30

82-40

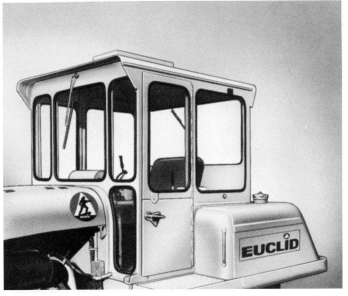

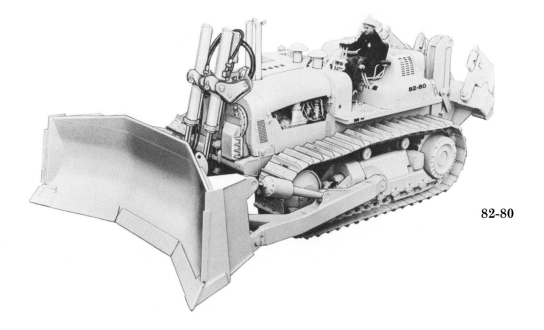

82-80

Late 1960s Crawler Line
After the 1968 reorganization of the Euclid Division into the Terex Earthmoving Equipment Division, the three crawler dozer models from Euclid were continued. *Vernon Simpson*

82-30

In 1966, Euclid renamed the C-6 the Model 82-30. Although much of the basic design of the tractor remained the same, horsepower from its GM 6-71N power plant was increased to 239 ghp and 225 fwhp, and its weight increased from 34,000 lbs. to 45,700 lbs. *Eric C. Orlemann collection*

82-30 FAM

Both Euclid and Terex won orders for military equipment including the 82-30 dozer, which was designated the 82-30 FAM. As with its civilian counterpart, the FAM was powered by a GM 6-71N engine with 239 ghp. The 82-30 FAM shown is packed and ready to go by rail to its U.S. Marine Corps receiving base. *Eric C. Orlemann collection*

Euclid 82-40

Euclid expanded its crawler line in 1966 with the addition of the 82-40, a model designed to fill the gap between the former C-6 (now 82-30) and TC-12 (now 82-80). The 82-40 is powered by a GM 8V-71N engine rated at 290 gross and 275 fwhp. *Vernon Simpson*

Terex 82-40

In 1969, Terex introduced models 82-40 DA (290 ghp/275 fwhp, naturally aspirated) and 82-40DAT (turbocharged version of the same engine with 308 ghp and 290 fwhp). The models 82-40 DA and 82-40 DAT were offered until 1973 when they were replaced by the 82-50. The two Terex 82-40s are seen in tandem push-loading a Euclid scraper. *Vernon Simpson*

82-50

Terex replaced the Model 82-40 with the 82-50 in 1973. It weighs 90,000 lbs. with blade and features a GM 12V-71T turbocharged engine. Sales literature lists horsepower of the 82-50 at 415 ghp and 370 fwhp. One 12V-71T engine now supplies more power than two 6V-71s in the first TC-12 dozer. The 82-50 remained in production through 1982. *Eric C. Orlemann collection*

82-80BA

In January of 1966 Euclid revamped its model numbering system, and the TC-12 became the Model 82-80BA. It had the same horsepower as the TC-12-3, with 454 ghp and 425 fwhp, and the same weight at 71,250 lbs. The last twin-engine crawler model with the Euclid name was built in 1967; production of the 82-80 series continued as the Model 82-80DA under Terex through 1974. *Historical Construction Equipment Association*

82-80

The 82-80DA produced 476 ghp and 440 fwhp from its twin 6-71N engines. Weight of the bare tractor is 73,000 lbs; with a ripper and blade attached, its weight increases to 105,260 lbs. It held the title of world's largest dozer until 1970, when Allis-Chalmers introduced the HD-41. *Eric C. Orlemann collection*

82-20B

Terex introduced its smallest crawler, the 82-20 in 1973. It was powered by a GM 6V-71T turbocharged engine with 180 fwhp and weighed 42,685 lbs. The 82-20 was upgraded to the 82-20B in 1976 with 205 fwhp from the same engine. Weight of the 82-20B was slightly heavier at 42,710 lbs. *Eric C. Orlemann collection*

Euclid 9FPM

This dozer was one of only six units built in 1955-56, but it never left Euclid's yard in Hudson, Ohio, finding employment in such mundane tasks as gravel spreading and snow removal. After Terex took over the facility, the tractor was sold to a junk dealer, and it was eventually acquired by its current owner, Lakeside Sand and Gravel Co. of Mantua, Ohio. Powered by a GM 6-71 diesel, the 9FPM tractor is rated at 218 ghp and 207 fwhp.

Euclid 1TPM

RIGHT. Euclid experimented with wheel dozers in 1949 and continued through the 1970s. However, it never sold any of the dozen or so models in large numbers. Wheel dozer development did lead to the company's rather successful line of wheel loaders. Many of the dozers were prototypes that Euclid tried to sell to the military. Such was the case of the 1TPM shown here in 1953. The all-wheel drive dozer was powered by a Cummins NHRS diesel rated at 300 fwhp and weighed 48,000 lbs. *Eric C. Orlemann collection*

Euclid 6TPM-G
An early 1960s prototype Model 6TPM-G dozer with 4-wheel drive is seen with a Euclid SV-18 hydraulic scraper. The pair was built as a demonstrator for bidding on some upcoming U.S. Army contracts. Euclid did not win the contract for the dozer, but was awarded a contract for the SV-18 scraper. The dozer was powered by a GM 8-71 engine with 280 ghp. *Historical Construction Equipment Association*

Euclid 11UPM
A four-wheel drive 11UPM dozer is being tested at Euclid's Hudson, Ohio factory. *Eric C. Orlemann*

Euclid 10FPM
The Model 10FPM was built in 1959 as an improved 9FPM. While also powered by a GM 6-71, its push arms and hydraulic cylinders were beefed up. *Eric C. Orlemann*

11UPM
Euclid built several Model 11UPM tractors in 1957-58 mainly for marketing for military contracts. The tractor is powered by a GM 4-71 engine with 127 ghp and 119 fwhp. *Historical Construction Equipment Association*

Terex PX-81
Based on the 72-81 wheel loader, the PX-81 was powered by a turbocharged GM 12V-71T engine with 500 ghp. The all-wheel drive dozer weighed 119,650 lbs. including its hydraulic ripper attachment. Although extensively tested, the PX-81 never went into production. *Eric C. Orlemann collection*

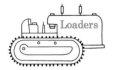

Euclid C-3 EXP
In 1956, the Euclid Division experimented with crawler loaders, starting with the C-3. Although far ahead of its time in its rear-engine design, only one such machine was built. Later, experimental models had the engine in front, but none were ever sold. The project was cancelled in 1957. *Eric C. Orlemann collection*

Terex 92-30 loader
Twelve years after the Euclid C-3 project, Terex decided to give the crawler loader another try. The first experimental machine, the Model 92-30, was built in late 1969 and was tested at the company's Milford, Ohio proving ground. Bucket capacities of the 92-30 ranged from 3 to 3.5 cu. yds., and it was powered by a GM 6-71T turbocharged engine rated at 250 ghp/225 fwhp. *Eric C. Orlemann collection*

Terex 92-20 loader
The 92-30 evolved to the 92-20 in 1972-73 with the same engine and bucket size. A third model, the 92-10, was also built and tested during this time. The 92-10 had 2.25 to 2.6 yard buckets and a GM 4-71N engine with 143 fwhp. By 1974, Terex realized the market was saturated and pulled the plug on the program. Caterpillar offered six crawler loader models during this time, Allis-Chalmers, Case, Deere and International Harvester each had four or five models, and Komatsu had just started to enter the U.S. market as well. *Eric C. Orlemann collection*

DONALD MILLS

CHAPTER SIX

INTERNATIONAL HARVESTER COMPANY

International Harvester was formed in 1902 with the merger of the McCormick and Deering harvester companies, along with several smaller firms. McCormick founder Cyrus McCormick is credited with the development of the first mechanical reaper in 1831 in the Shenandoah Valley of Virginia. The reaper was the first of a series of innovations that revolutionized agriculture during the 19th century, making it possible for a few farmers to feed masses. As sales grew for the new machine, McCormick moved his shop to the Chicago area in 1848 to be closer to the Midwestern farm markets.

The Red Team

An International TD-18 tractor is seen pulling a Bucyrus-Erie S-series scraper. Introduced in 1939, the TD-18 was rated at 97 fwhp, placing it in the top four most powerful crawlers at the time (with the Allis-Chalmers HD-14, Caterpillar D-8, and Cletrac FD). International Harvester started painting its crawler tractors Harvester Red in 1936 and continued the color until 1959. Most of the tractor attachment makers affiliated with IH such as Bucyrus-Erie, Heil, Isaacson and Austin-Western used the color scheme as well.

After the formation of IH, the company quickly moved into the tractor business, offering its first 20-hp friction drive unit in 1905. IH marketed early tractors under the name McCormick-Deering until the late 1930s, when the name International came into use.

International differed from the other crawler tractor builders in that it did not purchase an existing manufacturer or design, but rather based its first crawlers on its wheel tractor designs. The earliest IH crawler tractors were modified wheel tractors with full or half tracks offered by affiliated manufacturers such as Trackson, French & Hecht, Hadfield-Penfield, Moon Track and Mandt-Freil. These conversions were done either by the dealer or by individual owners.

As crawler tractors gained acceptance, particularly by farmers, IH developed its own version in the mid-1920s. This was a McCormick-Deering Model 10-20 wheel tractor with French & Hecht crawler tracks added; IH called it a "TracTracTor." Satisfied that the crawler was sound, the company designed and built its own undercarriage for the TracTracTors. The new crawlers were first offered in 1928 and were built side by side with wheel tractors at the IH Tractor Works in Chicago. The 10-20 TracTracTor weighed 6,250 lbs. and had about 25 belt hp. A slightly more powerful crawler, the Model T-20, was developed in 1931.

In 1932, the 40 series of crawlers was launched including the TA-40 (all fuel – gas, kerosene, distillate) and TK-40 (kerosene) TracTracTors, and IH's first diesel crawler, the TD-40, appeared the following year. The D-40 engine, IH's first diesel, was a 4-cylinder, 460-cu.-in block rated at 53.5 bhp (see sidebar p. 132). The diesel was started with gasoline, then switched to diesel fuel, a system that the company would continue for the next 30 years. The TD-40 was launched only a year and a half after Caterpillar introduced the first diesel-powered crawler tractor, its Diesel Sixty. IH added the T-35 (gas) and TD-35 (diesel) TracTracTor models in 1937.

In 1938 IH hired the famous industrial designer Raymond Loewy to redesign its entire tractor line including the crawlers. The company switched paint colors in 1936 to Harvester Red, and Loewy designed a new company logo with the "I" and "H" combined as block letters. In 1939 and 1940 the new-styled TracTracTors were unveiled with the well-known grills with horizontal lines created by Loewy. Three models were available with either gasoline or diesel power (TD- and T-6, TD- and T-9, and TD- and T-14), while the TD-18 came only with a diesel engine.

The TD-24 was introduced in 1947, the first of a series of moves by IH to become a major player in the construction equipment business. With 180 gross hp, it was touted as the world's most powerful crawler tractor, and it contained many advanced features such as planetary power steering. However, some of the early TD-24s were mechanically unreliable and tarnished the company's reputation in the crawler tractor field.

In the mid-1950s, IH again redesigned the crawler line and launched the first integrally-built crawler loader. The company added the TD-15 (150 series) and TD-20 (200 series) tractors in 1958. The

Melrose Park, Illinois Factory
Purchased in 1945, the factory became the manufacturing center for International's construction equipment and diesel engines. It is now headquarters for International's Truck Engine Group.
Don Heimburger

next year was a banner year for the crawler line, with introduction of the big TD-25 (230 ehp), the small T-4, T-5, TD-5, T-340 and TD-340 tractors, and IH's first wheel dozer, the D-500, rated at 600 hp. Five additional wheel dozer models were offered, with one lasting through the Dresser era. The largest IH-built crawler, the 320-fwhp TD-30, appeared in 1962 but was dropped in 1967.

IH had tried the construction equipment field as early as 1912 when it offered the Titan Type D road roller. However, most of the construction and forestry-related attachments were provided by affiliated suppliers such as Bucyrus-Erie (blades and scrapers), Heil (blades and scrapers), Drott (loaders and blades) and Hough (loaders). The Bucyrus-Erie affiliation allowed B-E attachments to be sold exclusively by IH dealers and lasted from 1935 to 1953. Several equipment makers like Galion, Adams, Austin-Western and Ingram used IH engines in most of their products, and IH dealers often carried and serviced these makes.

With the establishment of a construction equipment division in 1944, the company seriously committed to building a diversified line of earthmoving machinery. After purchase of the Frank G. Hough Co. in 1952, the scraper line from Heil the next year, and the Bucyrus-Erie attachments in 1953, IH designed and manufactured its own attachments and allied equipment such as bulldozer blades, cable control units, front-end loaders and scrapers.

By 1957, the company offered an impressive array of construction equipment: five crawler tractor models, six wheel loaders, two motor scrapers, two off-road dump trucks and one crawler loader. As other crawler manufacturers had or would soon do, IH switched to yellow paint for its products in the late 1950s.

Dresser Industries purchased the IH construction equipment line (Payline Division) in 1982 and continued building most of its products. The new company introduced the TD-40 dozer in 1985 with a 460-hp Cummins engine and a weight of over 134,000 lbs. Dresser became a part of Komatsu America International Co. (KAIC) in 1990, and in 1998, KAIC formed a joint venture with Huta Stalowa Wola of Poland. The new entity is called Dressta Co. Ltd., and it currently offers 10 crawler tractor models. All retained the "TD" prefix.

10-20 TracTracTor
The 10-20 was International Harvester's first crawler tractor. Production of the 10-20 started in 1928 and continued through 1931. The 10-20 was tested at the Nebraska Tractor Test Lab in 1931. The 6,250-lb. machine achieved power ratings of 24.8 bhp and 19.6 dbhp.

10-20 TracTracTor
This Model 10-20 shows the two "camel hump" steering clutch housings in front of the engine firewall.

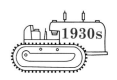

T-20 TracTracTor

IH continued to make improvements on the 10-20 and in 1931 replaced it with the T-20. A larger engine resulted in increased power to 26.6 bhp and 23.3 dbhp.

T-20 TracTracTor

The T-20 weighed 7,010 lbs. and was available with 41½-inch or 51-inch track gauges.

T-35 TracTracTor

Although the T-35 and TD-35 TracTracTors were available for only three years, 1937 through 1939, a total of 5,585 T-35s and TD-35s were sold. The 10,600-lb. gasoline-powered T-35 was tested at the University of Nebraska at 44.4 bhp, 36.6 dbhp and a maximum drawbar pull of 8,053 lbs. The dozer shown was built in 1939, its last year of production.

TD-35 TracTracTor

The diesel TD-35 tested at 42 belt hp, 37 drawbar hp, and pulled 8,243 lbs. Weight of the TD-35 is 11,245 lbs. Dimensions of both the T-35 and TD-35 are 132 in. long and 59.5 in. wide. Photo taken at Dyersville, Iowa. *Don Heimburger*

TA-40
This 1933 TA-40 TracTracTor belongs to the National Construction Equipment Museum of the Historical Construction Equipment Association in Bowling Green, Ohio.

INTERNATIONAL HARVESTER'S FIRST DIESEL

D-40 engine *Michael Androvich*

According to a paper presented by D.B. Baker, International Harvester's manager of engineering, Industrial Power Division, to the Society of Automotive Engineers in 1947, IH's diesel program began in 1916 after approval by its New Work Committee.

A single cylinder diesel that produced 10 bhp was built in 1918 and experimental two- and four-cylinder diesels were tested during the 1920s. The company sent several teams of engineers to Europe to study the new diesels produced in Germany and Switzerland, and a German Dorner diesel engine was shipped back to Chicago for testing and evaluation.

It was on this design that IH based its own diesel which was lab tested in 1928. The new engine had a four-cylinder block with 4 1/2 in. bore and a 6 in. stroke. It was installed on a tractor and sent to Phoenix, Arizona in 1929 for field testing. Three other diesel engines were built in 1930-32 with slightly larger bore and stroke: 4 1/2 in. x 6 1/4 in. These were also extensively tested on crawler tractors.

The final version was made in late 1932. It had a 4 3/4 in. bore, 6 1/2 in. stroke and a volume of 460 cubic in. It was initially rated at 53.5 bhp, but later increased to 65, then 76, and finally 95 bhp by 1957. The engine was first installed on the TD-40 TracTracTor and released for sale in April of 1933.

It also powered the first diesel wheel tractor (WD-40) and was sold as a separate power unit called the PD-40 engine. The TD-40 remained in production until 1939, when the styled TracTracTors appeared. However, the 460-cu. in. PD-40 engine was available for 20 more years as the UD-14, UD-14A, and D-460 engines in the TD-14, TD-14A, TD-14 (141) and TD-14 (142) crawlers.

132

Illust. 12. McCormick-Deering Diesel-40—Lower Cost tractor power.

TD-40

Introduced in 1933, the TD-40 TracTracTor was IH's first diesel-powered product. The tractor's four-cylinder D-40 engine produced 53.5 bhp and 48 dbhp on a 1938 Nebraska Tractor Lab test. *Jere Wissler*

TA-40/ TK-40/ TD-40 TracTracTors

In 1932, IH decided to enter the larger crawler tractor field with its "40" family of machines. These included the TA-40 (all fuel) with an engine that could run on gas, distillate or kerosene, and the TK-40 with an engine that ran on kerosene or distillate (kerosene is the first-cut product produced at a boiling point range of 350° to 550°F; distillate, or "white kerosene" is a second-cut product produced between 500° and 700°F). IH added the diesel TD-40 to the family in 1933 and a gas-powered T-40 in 1936. The "40s" were built until 1939 with a total of 8,376 units sold. The TA and TK models had six-cylinder engines, while the TD used a four-cylinder engine. The Nebraska Tractor Test Lab rated the TD-40 at 53.5 bhp, 51 bhp for the TA-40 and 49 bhp for the TK. IH advertised that the "40-Series" crawlers were capable of pulling 6 to 8 fourteen-inch plows. The weights of the 40-series tractors range from 12,000 to 12,750 lbs.

TD-40

A TD-40 with a Bucyrus-Erie angle blade pushes blasted rock in a mine. *Jere Wissler*

TD-40

A TD-40 makes a road cut with an unidentified make hydraulic dozer. *Jere Wissler*

Late 1940s Diesel Crawler Lineup

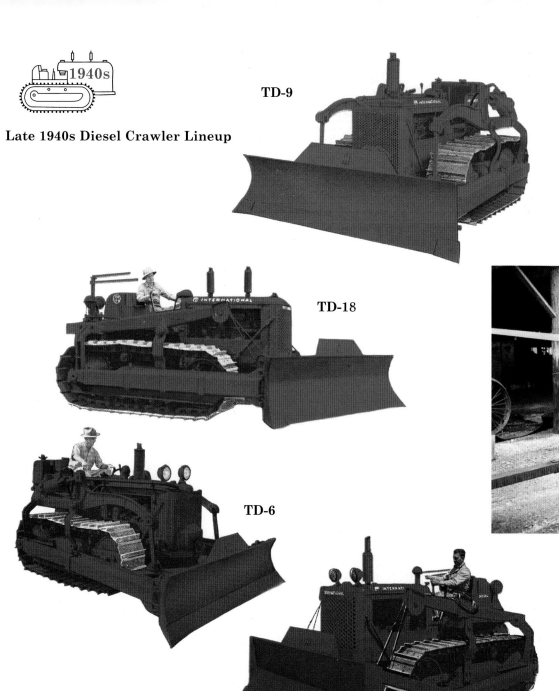

TD-9

TD-18

TD-6

TD-14

TD-24

T-6

IH launched the gasoline-powered T-6 in 1940, and it remained in the product line with very little change through 1956. Although designed primarily as an agricultural tractor, the T-6 also found its way into construction and logging use as well. The tractor was tested by the Nebraska Tractor Test Lab at 36 bhp and 30 dbhp and weighs 7,130 lbs. without attachments.

TD-6

Like the T-6, the diesel TD-6 was also produced from 1940 to 1956. Although a little heavier at 7,210 lbs., the TD-6 had slightly lower power ratings with an initial bhp of 31 (eventually increased to 40 bhp) and 28 dbhp.

TD-9

RIGHT. The TD-9 was produced from 1940 to 1956 and was International Harvester's all-time best selling crawler tractor, with nearly 60,000 units sold. Another 11,000 units of its gasoline-powered twin, the T-9, were also built. The TD-9 was available in 44 in. and 60 in. track gauges. Powered by a four-cylinder UD-9 diesel, the tractor was advertised at 44 bhp and 39 dbhp. The TD-9 weighs between 9,900 and 11,650 lbs. without attachments.

TD-18

International Harvester's diesels used a unique starting system. By opening a set of valves, auxiliary combustion chambers in each cylinder fitted with its own spark plug were activated. This reduced the compression pressure and the engine operated as a gasoline engine. When the motor was warm, the valves were closed and the engine operated as a diesel. Power for the TD-18 is provided by a six-cylinder diesel tested at 97 bhp and 80 dbhp. The tractor weighs 23,360 lbs. The TD-18 was available from 1939 to 1949, during which time more than 22,000 units were built. Many of these machines served time in the military during WWII. *Don Heimburger*

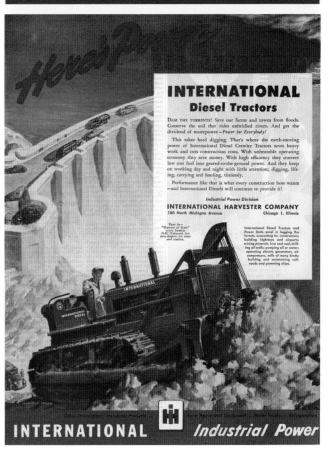

TD-14

OPPOSITE PAGE. The TD-14 was introduced in 1939 and remained in production until 1949. It has a 460-cubic-in., four-cylinder diesel engine with 72 bhp and delivers 57 dbhp. The TD-14 was available with either 56- or 74-inch track gauge and weighed between 16,400 and 17,595 lbs. without attachments. *Pit and Quarry*

TD-24

The TD-24 marked IH's entry into the heavy construction business, as the big crawler was designed for heavy duty pulling and dozing. Introduced in 1947, it was shown along with a two-story-high wooden replica of the machine at the 1948 Road Show in Chicago. At 180 ghp, a fwhp rating of 167 and 140 dbhp, the TD-24 took the crown of largest crawler away from A-C's HD-19, released just a few months earlier.

The engine for the TD-24 was also a new model from International, the UD-24. It was a six-cylinder diesel with 1,091-cubic inch displacement. The TD-24 featured "Planetary Power Steering," a system that combined hydraulically-controlled steering clutches with a two-speed range, similar to Allis-Chalmers' Torque Converter. The two-speed range unit could be engaged on the fly to allow shifting under power, and the unit was linked to a four-speed synchromesh transmission, providing eight speeds forward or reverse. The two-speed range could be used for gradual turns by placing one track into "low" and the other into "high" gear, allowing both tracks to turn under power. Unfortunately, this advanced transmission was not built to withstand the rigors of heavy duty construction work and broke down frequently, hurting IH's reputation for earthmoving machinery.

TOP. Gary Hirschlieb's 1948 TD-24 "hardnose" with Bucyrus-Erie cable blade is in action at the 1998 HCEA National Show, Lapeer, Michigan.

BOTTOM. A 1949 "softnose" TD-24 is equipped with a Bucyrus-Erie push block for loading scrapers.

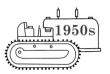

TD-24

International Harvester continued production of the TD-24 through 1954 with relatively few changes. In spite of frequent mechanical problems, the TD-24 sold well with more than 7,500 units built. This is a 1952 TD-24 with a Bucyrus-Erie cable blade in action on a small dam project in Nebraska.

TD-9A

An operator's-eye view of the TD-9A. At far left is the master clutch; next is the left brake pedal and steering clutch lever. The large red lever is the throttle, and the gear shift is just in front of the seat. The right steering clutch and brake pedal are next on the right, and the hydraulic blade lever is on the far right.

TD-6

TOP. Production of the original TD-6 Model continued to 1956 when the TD-6 Series 61 was offered. Power from the four-cylinder diesel was increased to 50 ehp, giving the tractor 42.5 dbhp. In 1959, the Series 61 was replaced by the Series 62 which remained in production to 1970. The Series 62 boasted 52 ehp from its 282-cu.-in., six-cylinder diesel engine.

TD-9A

BOTTOM. An IH ad in 1950 promoted a number of upgrades for the TD-9 including increased power to 51.5 fwhp and 40.5 dbhp. The power increase on the four-cylinder UD-9 engine was obtained from a redesigned combustion system with new pistons, an improved pre-combustion chamber, simplified injection nozzles, a new fuel pump and a higher compression ratio of 15.7 to 1. This 1953 TD-9A with a Bucyrus-Erie blade belongs to Buck Guyther of Mechanicsville, Maryland.

Mid-1950s Crawler Line

TD-6 (Series 61)

TD-9 (Series 91)

TD-24 (241 Series)

TD-14 (Series 142)

TD-18 (Series 182)

TD-9 (Series 92)

In 1956, International upgraded the TD-9 to the Series 91 with a 350-cu.-in. engine that produced 66 bhp and 55 dbhp. The Series 92 appeared in 1959 and was sold through 1962. It featured a new 282-cubic-in., six-cylinder diesel rated at 66 ehp and delivering 56 dbhp. *Roger Amato collection*

TD-14 (Series 141)

The Series 141 was only produced in 1955 and 1956. The tractor developed 83 bhp and 61 dbhp and weighed 25,345 lbs. The Series 141 was available with International's new line of hydraulic and cable-operated blades. This 1956 Series 141 with brush rake and blade skids is owned by dozer collector Alan Smith of McHenry, Illinois.

TD-14A

The TD-14A was offered from 1949 through 1955. Powered by an International UD-14A diesel, it is rated at 76 bhp and produces 65 dbhp. The machine weighs 18,465 lbs. without attachments. The TD-14A with a canopy in the photograph was built in 1952.

TD-14 (Series 142)

LEFT. International Harvester replaced the Series 141 with the 142 in 1956, and it was offered through 1958. Horsepower increased to 95 at the belt and 78.5 at the drawbar. The dozer shown is a 1957 model with a hydraulic blade.

TD-15 (Series 150)

BOTTOM LEFT. The TD-14 (142) was replaced by the TD-15 (Series 150) in 1958. It is powered by a D-554 six-cylinder diesel with 105 ehp and delivers 77 dbhp. A Series 150 dozer stockpiles sand and gravel at a New Jersey pit and screening plant. *Pit and Quarry*

TD-14 (Series 142)

A pair of Series 142 dozers work on a road construction project. *Pit & Quarry*

TD-18A

The TD-18A was offered until 1955 when replaced by the TD-18 (Series 181). The TD-18A is powered by a D-691 engine with 125 fwhp and produces 89.3 dbhp. This TD-18A was on display at the Field Day of the Past tractor show in Manakin, Virginia.

TD-18A

TD-18A

A TD-18A with Bucyrus-Erie sidearm cable blade operates in a surface coal mine. The big dozer weighs around 14 tons with blade. *Doug Frey*

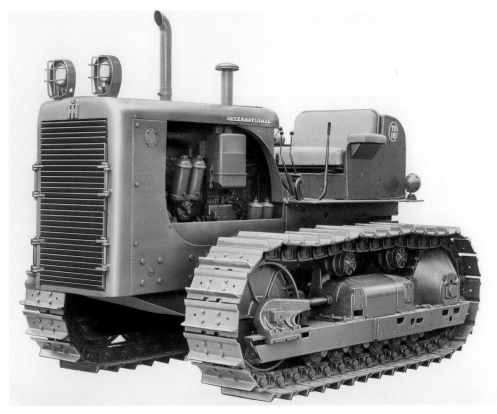

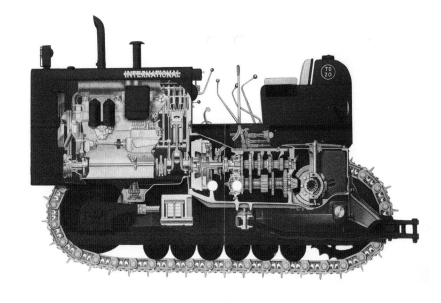

TD-18 (Series 182)
International offered the TD-18 (Series 182) from 1956 through 1958. It produces 128 ehp from a six-cylinder D-691 diesel engine. *Doug Frey*

TD-20 (Series 200)
The TD-18 (182) was replaced in 1958 with the TD-20 (Series 200) tractor. It was rated at 134 bhp and 111 dbhp. This cutaway view shows the tractor's engine, transmission final drive and undercarriage. *Doug Frey*

TD-18 (Series 182)
RIGHT. A Series 182 tractor clears large rocks at a surface mine with its IH cable-operated blade. *Pit & Quarry*

TD-24 (Series 241)
In 1955, the original TD-24 was replaced by the Series 241. An updated engine, the six-cylinder D-1091, produced 190 ehp and 161 dbhp for the gear-drive tractor. A torque converter version was also offered with 202 ehp. *Pit & Quarry*

T-4, T-5 and TD-5
ABOVE. In 1959, International entered the small crawler market. The company offered three models designed for farm applications (T-4, T-5 and TD-5) and two models for construction use (T-340 and TD-340). The gas-powered C-123 four-cylinder engine in the T-4 was rated at 34 fwhp, and it delivered 26.3 dbhp. The T-5 had a slightly more powerful C-135 gas engine with 40 fwhp and 30.9 dbhp. The T-4, 5 and TD-5 were available with 38-, 48- or 68-in. track gauge. The diesel-powered TD-5 produced 37 fwhp and 29.6 dbhp from the four-cylinder B-275 engine. The tractor was available with either four or five roller tracks. *Don Heimburger*

TD-25 (Series 250)
LEFT. The TD-25 (250) superceded the TD-24 (241) in late 1959 as the "super dozer" of the International product line. The Series 250 is powered by a DT-817 turbocharged diesel engine. With its 817-cu.-in. cylinder displacement, it produced 220 bhp. *Jere Wissler*

INTERNATIONAL
T-340
CRAWLER TRACTOR

T-340

This is a T-340 with a 7-ft.-wide "Bullgrader" hydraulic blade. More than 8,000 340-series crawlers were sold, thanks in large part to a military contract. *Jere Wissler*

500

International replaced the T-340 and TD-340 with the Model 500 in 1965. The Model 500 dozer was available with a four-cylinder diesel that developed 47 ehp and produced 31 dbhp, or a four-cylinder gasoline engine with the same rating. The Model 500 was upgraded to the 500C in 1969 and the 500E in 1975.

1960s

T-340 and TD-340

LEFT. The T-340 and TD-340 tractors appeared in 1959 and remained in production through 1965. The tractors weigh 5,532 and 5,821 lbs. respectively and were available in either 38- or 48-inch track gauge. The T-340 is powered by a C-135 gas engine rated at 35 bhp and 31 dbhp. The TD-340 has a D-166 engine with 36 bhp and 32 dbhp. *Don Heimburger*

TD-7C

LEFT. In 1969, IH unveiled a new line of small dozers: the T-7 and TD-7 Series C and the TD-8 Series C models. The T-7 and the 500 were the last gasoline-powered crawlers offered although no factory records indicate that the T-7 went into production. The diesel-powered TD-7C with gear drive was rated at 54 ehp and weighed 12,410 lbs.; the powershift version had 60 ehp and weighed an additional 100 lbs. The T-7C had a 60-ehp rating with powershift and had 54 ehp for the gear drive version.

TD-9B

RIGHT. The TD-9 Series B was offered between 1962 and 1973 with either a powershift or gear drive transmission. The dozer proved to be a good product for IH with more than 10,000 units sold. The powershift model had 75 ehp; the direct drive had 66 ehp from the tractor's DT-282 six-cylinder engine. *Pit & Quarry*

TD-8C

LEFT. IH's TD-8 Series C was introduced in 1969 with a four-cylinder 67-ehp diesel engine and gear drive transmission. Power was increased to 74 ehp with a powershift transmission. In 1974, it was replaced by the TD-8E with 78 ehp.

TD-20B

RIGHT. The Series B replaced the TD-20 Series 201 in 1963, and it remained in production through 1970. It was powered by a DT-691 turbocharged engine rated at 150 ehp and was available with a two-range (high and low) power-shift transmission with variable speeds in each range. Weight of the tractor is 30,300 lbs. *Jere Wissler*

TD-30

ABOVE. With its 320 ehp and weight of more than 30 tons, the TD-30 was well suited for push-loading scrapers. *Doug Frey*

TD-25 Series B and C

RIGHT. The TD-25 Series 250 was replaced by the TD-25 Series B in 1962 with a DT-817B engine and 10 more horsepower. The Series C was introduced in 1968 with a 285 ehp DT-817C engine and an upgraded 310-fwhp version (Series E) appeared in 1979. *Pit & Quarry*

TD-30

The TD-30 made its debut in 1962 and was offered through 1967. Weighing in at 61,000 lbs., it was International's largest crawler tractor and was designed to compete with Caterpillar's D-9 and the Euclid TC-12. The TD-30 could be ordered with either a DT-817 engine with 280 ehp and gear drive transmission or a 320-ehp DTI-817 engine with powershift; the additional 40 hp was gained by use of an intercooler. *Pit & Quarry*

Hough-International D-Series Paydozers

D-400 Paydozer

ABOVE. The Model D-400 Paydozer first appeared in 1963. It is basically the same machine as the 10-yd. Hough H-400 wheel loader. Two engine options were offered: a Cummins VT-12-525-CI or a GM 12V-71. Both were rated at 400 fwhp. The articulated-frame D-400 weighs 105,000 lbs. *Historical Construction Equipment Association*

D-500 Paydozer

LEFT. In 1961, the Hough Division of IH expanded from wheel loaders to wheel dozers. The first product in this new line was also the company's largest, the Model D-500 Paydozer. The giant tractor is built on an articulated frame and weighs 128,000 lbs. Optional equipment increased weight to 70 tons. Power options were either a Cummins VT-12-700 CI engine with 600 ghp or a GM 16V-71 with 635 ghp. The D-500 push-loads an IH scraper. *Historical Construction Equipment Association*

D-120C Paydozer

The D120C, launched in 1964, was an articulated frame dozer that weighed between 66,900 and 68,000 lbs. Two 6-cylinder engines were offered: an IH DT-817B with 375 ghp and 285 fwhp and a Cummins NT-855C with 335 ghp and 275 fwhp. *Vernon Simpson*

D-100 Paydozer

Hough offered two versions of the D-100: a rigid frame model in 1961 and an articulated model in 1964 called the D-100B. The D-100 dozer is similar to the 3 1/2-yd. Hough H-100 wheel loader. The rigid frame model is powered by a 220 ghp IH D-817 engine and weighs 40,000 lbs. The articulated version could be ordered with either a Cummins NH-220-CI with 220 ghp or a GM 6V-71 engine with 218 ghp. *Historical Construction Equipment Association*

H-400C Coal Dozer

After phasing out the D-series Paydozer line in 1974, IH continued the wheel dozer line by offering a coal blade for the H-400C Payloader. The H-400C Coal Dozer was powered by either a Cummins VT-1701C with 580 fwhp or a Detroit Diesel 12V-71T with 500 fwhp. The 20-ft.-wide blade can move 42 cubic yards of coal in one pass. The H-400C was available from 1975 through the 1982 purchase by Dresser.

D-90C Paydozer

The D-90C Paydozer is mounted on an articulated frame like its cousin, the H-90C Payloader. Power options were a GM 6V-53 engine (164 fwhp), a Cummins V6R-180 (162 fwhp), or an IH DT-573 engine (165 fwhp). The D-90C was available from 1964 through 1968 and weighs 44,000 lbs. *Historical Construction Equipment Association*

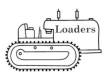

Drott 6K3 Skid Shovel

LEFT. The 6K3 loader on a TD-6 tractor has a 1 yard bucket and breakout force of 8,500 lbs. The TD-6 tractor produces 50 ehp and weighs 14,459 lbs. with the Skid Shovel attachment. *Dave Werner*

Drott 9K3 Skid Shovel

LOWER LEFT. The Drott 9K3 loader bucket has a capacity of 1½ yards and a breakout force of 11,500 lbs. This 9K3 Skid Shovel is on a 1954 TD-9 tractor rated at 51.5 fwhp.

Hough hydraulic loader

BELOW. Hough, while best known for its wheel loaders, also offered ½ yd. hydraulic loader attachments for the T-6 and TD-6 tractors, 1 yd. loaders for the T-9 and TD-9 and a 2 yd. loader for the TD-14 before it became part of International Harvester. These attachments, called Tractor Shovels, may have been the nucleus for the H-12 loader offered by IH's Hough Division in the late 1950s.

International 175C

The Model 175 loader was first offered by IH in 1963. It came with either a standard bucket or a Drott 4-in-1bucket. The loader was powered by a 115-ehp diesel and weighed 25,900 lbs. The 175 was upgraded to the 175B with a 2 yard bucket in 1965 and the 2 yard 175C with 134 fwhp in 1975. The 175C survived through the Dresser acquisition and is still manufactured by Dressta of Poland.

International 250

The 3 yard Model 250 was IH's largest crawler loader. The 150-fwhp integrally-built 250 loader replaced the TD-20 with the Drott Skid Shovel in 1963. It was upgraded to the 250B in 1966 with 160 fwhp and to the 250C in 1970 with 190 fwhp, all with powershift transmissions. The 250 weighs 20 tons. *Richard Yaremko*

Hough H-12 Crawler Payloader

Hough introduced the Model H-12 Payloader in 1957. The integrated loader featured a rear-mounted engine that could raise itself up to 30^0 for ease of maintenance and repair. Although the design of the H-12 was far ahead of its time, Hough sold only 235 units between 1957 and 1960. The loader comes with a 1¾ yard bucket and weighs 22,400 lbs. Power is supplied by an International UD-350 diesel rated at 91.5 bhp. This 1959 H-12 works on a small earthen dam near Seward, Nebraska.

Drott 14K3 Skid Shovel

A 1958 International TD-14 (Series 142) Tractor is equipped with a 2½ yd. Drott 14K3 Skid Shovel. The Series 142 is rated at 95 fwhp and weighs 32,900 lbs. with the Skid Shovel. In 1959, IH bought the rights to Drott's Skid Shovels which led to a new line of integrally-built crawler-loaders, launched in 1962: the Models 150, 175 and 250.

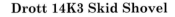

MERRILL MILL CO.
PATTEN 19..

CHAPTER SEVEN

OTHER CRAWLER MANUFACTURERS

Tractor manufacturing literally mushroomed during the first two decades of the 20th century. From the two earliest builders, Lombard Traction Engine Co. in 1900 and Holt in 1904, more than 40 crawler companies were in business by 1920. However, these companies built a combined total of less than 4,000 machines that year. Many of the companies made only one or two models and lasted only a few years. Some, like Monarch and Bates, merged with larger firms, while others which didn't build very reliable machines, couldn't sell their products, or lost patent infringement suits, went out of business.

The Great Depression weeded out many of the others remaining in the industry. By 1930, the pack had been reduced to about a half dozen firms, among them Allis-Chalmers, Caterpillar, Cleveland Tractor and International Harvester. That remained the case until after World War II, when American Tractor (later, Case), Deere and Euclid entered the crawler market. A few other companies like Minneapolis-Moline and Massy-Ferguson also tried to compete in the crawler arena, but their efforts were short-lived.

Last, a number of mini-crawlers (less than 30 hp) and micro-crawlers (less than 10 hp) have been offered over the years from both major and minor manufacturers. Some have been ready to run, while others came in kit form.

Lombard
A Lombard steam-powered Log Hauler pulls a train of log sleds in the Maine woods. *The Lumbermen's Museum*

Lombard Traction Engine Co.

Alvin O. Lombard (1856-1937) and the Lombard Traction Engine Co. are credited for producing the first commercially successful crawler tractor in 1900. Lombard was a mechanic and millwright and ran a small shop in Waterville, Maine catering mainly to the local lumbering industry. In conjunction with the Waterville Iron Works, Lombard built a steam-powered crawler tractor resembling a locomotive to haul logs out of the Maine woods over snow-packed trails during the winter and mud trails in the summer. The machine, called the Log Hauler, was tested in 1901 and 1902 and various improvements were made.

Lombard received a patent for his Log Hauler in May 1901, the second-known U.S. patent for an endless track or crawler tracked machine (the first was issued to Warren Miller of Marysville, California in 1859, but it was never produced commercially). The first Lombard Log Hauler was sold in 1903, and it appeared in many of the forests of the Northeast during the next decade.

RIGHT. The unique, strange-looking steam-powered Lombard Log Hauler with crew and log sled. *The Lumbermen's Museum*

BELOW. A gas-powered Lombard tractor pulls log sleds through the snow. *The Lumbermen's Museum*

LOMBARD TRACTORS

The early versions of the Lombard were operated by an engineer and fireman in the rear cab and steered by a tillerman in the front cab. A front-mounted tiller wheel was used in the summer and a set of skis was used for steering during the winter. On long sled trains, a conductor rode on the end and communicated with the cab by a bell and rope which ran along the side of the sleds.

Lombard log trains averaged eight or nine sleds, but on well maintained haul roads, trains of 10 to 12 cars were run. One Lombard could haul up to 300 tons of logs. Lombard tractors used a three-clutch system for steering the tracks, a master clutch and steering clutches for each track, much like the steering system in Holt's crawlers. The tractor measured 30 ft. long, 8 ft. 2 in. wide, 9 ft. tall and weighed 18 tons.

Lombard's first tractor had an upright boiler and two upright steam engines. By using an engine working independently for each track, the operator could avoid using a differential. This worked fine for compensating differences in speed, but when the two engines were in step, the vibrations were too great and the design was dropped in favor of horizontal cylinders connected to a differential. The steam engine was rated at 100 hp and was operated at 200 p.s.i. pressure. Maximum speed of the log hauler was 5 mph, but the log train could go as fast as 20 mph downhill.

The early models experienced frequent breakdowns, especially in the frames and undercarriages; mud, dirt, and rocks protruding from the snow-packed roads and trails were particularly hard on the track plates and the rest of the undercarriage as well. In spite of the name, Log Haulers were used for numerous other purposes such as hauling sand and gravel, moving wagons with ore and waste rock, pulling heavy blocks of stone in quarries, snow-plowing, and even hauling mail and passengers over remote snow-covered roads. A small snow-plow or "scraper" mounted beneath the frame was available to help level and maintain the snow-packed roads and trails.

Beginning in 1906, Lombard licensed the Phoenix Manufacturing Co. of Eau Claire, Wisconsin to build steam-powered crawlers under its Centiped line. Phoenix sold its machines mainly in Wisconsin, Minnesota, the Pacific Northwest and Alaska and some were even shipped to Russia.

In 1909, a four-cylinder 75-hp gasoline engine was offered as an option and after 1917, Lombard tractors used gasoline engines exclusively. During the late teens and 1920s, 110-hp and 140-hp gasoline engines were added to the line. Steam still remained the power of choice for pulling the longer sled trains; on roads where steam could haul 10 to12 sleds or cars, gasoline-powered Lombard tractors could only pull 5 to 6. The gasoline tractors were usually assigned to the shorter runs and moving cars in the loading and unloading yards. A Fairbanks-Morse diesel was offered as an optional engine in 1934.

However, the development of the truck and an expanded road system for hauling lumber made the Log Hauler obsolete and Lombard's sales began to slump. An electric-powered Lombard tractor was also built with a three-mile haul road equipped with overhead trolley lines. Unfortunately, heavy snows caused short-circuiting of the electric lines and the project was abandoned.

Two examples of Lombard tractors have been preserved in The Lumbermen's Museum, located in Patten, Maine. One is steam-powered and the other has a gasoline engine.

A steam-powered Lombard and its crew of four pose for the camera. *The Lumbermen's Museum*

YUBA BALL TREAD TRACTORS

The Ball Tread tractors were steered by a tiller wheel and a transmission that allowed each track to be operated independently. The Model 12-25 was rated at 12 dbhp and 25 bhp and weighed 7,600 lbs. It was followed by the Model 18-35, rated at 18 dbhp and 35 bhp. Both were powered by four-cylinder Wisconsin gasoline engines.

At least six crawler models are known to have been offered by Yuba including several larger models such as the 40-70 with 70 bhp and weight of 21,000 lbs. and the 25-40 with 40 bhp. Stearns, Waukesha and Wisconsin four-cylinder engines were used in the Yuba tractors during the 1920s. Yuba followed the plight of many other tractor builders after the Great Depression and went out of business by 1931. However, the gold mining arm of the company remained solvent and became the Yuba Consolidated Gold Mining Co.

Yuba's Ball Tread Tracks
This close-up view shows the Ball Tread system developed by Yuba. Instead of running the machine over the track with wheels on rails, most of the tractor's weight is carried by large (2¼ in. diameter) steel balls packed together in a ball race. The balls distribute the weight evenly over the entire ground-bearing area of each tread. The system allows the tractor to operate over very soft ground without packing it down. *Jeff Huff*

Yuba Model 12-20
Yuba introduced the Model 12-20 in 1916. It was rated at 20 bhp and delivered 12 dbhp from its 429-cu. in. engine. The Model 12-20 weighed 6,750 lbs.

Yuba Model 25-40
Available from 1922 to about 1930, the 25-40 was Yuba's last tractor model. Weighing 10,250 lbs., the tractor produced 40 bhp and 25 dbhp.

Acme Harvesting Machine Co.

For a short while, Acme was one of several Peoria, Illinois-based tractor companies. It introduced the Acme 12-24 in 1918 which was available with either front and rear steel wheels or a pair of tracks on the rear and was rated at 12 dbhp and 24 bhp.

Agricat / Joost Machinery Co.

Joost Machinery of Berkeley, California launched the Agricat mini crawler line in the late 1940s. Founder Earl H. Pence designed the machines and ran the company with subassemblies provided by Western Transmission Corp.

Initially, two steel-track models were offered: a short-track priced at $965 and a long-track at $1,091; both were also available with rubber tracks. Both models had a single-cylinder 6-hp Wisconsin engine and were available with dozer blade and loader attachments. Weight of the Agricat tractors ranged from 1,160 to 1,450 lbs.; with blade and ripper, the weight was over 4,000 lbs. Later models had Briggs & Stratton engines ranging from 9- to 12-hp and a 12-hp Wisconsin diesel was also available.

The tractors sold well through the 1950s and several attachments were offered including small hydraulic bucket loaders (4 to 6 cu. ft.), power dozer blade, ripper and a 7-ft. backhoe. The name of the manufacturer was changed to the Earl H. Pence Co. in the late 1950s and the facilities were moved to San Leandro, California. Around this time, the name "Agricat" caught the attention of Caterpillar Tractor Co., which sued Pence over copyright infringement. Pence lost the case and had to change the name to AgriTrac.

Western Transmission took over the AgriTrac line in 1965, and it was in turn purchased in 1967 by Freuhauf, the truck trailer manufacturer and maker of a rival mini crawler called the Trackmaster. Not long after that, skid-steer loaders gained popularity and the mini crawler market disappeared.

Alligator Tractor Co.

Alligator Tractor of St. Louis, Missouri offered a mini crawler during the 1960s with 18 different attachments including a dozer blade and a loader bucket. The tractor weighed an even ton and could be ordered with an 18-hp Wisconsin gasoline engine or a Duetz diesel. Alligator also manufactured chain saws, tillers and power mowers.

F. C. Austin Co.

F.C. Austin of Chicago, Illinois, introduced its first crawler, the Multipedal 18-35 in 1917 with a 4-cylinder engine. The company stopped production of the tractor in 1920.

Auto-Track Syndicate

Auto-Track Syndicate of San Francisco, California, offered the Auto-Track 30-50 from 1921 to 1924. It was powered by a Buda four-cylinder engine and weighed 9,875 lbs.

Ball Tread Co.

The Ball Tread Co. was established in 1911 in Detroit, Michigan by Clarence A. Henneuse, a former employee of C.L. Best Tractor Co, and several partners. The company developed an unusual concept of

Agricat A
This tractor weighs 1,160 lbs. without attachments and has two forward speeds and one for reverse. This Model A was built in 1949 and sold for $965.

Agricats
From the left are an Agricat Model B dozer, a Model B loader with a 4-cu. ft. bucket, and a Model A dozer. All were built in the late 1940s.

using large roller bearings in the undercarriage of its crawler tractors for smoother operation and less wear. The tractor's crawlers ran on two sets of steel balls which moved in channels on the inner surface or rail of each track, thus the name Ball Tread. The company advertised that the interior of its tracks were virtually frictionless.

Ball Tread introduced its first crawler tractor in 1912, the Model 12-25 along with a second model, the 18-35 later that year. Ball Tread was acquired late in 1912 by Alfred Johnson, James McCollough and Fred Calkins, and manufacturing was moved to San Jose, California. In 1914, the Ball Tread Co. was purchased by Yuba Construction Co., a Marysville, California dredge builder and contractor. Yuba operated a number of gold dredges on the Yuba River in northern California. The company's name was later changed to Yuba Manufacturing Co. and the tractor plant was moved to Benicia, California. (See sidebar on Yuba Ball Tread tractors.)

Bates Machine and Tractor Co.

Bates was an early entrant into the crawler tractor business with the introduction of its first Steel Mule in 1915. This was powered by a 20-belt hp gas engine, and it barely made it into the crawler tractor category, with two front steering wheels and a single crawler in the rear. Like the horse or mule it replaced, it came with no seat, utilizing the seat of the attachment it was pulling. The manufacturer was originally called the Joliet Tractor Co. of Joliet, Illinois, which became the Bates Machine and Tractor Co. in 1919.

Between 1929 and 1935, Bates was taken over by Foote Brothers Gear and Machine Co. which offered five tractor models ranging from 30 to 80 hp including a Waukesha-built diesel. Bates reorganized again in 1935 as a separate entity, the Bates Manufacturing Co., but went out of business for good in 1937.

Bear Tractor, Inc.

The New York City-based Bear Tractor Co. offered its Model B 25-35 in the early 1920s. With a Stearns 4-cylinder engine, it was first tested in late 1923 at the Nebraska Tractor Test Lab at 49 bhp/35 dbhp and retested in 1924 at 55 bhp and 44 dbhp. Weight of the tractor was 5,500 lbs. Bear Tractor was acquired by the Mead-Morrison Manufacturing Co. of Boston, Massachusetts in 1924.

Belle City Manufacturing Co.

Belle City Manufacturing of Racine, Wisconsin, introduced its 22-hp Track Pull crawler in 1926. It was basically a Fordson tractor with crawlers.

Belt Rail Tractor Co.

Based in St. Paul, Minnesota, Belt Rail produced a small crawler between 1917 and 1920. The Belt Rail B was powered by a four-cylinder Waukesha engine with 20 bhp and 12 dbhp. The tractor had two large steel wheels in front and a single track in the rear.

Bullock Creeping Grip
Dating from 1910, the Creeping Grip was one of the earliest crawler tractors on the market. Bullock continued the line until 1920, when it merged with Franklin Tractor Co.

Bates Model 45
Like the Model 35, the 45 had a Waukesha six-cylinder engine. The Model 45 boasted power of 66 bhp and 54 dbhp and weighed 13,509 lbs. It was available from 1930 to 1937, when Bates went out of business.

Bates Model G

ABOVE. Similar to the Model D, the G had two steel front wheels and a pair of crawler tracks on the rear with a large sprocket and two successively smaller idler wheels. The Model G was offered from 1921 to 1928 and was powered by a 4-cylinder Midwest gas engine with 35 bhp and 25 dbhp. It weighed 3 tons. *Jeff Huff*

Bates Model 35

BELOW. The Model 35 was sold from 1929 to 1937. It is powered by a Waukesha six-cylinder gas engine with 47 belt and 33 drawbar hp. Weight of the tractor is 10,750 lbs. The machine in the photo is owned by tractor collector Harold Radandt of Manitowoc, Wisconsin.

Bear

The Bear Model B25-35 with its Stearns four-cylinder engine was rated at 55 bhp and weighed 5,500 lbs. *Jeff Huff*

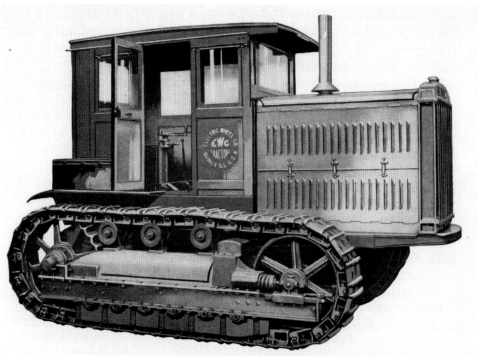

EWC 80
Introduced in 1928, the EWC 80 was powered by a Waukesha engine rated at 110 bhp. *Historical Construction Equipment Association*

Leader
Introduced in 1916, the half-track Leader 25-40 was rated at 40 bhp from a 4-cylinder engine. It is displayed at the Heidrick Ag Museum in Woodland, California.

Clark CA-1
Built for the U.S. Army as an airlifted dozer, the Model CA-1 was powered by a four-cylinder Waukesha engine with 28 bhp. Equipped with a blade and winch, the CA-1 weighed 4,350 lbs.

Ford Motor Co.
This nicely-restored 1926 Rigid X Model Fordson features a Hadfield-Penfield track conversion. The Fordson was tested by the Nebraska Tractor Testing Lab in 1926 at 22 bhp and 12 dbhp. The tractor belongs to Fordson collector Ed Bezanson of Waterford, Connecticut. *Edward Bezanson*

Fruehauf

Fruehauf renamed the Agri-Trac mini-crawler line it bought from Western Transmission as the Trackmasters. The line included dozer and loader attachments.

Westrak

Although only two prototypes were built, this one owned by Hewitt Brothers Logging has amazingly survived. This Westrack is powered by a Waukesha 4-cylinder engine.

Blewett Tractor Co.

Blewett Tractor of Tacoma, Washington, produced several crawler tractor models between 1919 and 1922. These were marketed under the Webfoot brand and ranged from 25 to 53 hp.

Bradley Tractor Co.

The Portland, Oregon-based firm produced a small crawler called the Angleworm 10 during the mid-1930s. The tractor weighed 2,600 lbs. and was powered by a Continental four-cylinder engine.

Buckeye Manufacturing Co.

This Anderson, Indiana firm began making crawler tractors in 1916 with its half-track Buckeye Junior. A 32-bhp full track model was offered the following year. In 1918, Buckeye introduced its Trundaar crawlers rated at 35 and 40 bhp. The company stopped building crawlers in the mid-1920s.

Bullock Tractor Co.

Bullock Tractor acquired the Western Implement & Motor Co. of Davenport, Iowa in 1912. Western introduced its Creeping Grip tractors in 1910 but lacked the financial backing to continue building its machines. The Creeping Grip had a 4-cylinder Waukesha engine with 12 dbhp and 20 bhp. Bullock moved the operation to Chicago and continued making the Creeping Grip line until its merger with Franklin Tractor Co. in 1920. Franklin-Bullock continued building crawlers through the 1920s.

Clark Equipment Co.

A product of the U.S. Army's engineers in World War II, the CA-1 Airborne Dozer was built under contract by the Clark Equipment Co. beginning in 1942. The machine was designed to be airlifted to remote locations to build small airstrips and other military facilities. The dozer was powered by a four-cylinder, 133-cu. in. Waukesha gas engine rated at 28 bhp. Clark had built nearly 400 CA-1 dozers when its plant was destroyed by fire. The remainder of the contract was then completed by the American Machine and Metals Co. of East Moline, Illinois. The bare tractor weighed 3,350 lbs., or 4,350 lbs. with a blade and winch. Other airborne attachments for the CA-1 were a single-drum sheepsfoot roller, an Adams pull-grader, Seaman soil stabilizer, and a LaPlante-Choate hydraulic pull-scraper.

Diamond Match Co.

The Chico, California match company assembled crawler tractors from parts supplied by other manufacturers from 1914 for at least a few years.

Drott Manufacturing Co.

Though best known for its crawler attachments, the Milwaukee, Wisconsin manufacturer briefly dabbled in crawler tractors. It produced a crawler called the Highlift from 1925 to 1929.

E.F. Townsend Tractor Co.

E.F. Townsend of Los Angeles, California built its EFT crawler in 1921 and 1922. Powered by a four-cylinder engine, the tractor had two small steel wheels in the rear to support the tail seat for the operator.

Electric Wheel Co.

The Electric Wheel Co. of Quincy, Illinois was founded in 1851 and began building wheel tractors in 1904. The company introduced its first crawler tractor, the All Work 25-35 in 1925. The All Work 25-35 became the EWC 5-Ton in 1927 and two other models followed, the EWC 4-Ton and the EWC 80 in 1928. The EWC 80 was Electric Wheel's largest model with power supplied by a Waukesha four-cylinder engine with a 6 ¾-in. bore and an 8-in. stroke. The engine was rated at 110 bhp, making it one of the more powerful crawler tractors at the time. Fierce competition among tractor makers in the late 1920s and the 1929 stock market crash forced Electric Wheel to stop crawler tractor production at the end of 1929.

Ford Motor Co.

Although Ford Motor did not offer a crawler tractor model, many manufacturers offered after-market track conversion kits for its Fordson wheel tractors, including the Hadfield-Pennfield Steel Co. A Fordson was tested by the Nebraska Tractor Testing Lab in 1926 at 22 bhp and 12 dbhp.

Franklin Flexible Tractor Co.

In 1920, Bullock Tractor and Franklin Flexible merged to become the Franklin-Bullock Tractor Co. The new firm launched its Model 18-30 in 1920 featuring a front-mounted winch designed for logging applications. Several other models followed from the Greenville, Ohio company.

Fruehauf Corp.

Indianapolis, Indiana-based Fruehauf Corp., pioneer of the truck trailer, also made a mini-crawler called the Trackmaster in the late 1960s. In 1967, Fruehauf purchased the Western Transmission Co. and its Agri-Trac line, which was the AgriCat line Western had acquired two years earlier. This turned out to be a poor decision by Fruehauf, as by the early 1970s, skid-steer loaders had gained popularity to the point that the mini-crawler market dried up.

General Tractor Co.

General Tractor of Seattle, Washington, offered the Westrak, a small crawler in 1948. It was available with either a 24-bhp Waukesha or a 29-bhp Hercules gasoline engine and weighed about two tons. Unfortunately, the founder of the company passed away after only a few tractors were built and the company folded.

Gile Tractor and Engine Co.

Gile of Ludington, Michigan, began making tractors in 1913 and launched its only crawler, the Model K in 1916. It had a two-cylinder engine, was rated at 20 bhp, 12 dbhp and weighed three tons.

Henneuse Tractor Co.

Based in Sacramento, California, Henneuse was a short-lived company, producing only a few tractors in 1921 and 1922. Its one model was the Rigid-Rail 25-40 with a Stearns four-cylinder engine. It bore a close resemblance to the Ball Tread tractor developed by C.A. Henneuse in 1912.

Massey Ferguson

The late 1960s crawler line from Massey Ferguson included four models that were configured as either a dozer or a loader. *Jeff Huff*

Mead-Morrison 55
The MM 55 open model was rated at 55 bhp and 45 dbhp and weighed 9,200 lbs. *Jeff Huff*

Mead-Morrison 80
The MM 80 was advertised at 80 bhp and had a weight of 15,000 lbs. The enclosed cab and lights were some of the optional features available.

Hicks Tractor Co.

Hicks produced only one tractor model, the 12-25 in 1917. It had a Buda four-cylinder engine and weighed 4,750 lbs. The firm started in Minneapolis, Minneapolis, then moved to Milwaukee, Wisconsin and lasted until about 1919.

Hicks-Parrett Tractor Co.

Hicks-Parrett of Chicago, Illinois built wheeled tractors and offered a crawler in 1921 called the Model 18-30 Crawler. It had a single track in the rear and steel wheels in front. It was powered by a Buda four-cylinder engine and weighed 5,250 lbs. The company went out of business in 1922.

H.W. Leavitt Co.

H.W. Leavitt, Waterloo, Iowa, briefly (1912-1913) made crawler track conversions for the Waterloo Boy Model R wheel tractor. The Waterloo Boy was made by the Waterloo Gasoline Engine Co., also of Waterloo, Iowa. The crawler was called the Leavitt Catapillar and had a two-cylinder, kerosene-fueled engine rated at 24 bhp and 12 dbhp. Waterloo became part of John Deere in 1918, the beginning of Deere's long tradition as a tractor builder.

J-T Tractor Co.

J-T of Cleveland, Ohio, launched its first crawler in 1918, the Model N (16-30) with a four-cylinder Chief engine and a weight of 7,000 lbs. It was followed by the Model 40 in 1920, also with a Chief 4-cylinder engine. J-T introduced its Model 25-40 with a Climax KU engine in 1925 and its last crawler, the Model 30-45 in 1928. The 25-40 weighed 9,800 lbs. and the 30-45 weighed 10,000 lbs. The company folded in 1929 or 1930.

John Bean Spray Pump Co.

John Bean, located in San Jose, California, produced at least two small crawler models under its Trackpull brand between 1915 and 1921. Alfred Johnson and James McCollough, formerly of the Ball Tread Co., worked on the design and production of the John Bean crawlers. The tractors had a single front-mounted crawler track and a pair of wheels in the rear to support the tail seat and were designed for spraying orchards and vineyards. Power came from a LeRoi four-cylinder engine rated at 10 bhp and 6 dbhp.

Joliet Oil Tractor Co.

This Joliet, Illinois-based company offered four crawler models from 1913 to 1919. The two earliest models had two steel wheels in front and a single track in back and could be operated either by reins or a set of three small steering wheels. Bates Tractor Co. purchased Joliet in 1919 and used the factory to produce its "Steel Mule" crawlers.

Keystone Iron & Steel Works

Keystone was a Los Angeles, California firm that began building wheel tractors in the early 1900s and offered a crawler in 1921. The Keystone Model 30 had a 4-cylinder Waukesha engine and an unusual undercarriage design, with a large drive sprocket in the center and two idler wheels on each end. The tractor weighed 7,800 lbs.

Killen-Walsh Manufacturing Co.

The Appleton, Wisconsin firm introduced its first crawler in 1914, known as the Straits 30-50 Tractor, named after its designer. It was rated at 50 bhp and weighed 9,000 lbs. Instead of a front tiller wheel, the Straits used a small single crawler track for turning, presumably for better flotation. A second smaller model, the Straits No. 3, was introduced in 1916. It had 25 bhp and weighed 6,000 lbs.

Laughlin-Homer Engine Corp.

Another Los Angeles, California tractor builder, Laughlin-Homer produced the Model 8-20 crawler in 1919 and 1920. It used a Laughlin 4-cylinder engine rated at 10 dbhp and 20 bhp and weighed 7,000 lbs.

Leader Engine / Dayton-Dick Co.

The Leader Engine Co. of Detroit, Michigan started building wheel tractors in 1913 after its merger with Dayton-Dick Co. of Quincy, Illinois. In 1916, the company produced two crawler tractor models with steel front wheels, the Leader 18-36 and Leader 25-40, and it introduced a full-track crawler, the Model GU in 1919. That year, the firm became the Dayton-Dowd Co. which continued making tractors until 1923.

Lennox Machine Co.

Des Moines, Iowa-based Lennox offered two models of its KittyTrack mini-dozers during the 1960s: the KittyTrack 600 with 6 hp and the KittyTrack 800 with 8 hp. Both had Briggs & Stratton engines.

Massey Ferguson

Massey Ferguson was best known as an agricultural tractor and implement manufacturer, but in 1967 tried its luck in the construction equipment business. Massey Ferguson offered four dozer and four corresponding crawler loader models. These were the MF 200 with 44 fwhp, MF 300 with 65 fwhp, MF3366 with 76 fwhp, and MF500 with 136 fwhp. Bucket capacities of the loaders ranged from ¾ to 2 ¼ cubic yards and dozer blade widths ranged from 6 ft. 8 in. to 10 ft. During the 1970s, MF became affiliated with Hanomag of Germany and offered four dozer and crawler loader models with bucket capacities up to 2.8 yards. The dozers were the MF 300 (69 fwhp), MF D400C (90 fwhp), MF D600C (144 fwhp), and MF D700C (180 fwhp).

Mead-Morrison Manufacturing Co.

Mead-Morrison produced a variety of construction equipment during the teens and 1920s including power shovels, cranes and crane attachments, hoists, winches, snowplows and dozer blades, and two crawler tractor models. The Boston, Massachusetts firm took over Bear Tractor Co. in 1924 and continued building crawler tractors through the 1920s. Mead-Morrison offered the Bear Model B 25-35 until 1925, when it replaced it with the MM 55. The MM 55 had the same Stearns four-cylinder engine with 55 bhp, 43 dbhp and weighed 9,200 lbs. In 1927, the MM 80 was added to the line with a rated 80 bhp, 65 dbhp and weight of 15,000 lbs.

Both tractors had steering wheels instead of clutch levers and featured the same unique shock-absorbing system from Bear Tractor with a torsion bar (and later, leaf springs) mounted under the radia-

Mity Kat
The Mity Kat mini-dozer was powered by a Hercules four-cylinder engine with about 20 hp.

KittyTrack
The KittyTrack was made by the Lennox Machine Co. of Des Moines, Iowa during the 1960s. Two models were offered: the 600 with 6 hp and the 800 with 8 hp, both with Briggs & Stratton engines. The mini-dozer shown is a Model 800.

tor holding double-compression coiled springs attached to outside-mounted track frames. The spring coils kept the lower half of each track under constant pressure by means of three equalizing rollers. As the tracks move over rough ground, the front idler and rear sprocket wheels are raised or depressed, enabling the track to hug the ground along its entire length. Open and enclosed cab versions were sold for both models, so they could be kept busy all year round.

Many of Mead-Morrison's tractors were used by counties and municipalities in New England for grading roads in the summer and plowing snow in the winter. There is no record of tractor production by the company after 1930.

Minneapolis-Moline Co.

Minneapolis Moline Power Implement Co. was formed in 1929 by the merger of Moline Implement Co., Minneapolis Threshing Machine Co. and Minneapolis Steel & Machinery Co. From MS&M's Twin City tractor line, Minneapolis-Moline developed a large and successful line of wheel tractors. However, in what is one of the shortest crawler tractor runs, the company offered dozer and loader models between 1958 and 1961. The machines, called MoTracs, were based on the company's Jetstar tractors and were available with the same four-cylinder gas and diesel engines.

Mity Kat Corp.

Mity Kat of Medford, Massachusetts produced mini-crawler tractors during the 1960s and 70s. The tractors used a Hercules ZXB-3 four-cylinder gasoline engine and an Oliver transmission and rear differential.

Moon Tractor Co.

San Francisco, California-based Moon introduced the Pathmaker 12-25 tractor in 1920. It was powered by a Buda four-cylinder XTU engine with 25 bhp and weighed 7,500 lbs.

National Brake and Electric Co.

This Milwaukee, Wisconsin-based firm offered its Model 25 crawler from the mid-1920s to the early 1930s. Powered by a Continental four-cylinder engine with 38 bhp, the tractor weighed 5,200 lbs. National Brake became the Franco National Tractor Co. during the 1930s, offering two models: Model A and the smaller Model E, available in standard and orchard configurations. The E was available with Waukesha gasoline, kerosene, or diesel engines rated at 35 bhp and 25 dbhp.

Oliver Tractor Co.

Not to be confused with the Oliver Farm Equipment Co. and the Oliver Corp., Oliver Tractor of Knoxville, Tennessee, introduced two crawler models in 1918. These were the Model A with 30 bhp and 15 dbhp and a Model B with 20 bhp and 12 dbhp. Both models had two steel front wheels and two crawler tracks on the rear.

Pan Motor Co.

This St. Cloud, Minnesota firm produced a crawler called the Pan Model 12-24 Tank-Tread in 1919 and 1920. Only a few were produced, and the company went out of business in 1920.

National
Available from 1925 to 1931, the Model 25 crawler was rated at 38 bhp and weighed 5,200 lbs.

MoTrac loader
Minneapolis-Moline offered loader and dozer versions of a crawler tractor based on its Jetstar wheel tractor from 1958 to 1961. With only about 250 units built over 50 years ago, this MoTrac loader is a rare piece. Minneapolis-Moline was acquired by White Motor Co. in 1963, which became part of AGCO Corp. in 1991.

Panther Tractor Corp.
Panther of Dallas, Texas, built a mini-crawler tractor with a unique center-drive sprocket from the late 1940s to the early 60s. Two models were available: the gasoline-fueled TG-4 and the kerosene-fueled TK-4. Both were powered by Waukesha four-cylinder engines rated at 16 hp.

Perrin Tractor & Implement Co.
Perrin, of Portland, Oregon, made a small crawler called the "Terra Trac-Tor" during the late 1940s. It was powered by an 8-hp single-cylinder engine and weighed 1,200 lbs.

Phoenix Manufacturing Co.
The Eau Claire, Wisconsin-based company began building Lombard-designed steam tractors called Centipeds in 1906 under a contract with the Lombard Traction Engine Co. Charles Tolles, a long-time engineer with Phoenix, was in charge of the Centiped project. The Phoenix machines were somewhat different in that they had four vertical cylinders rated at 336 rpm, while the Lombard-built tractors used only two cylinders rated at 250 rpm. In 1914, Phoenix launched a gasoline-powered Centiped with two front steering wheels. It was powered by a 4-cylinder engine with 50 bhp. More than 100 Centipeds were sold, with some shipped as far as Alaska and even Russia. There is no record of crawler production after the late 1920s.

Scientific Farming Machinery Co.
This Minneapolis, Minnesota manufacturer began in 1916 and introduced a crawler tractor in 1919. Called the Tank Tread X 25-50, it had two rear tracks with large rear sprockets and smaller front idler wheels, plus two steel wheels in front. The X 25-50 was powered by a Waukesha engine. The company folded in 1924.

Schramm Inc.
Though best known for its air compressors, Schramm Inc. of West Chester, Pennsylvania offered its Track Welder unit in the late 1940s to about the mid-1950s. A similar Model 60 crawler was available with a 60-cubic-foot-per-minute air compressor unit and a small hydraulic blade for back filling. Other manufacturers of air compressors including Ingersoll-Rand and Chicago Pneumatic also built crawler-tractor compressors during the 1930s, but they were offered for only a few years.

Scott Engineering Corp.
Scott, based in Charleston, West Virginia, introduced its Scott-Six crawler in the late 1920s. The tractor was designed as an industrial and construction machine and featured a double-drum winch attached on the rear as standard equipment. It was powered by a Continental Red Seal six-cylinder engine rated at 30 bhp and 20 dbhp and weighed 5,000 lbs. Scott was bought by Kanawha Manufacturing Co. in 1930, who continued producing the Scott-Six for a year or so longer. Attachments available for the Scott included a dozer blade, front and rear cranes, a cable-operated loader bucket, snowplow, and a telephone pole digger/installer unit.

Schramm
A 1948 Schramm Pneumatractor with a 60-cubic-feet-per-minute air compressor was on display at 2006 HCEA Show in Bowling Green, Ohio.

Panther
A 1947 Panther TG-4 tractor is shown with a 16-hp Waukesha gasoline engine.

Stockton Tractor Co.

Stockton Tractor of Stockton, California offered a crawler version of its wheel tractor in 1920 but dropped in it 1921. Called the Sure-Grip Model B, it had a four-cylinder Herschell-Spillman engine rated at 12 bhp and 8 dbhp. The tractor had steel front wheels and crawlers with elevated sprockets on the rear.

Sullivan Tractor Co.

Sullivan of Oakland, California offered one small crawler model in 1916. It was powered by a four-cylinder Beaver engine rated at 10 bhp, 8 dbhp, and it weighed 4,000 lbs. Production of the tractor was very limited and probably did not last past 1918.

C.F. Struck Corp.

Founded by Charles F. Struck in 1964, the Cedarburg, Wisconsin company has enjoyed the longest run of all the mini-dozer manufacturers. The first Struck crawler, the Mini-Dozer MD-34, was sold in 1967. It was followed by the MD-40, MD-45, MD-50, and MD-55 crawlers which were offered until 1975. Models MD-1200 and MD-1600 along with the MT-1800, the first of the Magnetrac series crawlers, were all made between 1975 and 1986. Until 1986, all Struck crawlers were belt-driven; those built after 1986 are hydraulically driven. From the late 1990s to 2005, Struck offered four compact crawler models: three Magnetrac models, the MH-4800, MH-5000 and the MH-6000, and one Mini-Dozer, the MD-750. Horsepower ranged from 15 bhp for the MD-750 to 28 bhp for the diesel-powered MH-6000; weight of these models ranged from 950 to 2,150 lbs. without attachments. In 2006, Struck narrowed its line to two models: the MH4800 with 25 hp and the MH7000 with 31 hp.

Tom Thumb Tractor Co.

Minneapolis, Minnesota-based Tom Thumb Tractor introduced its Model 12-20 in 1916. It had a four-cylinder Waukesha vertical engine rated at 20 bhp and 12 dbhp. The Tom Thumb used a drive chain to transfer power from the engine to the rear sprocket of its single rear crawler. Steering was accomplished by a steering wheel connected to two large steel wheels in the front.

Union Tool Co.

Union Tool, Torrance, California, built its Sure-Grip Model D crawler between 1914 and 1922. It was powered by a four-cylinder Union engine with 25 bhp, 12 dbhp and weighed 9,980 lbs.

Union Tractor Co.

One of several tractor makers based in San Francisco, California, the Union Tractor's Bulldog tractor was only offered in 1917 and 1918. It was rated at 30 bhp and 18 dbhp.

Western Implement & Motor Co.

Western Implement & Motor of Davenport, Iowa launched its Creeping Grip crawler in 1910. It was rated at 20 bhp and 12 dbhp. Western was bought by the Bullock Tractor Co. in 1912, and assembly of the Creeping Grip tractors was moved to Chicago.

Struck
A late 1960s Struck mini-dozer MD-34 is seen here with a 5-hp Briggs & Stratton single cylinder engine.

CHAPTER EIGHT

WHEEL DOZERS

BULLDOZERS ON WHEELS

During the early days of World War II, Army combat engineers quickly gained an appreciation of the bulldozer. As the war moved to remote locations such as jungles and small islands, the need arose for construction equipment that could be airlifted and dropped at places where there was no other access.

In 1943, the Army Corps of Engineers approached R.G. LeTourneau, Inc. to design and build a small wheeled tractor with a bulldozer blade and a 2 yard scraper. The weight of the machine would have to be within the limits of air transport and rugged enough to withstand an airdrop. The result was the LeTourneau D-4 Tournapull, a small dozer-scraper powered by a Continental gas engine with 45 hp and weighing 6,500 lbs. This first attempt at an integrally-built wheeled bulldozer proved to be underpowered for most chores, but it led the way to bigger and better machines.

Michigan Model 480 Tractor Dozer
With a rated 600 ghp from its Cummins engine, the Model 480 was by far the most powerful wheel or crawler dozer when it was released in 1958. *Vernon Simpson*

Of course, blades had been attached to wheel tractors, and even steam traction engines for many years. But no one had previously built such a machine from scratch that was dedicated to bulldozing. The wheel dozer represented a tradeoff between speed/maneuverability and traction. The Army was particularly interested in the former and continued experimenting with high-speed dozers after World War II.

The promise of large military orders also did much to encourage equipment manufacturers to do their own development of high-speed dozers. Other markets for the wheel dozer included surface mine operators and companies that maintained large stockpiles of raw materials like quarries, the paper pulp and chemical industries and coal-burning utilities.

Some of the engineering problems associated with building wheel dozers include difficulty of attaching the arms of the blade to the tractor frame, the tendency of the blade to tilt with the front axle when turning, and the need for a large turning radius when steering with the front wheels. Initially, most wheel dozers had outside-mounted blade side arms and had either front- or rear-wheel steering. Later models came with inside-mounted blade supports and either all-wheel steering or were articulated.

Right after the war, R.G. LeTourneau began work on a series of four larger wheel dozers ranging in power from 122 to 750 hp and weighing between 10 and 50 tons. The four dozer models were, from largest to smallest, the A, B, C and D. Announced in 1946, the dozers were skid steered and had cable-lifted blades with outside-mounted blade arms. The 750-hp Model A had a Packard marine engine which proved too powerful for the dozer's transmission, and only a few were sold. Two of these machines (Models C and D) remained in production through the 1960s under the Wabco brand after Westinghouse Airbrake Co. purchased LeTourneau in 1953.

Under the terms of the Wabco purchase, R.G. LeTourneau, Inc. was allowed to re-enter the earthmoving equipment business in 1958, and it introduced the first of its giant electric wheel dozers in the following year. By 1961, it was offering five models ranging in weight from 90,000 to 290,000 lbs. and with up to three diesel generators for a combined output of 1,260 ghp. Although none of the electric wheel dozer models sold in large numbers, a version was offered by successor Marathon-LeTourneau until 1985. LeTourneau, now part of the Rowan Companies, offered one wheel dozer model again in 2004.

LaPlant-Choate launched its TD-300 Motor Dozer with a 225-hp engine in 1948. Although the Motor Dozer did not sell well, it offered innovations far ahead of its time like hydraulic blade control, inside-mounted blade arms and all-wheel steering.

Always with an eye on the competition, Caterpillar started work on a dozer blade attachment for its DW-10 tractor. Called the DW-10/10S dozer, it was offered between 1951 and 1955. In 1952, Caterpillar offered a similar blade (20S) for the DW-20 tractor with a 225-hp engine. Both machines had front-wheel steering and used cable-operated blades. The company's next wheel dozer was the No.668/668S, an on-demand four-wheel drive tractor it initially built for the military in 1956. It was available with either hydraulic or cable blades, but was dropped from the product line two years later. During the early 1960s, Caterpillar developed a completely new wheel dozer line, introducing Models 824 and 834 in 1963 followed by the 814 in

Model 180
The Michigan Model 180 Tractor Dozer first appeared in 1955. Initially, the dozer weighed 27,000 lbs. and was powered by a Waukesha 135-DKBS engine with 165 ghp. Later versions offered a GM 6V-53 turbocharged engine rated at 170 ghp or a Cummins C-464-C with 162 ghp and weight increased to 40,000 lbs. The Model 180 had four-wheel drive with a powershift transmission and could move as fast as 27 mph. *Pit & Quarry*

Michigan Wheel Dozer
Model 180. *Vernon Simpson*

1970. Caterpillar's 800-series wheel dozers are still in production with five models in the current product line, including two models from its purchase of Tiger Engineering Pty's patented designs in 1997. They range in power from 240 to 800 fwhp.

Clark Equipment entered the wheel dozer business in 1955 with its Michigan Model 180, followed by larger models (280, 380 and 480) in 1957 and 1958. All of the Michigan dozers had rear-wheel steering and came with hydraulic blades. The Michigan dozer line proved popular with contractors; some upgraded models remained in production through the 1980s.

During the 1960s and 1970s, several other manufacturers tried their hands at the wheel dozer including International-Hough, Allis-Chalmers, M-R-S, Marion, FWD-Wagner and RayGo-Wagner. Each of these companies offered at least one very large wheel dozer (600 to 1,500 ghp) but relatively few units were sold, and all were out of the wheel dozer business by the mid-1980s.

The wheel dozers of Allis-Chalmers (see Volume I), Caterpillar, Euclid and International Harvester are described in the chapters for those manufacturers.

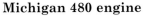

Michigan 480 engine
One of two engines available for the Model 480 was a Cummins VT-1710 diesel rated at 600 ghp, making it by far the most powerful dozer of its day. *Vernon Simpson*

Michigan Wheel Dozers
TOP TO BOTTOM. Models 280, 380 and 480. *Vernon Simpson*

Clark Equipment Co. – Michigan Wheel Dozers

Clark Equipment Company was established in 1903 as a drill bit manufacturer. By 1911, it had diversified to wheels and in 1916 started making axles and other specialty steel products. Clark first entered the construction business during World War II with a contract to build a small air-drop dozer, the CA-1 for the U.S. Army (see Other Manufacturers chapter).

In 1953, Clark acquired the Ross Carrier Co. and its Michigan Power Shovel subsidiary and formed a construction machinery division. It also hired Clarence Killebrew, an engineer with the Frank G. Hough Co. to help design a new line of wheel loaders with torque converters, powershift transmissions and planetary axles. The prototype loaders appeared promising, so Clark opened a new factory at Benton Harbor, Michigan.

The following year, Clark launched three wheel loader models under the Michigan name, the 75A, 125A and 175A. The machines proved popular, and in 1955 Clark offered the first of a series of wheel dozers, the Model 180 Tractor Dozer. Like its loaders, the Tractor Dozer had a rigid frame and rear-wheel steering.

By 1958, the Michigan Tractor Dozer had expanded to four models (180, 280, 380 and 480) ranging from 165 to 600 ghp. The wheel dozers were available with a variety of blade types including an angledozer, coal dozer, cushioned push-block, U-blade, heavy-duty mining blade, rear push-block for tandem push-loading and a snowplow.

In 1965, Clark redesigned its loader and wheel dozer line to include articulated machines. The Model 480 was dropped in 1966, and production of the 180 ceased a few years later. Clark experimented with an articulated version of the Model 180, but it never made it into the product line. Models 280 and 380 continued through a number of upgrades until 1994, when the wheel dozer line ended.

Clark Michigan formed a 50-50 joint venture with Volvo AB of Sweden in 1985. The new firm was called V.M.E. (Volvo-Michigan-Euclid) and operated as V.M.E. Americas in North America. In 1994, the name Michigan was dropped and in 1995, V.M.E. Americas became Volvo Construction Equipment, a subsidiary of AB Volvo headquartered in Belgium.

Model 380
Pit & Quarry

Model 380
The Model 380 first appeared in 1957. It was powered by either a GM or a Cummins engine with 375 ghp. The machine weighs 94,000 lbs. with blade attached. *Vernon Simpson*

Model 480
The Model 480 was offered with either a 12-cylinder Cummins VT-1710-C, initially with 600 ghp (later 635 ghp) or a 16-cylinder GM 16V-71N rated at 635 ghp. Introduced in 1958, the big dozer weighed 105,000 lbs. with its standard blade attached. This Model 480 pushes a load of broken rock on an interstate highway job in Indiana. Ralph Myers Contracting Corp. of Salem, Indiana is the contractor. *Pit & Quarry*

Model 380B
The articulated 380B is powered by a Cummins VT-1710-C engine that produces 635 ghp and 572 fwhp. Equipped with a 15-ft. 9-in wide blade and counterweights, the dozer weighs 122,950 lbs. This Michigan 380B spreads fill from scrapers on a Haverhill Contracting Co. highway project in Columbia, Maryland.

Model 290M
In 1962, Clark won a contract to build a specially-designed wheel dozer for the U.S. Army. The machine was based on the same specifications as the Caterpillar 830M wheel dozer, including an articulated frame, four-wheel drive and the ability to pull an 18 yard scraper. Unlike all of Michigan's other models, it had a front-mounted engine. The 290M was powered by a Cummins NT380 turbocharged diesel rated at 350 fwhp, and it weighed 54,190 lbs. with a blade. The dozer was relatively light for its size and power, and it could travel with a scraper in tow at 25 mhp. This 290M is part of the U.S. Army Engineer Museum collection at Fort Leonard Wood, Missouri.

R.G. LeTourneau, Inc.
(See company history in the Blade Manufacturers chapter)

Model D-4 Airborne Dozer-scraper
During the early days of World War II, R.G. LeTourneau, Inc. worked with the U.S. Army to develop an air-deployable earthmover that could be dropped into remote locations. Such a machine was particularly needed for the war effort in the Pacific, where landing strips and bases had to be built on many of the islands. The result was a combination wheel dozer and small scraper, and it was the first mass-produced integrated wheel dozer. The tractor was powered by a four-cylinder Continental gas engine with 45 bhp. The total weight of the unit was 6,500 lbs. The blade and the two-yard scraper were operated by a three-drum cable control unit behind the seat. The machine shown here is a 1944 version at the 2003 HCEA Show in Bowling Green, Ohio. *Historical Construction Equipment Association*

Model A
By far the most powerful dozer of its time (1947-49) and for a decade after, the Model A Tournadozer boasted a maximum 750 ghp from a Packard marine engine fueled with liquid butane. *Eric C. Orlemann*

Model C
The Model C was upgraded to the Super C in 1953 just before LeTourneau was sold to Westinghouse Air Brake Co. (Wabco). It remained in the Wabco Product line until 1972 and was by far the best selling Tournadozer model. Wabco offered a wide variety of attachments for the Super C including tree-stingers, push blocks, side-boom cranes, snowplows and even couplers for switching rail cars on paved sidings.

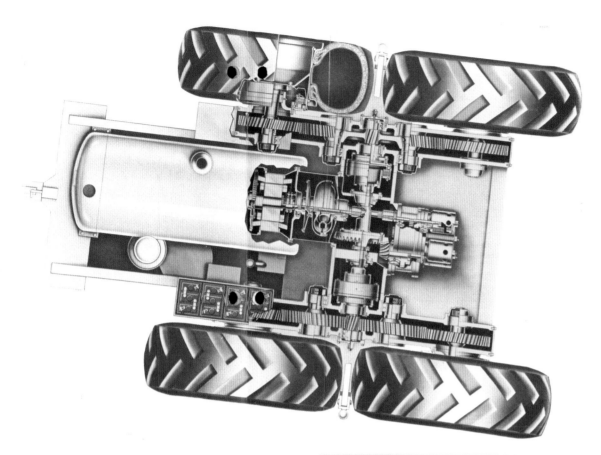

Model C

R.G. LeTourneau, Inc. announced a line of wheel dozers in 1946 that was matched to its motor scraper models. The wheel dozers included the Models A, B, C and D. The 750-hp Model A was largely experimental although a few were sold. The B was the largest production model with a 300-hp engine and weight of 25 tons. Next came the C shown here, offered initially with a 160 fwhp Buda diesel, but later given a GM 6-71 with 218 fwhp. The Model C weighed 30,000 lbs. *Vernon Simpson*

Model K-53

After developing a series of giant electric wheel scrapers, LeTourneau began work on a line of electric wheel dozers. Introduced in 1960, the K-53 was one of the first of these machines dubbed Pacemaker Tractors to be placed on the market. The K-Series dozers were numbered with the last digit reflecting the number of wheels; thus, the K-53 was a three-wheel dozer. The K-53 was powered by a GM 12V-71 diesel that turned a LeTourneau AC-DC generator set. The generator provided DC power to each of the three drive wheels and AC power for the steering and blade lifting motors and other tractor functions. Total weight of the dozer was 90,000 lbs. *Gary Hansen*

Model K-54

LEFT. Launched in 1960, the K-54 was a four-wheel articulated dozer with one GM 12V-71 diesel generator that produced 420 ghp for its DC electric drive wheel motors. *Eric C. Orlemann*

Model K-205

RIGHT. LeTourneau's largest Pacemaker dozer was the K-205. It was a five-wheel machine with three diesel generators producing a combined 1,260 ghp to its five wheel-mounted DC motors. The prototype machine had three Cummins V12-420 engines rated at 420 ghp each, but GM 12V-71s with the same horsepower were also available. The dozer was introduced in 1961 and put to work in 1962 at the Hubbard Creek Dam Project in Breckenridge, Texas where it was used to push-load 40-yard scrapers. The machine weighed between 120 and 143 tons depending on attachments and could be ballasted to 187 tons. Only one K-205 is known to have been built. *Eric C. Orlemann*

Model K-103

LEFT. The K-103 was a three-wheel dozer with two diesel generators – GM 12V-71s rated at a total of 840 ghp. The machine was first offered in 1961 and weighed 132,000 lbs. *Eric C. Orlemann*

T-Series Wheel Dozers

In 1966, LeTourneau replaced its K Series wheel dozers with the T Series starting with the T-300A and T-450A dozers. These were single-engine diesel electric articulated-frame machines with more of a conventional look than most of the K models, except the K-54, its 4-wheel predecessor. In 1969, the company started calling its wheel dozers Letro-Dozers. As with all of its previous wheel dozer models, only a few were produced.

Model T-450A

A T-450A pushes wood chips with its light-material blade. Originally introduced in 1965 as the Model K-54, the diesel-electric dozer uses a 475 ghp GM 12V-71N engine and weighs 41 tons. *Eric C. Orlemann*

T-600B

The T-600A was replaced by the B in 1969, and it was offered through 1970. Like the T-600A, it was powered by a GM 16V-71N diesel generator rated at 635 ghp and 609 fwhp. Weight of the machine is 136,440 lbs. *LeTourneau Inc.*

T-600A

LeTourneau announced the Model K-600A in December 1966, but changed it to the T Series as the T-600A in 1967. Each wheel of the articulated-frame dozer was powered by a DC electric motor tied to a generator run by a GM 16V-71 engine rated at 635 ghp and 605 fwhp. *Gary Hansen*

Model T-600A

As the model number on the machine shows, the T-600A was first called a K-600A when tested in 1967, but then renamed the T-600A in 1968, the first of the new T-series dozers. This T-600A with a push-block is powered by a 635-ghp GM 16V-71N diesel engine and weighs 135,000 lbs. *Eric C. Orlemann*

LeTourneau-Westinghouse Co. (Wabco)
Model C

After purchasing R.G. LeTourneau, Inc. in 1953, Westinghouse Air Brake Co. (Wabco) dropped the Model B but kept the C and D dozers in its product line. Two power options were available for the Wabco Model C: a 2-cycle GM 6-71 with 218 fwhp or a 4-cycle Cummins HBIS-600 with 200 fwhp. The Wabco Model C is equipped with a torque converter and a four-speed forward (2 reverse), constant mesh transmission and can move as fast as 17.2 mph (7.2 mph in reverse).

Model D

LeTourneau-Westinghouse or Wabco announced the redesigned Model D Tournatractor in 1956. It featured a 143-fwhp GM 4-71 diesel engine and a planetary steering system for full power while turning. The Model D was dropped from production in 1960. *Pit & Quarry*

Model Twin-C
The Twin-C was introduced in 1956 and was available through 1959. It featured two GM 6-71 diesels with 210 fwhp each for a total of 420 fwhp. The articulated push-dozer weighed just over 80,000 lbs. and could move as fast as 20 mph. The Twin-C here is push-loading a LeTourneau-Westinghouse Model B scraper. *Gary Hansen*

Marathon-LeTourneau Co.
D-800 LeTro-Dozer
Soon after Marathon Manufacturing Co. acquired R.G. LeTourneau, Inc. in 1970, it dropped the wheel dozer line to concentrate on diesel-electric wheel loaders. However, in 1978 the company gave wheel dozers another try in the form of the D-800 LeTro-Dozer. Two power options were offered: a Cummins KT2300-C 12-cylinder engine rated at 900 ghp and 820 fwhp or a GM 16V-92T 16-cylinder engine rated at 860 ghp and 800 fwhp. Weight of the machine ranges from 193,000 to 214,400 lbs, depending on dozer options: standard blade, coal blade or mine reclamation blade. *LeTourneau Inc.*

Peerless Manufacturing Co.
V-Con V-250 wheel dozer
In the late 1960s, Peerless Manufacturing Company's Vehicle Constructor (V-Con) Division of Dallas, Texas designed a large diesel-electric wheel dozer for reclaiming surface mines. The dozer, designated the V-250, was powered by a 1,000-ghp diesel generator that supplied power to DC electric motors in each wheel. Equipped with a 22-ft. wide blade, the machine weighed in at 250,000 lbs. Only one V-250 was built in 1970 and lack of additional orders caused the project to be cancelled. *Historical Construction Equipment Association*

LaPlant-Choate Manufacturing Co.
(See company profile in Blade Manufacturers chapter.)

TD-300 Motor Dozer
LaPlant-Choate tried to compete with R.G. LeTourneau's wheel dozers by offering the Motor Dozer in 1948. Distinct advantages of the Motor Dozer were its all-wheel steering and hydraulically-operated blade that could exert downward pressure when pushing dirt. The 47,000-lb. dozer came with a Buda diesel engine rated at 225 fwhp. Its two four-speed transmissions gave it a total of eight speeds forward and two in reverse. The top speed of the dozer was 22.5 mph. Only a few Motor Dozers were sold, and it was not continued after LaPlant-Choate was taken over by Allis-Chalmers in 1952. *Gary Hansen*

Marion Power Shovel Co., V-Con Division
V-220 wheel dozer
Marion Power Shovel Co. purchased the Vehicle Constructor (V-Con) line from Peerless Manufacturing Co. in 1974 and redesigned the V-Con V-250 into its own Model V-220 wheel dozer. It used a Detroit Diesel 16V-149T electric generator set to power the electric motors in each wheel. The engine was rated at 1,500 ghp, a 50% increase over the V-250. The weight was increased by 50,000 lbs. from the V-250 to 150 tons. The V-220 was outfitted with a 26-ft.-wide blade and was marketed for surface mine excavation and reclamation work. After only two units were sold, the V-220 was dropped from the product line. *Historical Construction Equipment Association*

M-R-S Manufacturing Co.
M-R-S 200

Mississippi Road Services, or M-R-S, built wheel tractors for industrial and construction applications in the early 1950s, most of which could be outfitted with M-R-S blades. In the early 1960s, the company started designing and testing a line of articulated wheel tractors and dozers, in part in anticipation of a large military contract. Scrapers and dump wagons were offered for each tractor/dozer model. In 1964, M-R-S was awarded a contract to build the Model 100M, a military version of its I-100 wheel dozer for the U. S. Navy and the Marine Corps. It weighed 24,000 lbs. and was powered by a 143-fwhp GM 4-71 engine. M-R-S offered several other wheel dozers including the Model 200 for civilian (shown here) and military use. The M-R-S 200 was equipped with a GM 8-71 engine advertised at 335 fwhp. At least 10 other M-R-S tractor models were available with blade attachments. M-R-S was acquired by Taylor Machine Works, Inc. of Louisville, Mississippi in 1986, and production of the wheel tractor-dozer line ended. *Pit & Quarry*

FWD Wagner, Inc.

Wagner offered small blade attachments for its Scoopmobile wheel loaders in the late 1940s. During the 1950s, the company expanded with a line of wheel tractors with optional blades called Dozermobiles. After becoming part of the FWD Corp. in 1961, it developed a larger wheel dozer, the WI-30, with twin Cummins engines and all-wheel drive. Blades and/or push-blocks were mounted on either end, and dual controls were placed in the cab so that "either direction is forward." An even bigger dozer, the WD-30 was sold in the late 1960s that featured double tires on all four wheels, and of course, all-wheel drive.

RayGo acquired Wagner in the early 1970s and expanded the wheel dozer line to eight models, nearly all with Cummins power ranging from 335 to 700 ghp. Three RayGo models, CHD-30, CD-1200 and 40/60 were successors to the WD-30; all had 700 ghp Cummins engines, powershift transmissions with torque converters and 60-ton shipping weights.

Model WD-30
Power for the WD-30 came from a Cummins diesel rated at 700 ghp. The 60-ton dozer was used mostly for material handling such as maintaining coal and wood chip stockpiles and strip mine reclamation. Hydro-inflation of the tires added another 18,000 lbs. for a total weight of 138,000 lbs. *Gary Hansen*

MODEL HD-15 — 102.0 DRAWBAR hp. — 27,500 lb.

190

CHAPTER NINE

BLADE MANUFACTURERS

The concept of the bulldozer goes as far back as the earliest civilizations that used oxen and other animals to push or pull small piles of earth and rocks. Ancient Egyptian drawings show animals pulling rope-drawn boards to level the ground, and the Romans used similar devices in the construction of their roads and buildings. In the 1800s, wooden blades were hitched to teams of horses or mules in the construction of canals, railroads and early turnpikes. These were usually attached to the tongue and front wheels from a wagon. Grader manufacturers like Russell and Western even offered such blades for sale in their equipment catalogs.

Blade builders

In this early 1950s scene, an Allis-Chalmers HD-15 (left) with a Gar Wood Industries cable-operated blade and an A-C HD-9 with a Baker Manufacturing hydraulically-operated blade team up to move a wide swath of dirt. A-C acquired Baker in 1955 and started its own integrally-built line of dozers with blades based largely on Baker's designs. Gar Wood continued building blades for Euclid until 1963, when it purchased the rights to blades and other crawler attachments from Gar Wood. By this time, nearly all of the major crawler tractor manufacturers had their own line of blades and other attachments, and Gar Wood had to focus on other lines of business.

As steam tractors came into being in the late 1800s, contractors experimented with attaching blades in front to move earth; a Holt steam-powered tractor equipped with a wooden plank blade bolted to the front was used to push debris and muck from the streets of Stockton, California after a major flood in 1902. But it was the development of the crawler tractor that enabled the bulldozer to reach its full potential. The crawler provided the power, grip, weight distribution and turning ability needed to move large volumes of rock, dirt and other materials.

Three types of blade designs were initially built: (1) backfiller, a light, low-profile blade similar to a snowplow used for pushing loose material back into excavations such as pipelines and basements; (2) bulldozer, heavier and higher in profile than a backfiller, which exerts at least some downward force by either its weight or by pressure from a hydraulic cylinder; and (3) angledozer or trailbuilder, a blade that can be set at angles up to 45° with the tractor and is used for opening hillside cuts or grading material to one side that is usually lower.

In the 1940s, specialty blades came on the market. These included coal and woodchip blades, root and brush rakes, rock and stump blades, tree-shearing blades, V-blades for bank grading, "U" and

LaPlant-Choate blade
An example of one of the earliest LaPlant-Choate hand-operated blades is seen on this 1925 Holt Model T-35 tractor in Canandaigua, New York.

ROBERT G. LETOURNEAU AND THE BULLDOZER

Robert G. LeTourneau started out as an excavating contractor in the San Francisco Bay area and in 1926 his firm had grown large enough to win a contract for a highway across Crow Canyon in the Dublin Mountains between Oakland and Stockton. Because of the size of the job and the company's limited finances, it was a make-or-break contract. Since deep cuts were required, LeTourneau decided that the quickest way to open the cuts would be with a blade attached to the front of a crawler tractor, rather than the traditional and more costly approach of using power shovels. Such blades were already in existence and were being used by the U.S. Forest Service and others, but they were small and attached to weak tractors.

In *Mover of Men and Mountains*, LeTourneau writes, "I have it on good authority that no one knows where the name bulldozer comes from, nor who invented it. But that's its name, and I'll put my name in with many others in claiming to have invented it. Up to now, with minor concessions, I've won all my arguments with other claimants to the title. Plowboards, or what we now call dozer blades, were used by the Mormons in the early days of Salt Lake City, and were later used with varying degrees of success with mule power and tractors. All had the same weakness. The blade couldn't be lifted out of the ground for turning or backing."

"Stuck up there in Crow Canyon, my contribution was the first practical blade

Robert G. LeTourneau (1888 - 1969)
LeTourneau University

192

"semi-U" blades, inside push-beam blades, and push blocks for scraper loading. During the 1950s and 1960s, the universal blade came into being that could be tilted forward and back, side to side and set at various angles. Case was the first with the power-tilt universal blade, which could be adjusted from the cab.

LaPlant-Choate Manufacturing Co. started making snowplows for wheel tractors in the 1910s and experimented with snowplows on a few crawlers. Competitor Mack Wooldridge mounted snowplows on Best tractors as early as 1918. One of the first recorded sales of bulldozers was to the City of South Milwaukee, Wisconsin in 1922. The city purchased several Best tractors with snowplow blades modified by the dealer to spread garbage at its dump. Some of the early crawler tractor makers like Best, Holt and Monarch experimented with their own blades during the teens and early twenties, but never produced any in quantity.

Another pioneer in adapting blades to crawlers was Ted Flynn of the U.S. Forest Service. As an engineer for several large National Forests in the Western U.S., Flynn saw the need for better logging roads and fire trails. As he recounted in his memoirs (see *Forest History*, Fall 1963), "(In 1923, I) was watching a little Cletrac (tractor)

pulling a small grader behind trying to open a new road up to Mt. Adams (Washington) on a very steep hillside, where the grader rolled over about 10 times that day. (Seeing that) gave me the idea of why not an angle blade in front of the tractor. Without funds, blacksmith Joe Meadows and myself built a counterbalanced, hand-lift, angle blade bulldozer using a worn horse (drawn) grader blade and scrap metal. We attached it to this little Cletrac tractor and put it to work on our Carson-Guler forest road. It was very good for side casting and moved as much material as three teams of horses with Fresnos. It fell off in a few days, but it proved an idea."

Commercially-made bulldozer blades came into being in the mid-1920s, and by the end of the decade, pioneer manufacturers such as LaPlant-Choate, Baker, Wooldridge and R.G. LeTourneau were turning them out in large numbers. LaPlant-Choate tried mounting a straight steel blade in front of a crawler tractor in the early 1920s and started offering them for sale in 1923. These early blades were raised and lowered manually, usually by a winch with a hand wheel.

In 1925, LaPlant-Choate introduced the first hydraulically-operated blade powered by the tractor's engine. Two years later, it offered the first commercial angledozer. Baker Manufacturing Co., another

that could be raised or lowered at will, with push-button controls... I put a steel scraper blade out in front of my new Best [Sixty] tractor, rigged it up with an electric cable winch, and wove the cable through some sheaves. A press of the button would lift the blade out of the ground for easy turning or backing up. Another touch of the button would shut off the power, and the blade would dig into the ground of its own weight. It was to change the course of heavy construction history, but all I knew then was that it was bulldozing me out of a tight spot."

After the success at Crow Canyon, LeTourneau continued to refine the cable-operated dozer blade. In 1928, he developed the first electric cable control unit for other attachments like rippers and scrapers, and he built the first direct-drive power control unit in 1930. LeTourneau began marketing cable-operated bulldozer blades in 1932 and offered the first angle-dozer in 1933.

A partnership was established with Caterpillar Tractor Co. in 1934 through which LeTourneau blades and other attachments were sold and serviced by Caterpillar dealers. This prompted LeTourneau to open a new blade and attachment factory a year later in Peoria, Illinois just across the river from Caterpillar's tractor plant. By 1936, the company was offering three styles of blade-lifting frames that were adaptable to nearly any tractor sold at the time. Although there were many other blade makers such as Baker, Wooldridge, LaPlant-Choate, Bucyrus-Erie and Gar-Wood, R.G. LeTourneau became the dominant blade producer during the late 1930s and 1940s.

The LeTourneau company built more than 14,000 blade units just for the military during World War II. Seventy percent of all earthmoving equipment used by the Allies during the war was all or partly constructed by LeTourneau. After the war,

LeTourneau designed and marketed the first heavy duty wheel dozers called "Tournadozers." Westinghouse Airbrake Co. (Wabco) acquired the earthmoving equipment division of LeTourneau in 1953, with a proviso that LeTourneau stay out of the construction equipment business for five years. Surprisingly, at age 70 LeTourneau reentered the business in 1958 and developed a line of giant electric wheel dozers and other construction machines in the late 1950s and 1960s.

LeTourneau was granted his first patent in 1923 at age 34, and he received his 299th and last patent at age 77, making him one of the top inventors of all time. There were other pioneers in the bulldozer business such as partners E.W. LaPlant and Roy Choate, Ted Flynn and Earl Hall of the U.S. Forest Service, and Mack Wooldridge, who had his own equipment manufacturing company, but none were as successful as LeTourneau in refining, promoting and marketing their inventions.

early snowplow maker, was close on LaPlant's heels offering a blade in 1924 for Monarch tractors that lifted up as the machine backed up. In 1926, Baker perfected a hydraulic lifting device for its blade. Because of the low power of the early hydraulic mechanisms, blades were mounted to beams that extended beyond the rear of the tractor to gain as much counter balance as possible.

LeTourneau opted for a cable-lifting system, as cables could lift more weight and were deemed more reliable at the time. At first the LeTourneau system used an electric motor to retract the cable, but it was dropped in favor of the less complicated winch that was powered directly from the tractor engine. This mechanism, called the power control unit or PCU, became an integral part of bulldozer operation. Until hydraulic control equipment achieved the power and reliability of the PCU, most large crawler tractors destined for the construction industry were PCU-equipped.

By 1928, LeTourneau was selling cable-operated blades for most makes of crawler tractors, and in the early 1930s, it became affiliated with Caterpillar Tractor Co. as a supplier of blades and other attachments. Some of the other blade builders followed suit and aligned themselves with tractor makers: LaPlant-Choate and Rome Plow with Caterpillar, Baker and Gar Wood with Allis-Chalmers, and Bucyrus-Erie with International Harvester. However, most of the 70+ blade makers remained independent, offering a unique type of blade, lower cost product, or they served a local geographic area.

Many small builders sprang up in the late 1930s and 1940s when farm crawlers were being replaced by wheel tractors. Those crawlers with life remaining were picked up by contractors and loggers and usually given a blade. Caterpillar was the first tractor manufacturer to build blades and other attachments for its own machines, offering cable blades in 1946 and hydraulic blades in 1948. This started the practice of building integrated bulldozers in which attachments and tractor were designed and assembled together.

Baker Manufacturing Co., Springfield, Illinois

M. W. Baker was among the handful of pioneer bulldozer blade makers. He founded Baker Manufacturing Co. in 1908 in Plano (near Aurora), Illinois. The company began with 12 employees assembling road grading machinery. As the firm grew, it moved to a larger facility in Springfield, Illinois in 1913. By the late teens, Baker had expanded its product line to snowplows, scrapers, sweepers and backfiller blades for wheel tractors.

After World War I, Baker experimented with backfillers and was one of the first companies to offer bulldozer blades as an off-the-shelf product. In 1924, the company attached a blade to a crawler tractor on a frame that was raised as the tractor backed up. Two years later, Baker came out with a manually-operated hydraulic lifting device for the blade and by 1928 was offering blades lifted by hydraulic power pumped from the tractor engine. After Monarch Tractor opened in Springfield, Baker tested its blades on the new crawlers and soon became an approved supplier of Monarch tractor attachments. In fact, it was on a Monarch 6-Ton tractor that Baker tested its first hydraulically-powered blade. With the purchase of Monarch by Allis-Chalmers in 1928, Baker became closely allied with A-C, a relationship that would last for nearly 30 years.

LeTourneau blade
A LeTourneau bulldozer with Type B cable frame on a Caterpillar Diesel Seventy-Five tractor.

LeTourneau blade
The LeTourneau blade with Type A cable frame on a Caterpillar D-8 tractor.

LeTourneau K-205 wheel dozer
Here is a close-up view of the blade and electrically-driven rack-and-pinion lifting mechanism for one of the earliest of R.G. LeTourneau's electric-drive wheel dozers. *Eric C. Orlemann collection*

Baker's Springfield plant soon grew to capacity, and the firm opened a second factory 50 miles west in Beardstown, Illinois. The Springfield plant had more than 500 employees, and the Beardstown plant grew to 65. In 1930, Baker developed the first twin-cylinder hydraulic lifting device for blades and by 1932 was offering the first double-acting cylinders that permitted downward pressure to be exerted on the blade. These evolved into the well-known vertical cylinders connected by a frame to form a high arch over the tractor engine. During the 1930s, Baker developed hydraulic blades for all A-C crawler tractor models.

In 1946, Baker and A-C engineers began work on a new bulldozer, the HD-19, which would be designed and built specifically for bulldozing. Baker made the hard-nose grill with side-mounted hydraulic cylinders for the HD-19, dropping the vertical-lift frame design it used since the early 1930s. It, along with Caterpillar's cable-operated D-6, D-7, and D-8, were the first integrally-built crawler bulldozers. At 163 fwhp and a weight of 20 tons, the HD-19 was the world's largest crawler tractor, though a few months later International's TD-24 grabbed the title. Following a trend set by Caterpillar and others to build blades and other tractor attachments in-house, Allis-Chalmers bought Baker Manufacturing in 1955. After that, all blades built by the company had the A-C logo.

Balderson, Inc., Wamego, Kansas

Founded in 1949 by Willard Balderson, the company built dozer blades, tree and rock clearing blades and rakes and loader buckets primarily for Caterpillar tractors. Balderson was famous for fabricating the 48-ft.-wide blade for the Caterpillar twin D-9 "Double Dude" surface mine reclamation dozers in the late 1960s.

LeTourneau blade
A LeTourneau Type C cable frame and blade on a Caterpillar Diesel 50 tractor.

BAKER AND THE X-DOZER

One of the most unusual ideas in blade design was the X-Dozer, which Baker introduced in 1952. The X-Dozer featured a blade attached directly to the front frame of the tractor which used mid-mounted hydraulic cylinders to raise and lower the tractor chassis and blade. Two models were offered: HD-9X for the Allis-Chalmers HD-9 tractor and HD-15X for the HD-15. The HD-9 was rated at 79 hp and weighed about 21,500 lbs. with a 9X blade, while the HD-15 had 118 hp and a weight of 34,600 lbs. with a 15X blade. The 9X blade could be pushed as deep as 13 inches below grade and lifted as high as 37 inches above ground; the 15X could go 15 inches below grade and 39½ inches above ground. Downward pressure on the blade always included the weight of the engine, and the extra weight of the side push arms was eliminated; the X-Dozer blade is about 1,500 lbs. lighter than a similar sized side-arm blade. Both the HD-9X and HD-15X dozers were eight feet wide, allowing them to be hauled without special permits.

The close blade mounting improved fine-grading capability, was better for cutting down slopes, and was easier to turn while dozing. Visibility was improved when the blade was lowered, but poor when raised. An oversized hydraulic system was needed to handle the engine weight, and it was difficult to use the tractor if the system was not functioning properly. Although the tractor's power was transmitted more directly to the front of the blade than with side-mounted push arms, stresses from dozing were transmitted more directly back to the entire tractor instead of the undercarriage. Baker advertised the X-Dozers as especially well suited for digging farm ponds and mud pits for oil wells. The closer position of the blade to the tractor allowed a steeper angle of approach for making deep cuts.

The X-Dozers were offered through 1955, when Baker became part of Allis-Chalmers and production of the HD-9 and HD-15 tractors ended. Although certainly not best sellers, the novel blade did lead to the inside push-beam dozer which is still in use on many models today.

Baker & Allis-Chalmers **team up to bring you the** *first radical change* **in bulldozer design since Baker pioneered the hydraulic control bulldozer in 1926!**

For Versatility Plus Haulability...

Baker HD-9X Dozer
An Allis-Chalmers HD-9 tractor converted to an HD-9X Dozer pushes dirt away from a creek bed for a new pond. *Gary Hansen*

Baker blade
Early Baker hydraulic blade on an Allis-Chalmers Model S tractor at the Vintage Tracks Museum.

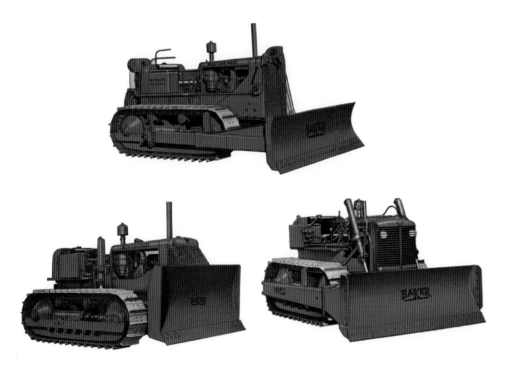

Baker blades
These are examples of Baker cable and hydraulic blades on Allis-Chalmers tractors available in the early 1950s. *Doug Frye*

Bucyrus-Erie Co., South Milwaukee, Wisconsin

Bucyrus-Erie was established in 1927 with the merger of the two steam shovel building companies. The merged company built hydraulic blades for International Harvester T- and TD-6, 9, 14, 18 tractors and cable blades for TD-18 and TD-24 tractors between 1938 and 1953. Bucyrus-Erie tractor attachments were sold exclusively by IH dealers. The B-E straight bulldozer blades and its "Bullgrader" angledozer blades were very popular with contractors in the 1940s and 1950s.

Case Corporation, Racine, Wisconsin

See company profile in Volume I. Case began building hydraulic dozer blades and loader buckets in 1957 for the crawler tractor line it acquired from American Tractor Co. Case continues to offer a full line of hydraulic blades for its crawler models.

Caterpillar Tractor Co., Peoria, Illinois

See company profile in Chapter 1. Caterpillar was the first tractor manufacturer to build blades and other attachments for its own machines, offering cable-operated blades for its larger (D-6, D-7 and D-8) tractors in 1946 and hydraulically-operated blades in 1948.

Continental Roll & Steel Foundry Co., East Chicago, Illinois

Continental offered hydraulic blades primarily for International Harvester TracTracTors during the 1930s. It became part of blade maker Gar Wood Industries in 1940.

Deere and Co., Dubuque, Iowa and Moline, Illinois

The Deere dozer line started in 1948 with a hydraulic blade attachment for its newly-released Model MC crawler and added the No. 61 blade for its Model 40 in 1952. Deere now produces a full line of hydraulic blades for all of its crawler tractor models. See company profile in Chapter 3.

Euclid Road Machinery Co., Euclid (Cleveland), Ohio

Euclid made hydraulic dozer blades during the 1920s and 30s for most of the popular makes of crawler tractors. Ironically, when Euclid entered the crawler business in 1954, it had to subcontract blades and lifting equipment to Gar Wood Industries. After GM purchased Gar Wood in 1963, Euclid and later Terex were able to produce their own blades. See company profile in Chapter 5.

Florida Land Clearing Equipment Co. (FLECO), Jacksonville, Florida

FLECO was a manufacturer of rock rakes, tree pushers and other land-clearing blades and rakes, including the "Stumper," a device resembling a push-block with teeth that mounted on the C-frame of the bulldozer. The company also offered the "V-Tree Cutter," a V-shaped blade with a sharp, serrated lower cutting edge. This blade was available for Caterpillar tractor models D-4, D-5, D-6, D-7 and D-8.

The Heil Co., Milwaukee, Wisconsin, and Hillside, New Jersey

Heil was established in 1901, and is still in the construction business, though it no longer makes blades. Heil built the hydraulically-operated (Trailbuilder) and angledozer blades for International Harvester TD-6, 9, and 14 tractors and cable blades for larger IH tractors

Balderson
Balderson BD-16C inside-mounted blade is on a Caterpillar D-6C tractor. *Pit & Quarry*

Balderson
A 14-ft.-wide Balderson BB9-14 Bowldozer Blade is attached to a Caterpillar D-9 tractor. *Pit & Quarry*

Bucyrus-Erie blade
A B-E hydraulic blade on an International Harvester TD-14A tractor is seen at work near Richmond, Virginia.

including the TD-18 and 24. Heil also offered blades for Cletrac tractors including the Model HD-60 blade for Cletrac DD and DG crawlers and the Model HT-35 for the Cletrac BD and BG crawlers. Heil's blades were up to 14 ft. wide.

International Harvester Co., Melrose Park, Illinois

See company profile in Chapter 6. IHC relied on Bucyrus-Erie, Isaacson, Heil, Continental and other attachment manufacturers to supply blades for its tractor line and began a joint marketing venture with Drott Manufacturing Corp. in 1950 for front-end loaders. After the mid-1950s, International offered its own cable- and hydraulically-operated blades.

Isaacson Iron Works, Seattle, Washington

Issacson Iron Works was organized in 1907 and became a popular blade manufacturer during the 1930s and 1940s. The company built "Circle I Brand" Trac-Dozer cable and hydraulic blades primarily for International Harvester tractors. Isaacson offered both front- and rear-mounted power control units for its blades and to operate its pull-scrapers. It also sold a line of "Klearing-Dozer" brush rake blades.

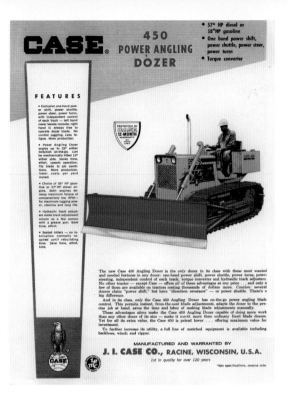

Case blade
An example of Case dozer blades is the Power-Angling Dozer on the Model 450 Tractor, which was released in 1965. *Case Corporation*

Bucyrus-Erie blade
A B-E cable-operated blade is on an International Harvester TD-24 tractor.

LaPlant-Choate Manufacturing Co., Cedar Rapids, Iowa

Nephews E.W. LaPlant and Roy Choate started by building horse-drawn stump pullers in Cedar Rapids in 1911. The pair soon got into other types of logging and construction equipment such as horse- and tractor-drawn logging wheels and dump wagons. In 1923, LaPlant-Choate became the first to make hand-operated bulldozer blades for crawler tractors on a production basis.

Prior to this, blades had been built on a made-to-order basis or fabricated by contractors for their own use. LaPlant-Choate had been testing their new blades on tractors from Best and Holt, and after the formation of Caterpillar Tractor in 1925, became one of its affiliated suppliers of blades and allied equipment.

The year 1925 also marked LaPlant-Choate's introduction of the first hydraulically-operated dozer blade. This early dozer was readily identified by the rectangular frame and round hydraulic oil tank behind the operator. The push frame for the blade was mounted with a fulcrum near the center of the tractor's track frame. The hydraulic pump was driven by a power take-off shaft from the engine. A hydraulic cylinder pushed down on the back of the push frame to raise the blade. Under this arrangement, the operator could not exert downward pressure on the blade. The high mounting of the pump and cylinder left the drawbar free for towing equipment without disconnecting the blade.

LaPlant-Choate incorporated in 1927 and expanded its Cedar Rapids factory. During the 1930s, it developed hydraulic blades for all models in the Caterpillar lineup and cable blades for the larger models. In 1940, LaPlant-Choate started building hydraulic scrapers for Caterpillar's new DW-10 wheel tractor and also started offering a wide variety of dozer blades for land clearing and logging operations. During World War II, the company was a major supplier of hydraulic blades for the U.S. military and the Allies. In 1943, LaPlant-Choate was awarded a contract to supply hydraulic blades for the Army's new Tankdozer, a specially designed tank for penetrating barriers and clearing land mines and debris. The Tankdozer turned out to be a significant war machine in the invasion of Normandy.

After the war, the company began a line of motor scrapers and built a 225-hp wheel dozer called the TD-300 Motor-Dozer. The company also pioneered the mounting of a hydraulic ripper on the back of a tractor, an attachment that is nearly as common today as a blade. LaPlant-Choate was purchased by Allis-Chalmers in 1952.

Caterpillar blade
MIDDLE RIGHT. Caterpillar No. 25 rear-mounted cable control unit and 6A (angle) blade, are seen on an early D-6 (9U) tractor. *Richard Yaremko*

Caterpillar blade
BOTTOM RIGHT. In addition to the straight hydraulic blade shown, an angle dozer, a universal dozer (for coal and other soft materials), a rip dozer (ripping shanks mounted at each end), and a cushion blade were available for the D-9G. *David Werner*

Caterpillar blade
A No. 24 front-mounted cable control unit and 8S (straight) blade are mounted on a D-8 tractor.

GAR WOOD INDUSTRIES, INC.

Gar Wood Industries, Inc., of Detroit, Michigan and Findlay, Ohio, was founded by inventor Garfield "Gar" Wood and his eight brothers in 1913. Wood is accredited with the invention of the hydraulic lift for dump and other types of truck bodies. Gar Wood was an avid motorboat designer and racer, and his company also produced a line of speedboats through the 1940s. He was highly regarded as a boat racer, winning numerous races and holding several water speed records.

The company began as the Wood Hydraulic Hoist and Body Co. in the Detroit area and changed its name to Gar Wood Industries in the late 1930s. During the 1940s, Gar Wood became a major manufacturer of construction equipment including dozer blades, rippers, scrapers, spreaders, sheepsfoot rollers and even cranes and shovels. The firm was an allied supplier for Allis-Chalmers during the 1940s and early 1950s, supplying cable blades for the larger HD-series tractors and hydraulic blades for the smaller tractors. Gar Wood also made hydraulic and cable "BullDozer," "DozeCaster" and "TipDozer" blades for Euclid C-6 and TC-12 tractors, and its blades were even installed on Caterpillar, Cletrac and International crawlers. The GM Euclid Division purchased Gar Wood's blade line in 1963.

Gar Wood purchased the Buckeye Traction Ditcher Co. of Findlay, Ohio in 1945 and maintained a factory in Findlay into the early 1970s when the company left the construction equipment business. Garfield Wood retired from the company in 1940 and moved to Miami, Florida where he continued his interest in motorboat racing.

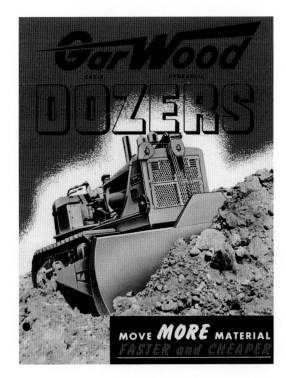

Gar Wood blade
A Gar Wood cable-operated blade is shown on an Allis-Chalmers Model HD-20 tractor. *Doug Frye*

Gar Wood blade
During much of the 1950s and 60s, Gar Wood was the sole supplier of hydraulic and cable Dozecaster blades for Euclid's C-6 and TC-12 (shown) tractors. Gar Wood also made a hydraulically-adjustable Tipdozer, full U-Dozer, modified U-Dozer, inside push-beam, C-frame push blocks, brush rakes and hydraulic rippers.

Gar Wood blade
A Model HB-53 hydraulic blade is attached to an Allis-Chalmers HD-5 tractor. *Doug Frye*

602 BULLDOZER

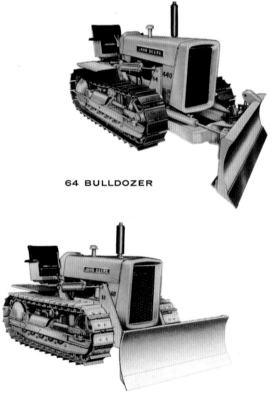

64 BULLDOZER

63 BULLDOZER

Pacific Car and Foundry Co., Renton, Washington

Founded in 1905, Pacific Car and Foundry, now known as Paccar, first offered a cable winch unit for tractors in 1932 under the Carco line. The Carco line was expanded during the 1930s to include blades, brush rakes and logging arches. Although Carco was an affiliated attachment vendor to Allis-Chalmers from the late 1930s to the mid-1950s, it offered blades and other implements for other makes of crawler tractors. The company stopped building blades in the late 1950s, but Carco winches are still made by Paccar.

Rockland Manufacturing Co., Bedford, Pennsylvania

Rockland started in the early 1950s making land-clearing attachments including brush rakes and expanded to other specialty dozer blades. The company is still in the blade and loader bucket business.

Rome Plow Co., Cedartown, Georgia

The Rome Plow Co. was established in 1932 by Tom Mullen and Jack Leamann as a builder of agricultural implements including heavy-duty plows. Mullen, at the time, held the Caterpillar dealership for the Honduras and wanted to offer tillage and land-clearing attachments for the tractors he sold. The partners acquired Towers and Sullivan Plow Co. of Rome, Georgia and started producing attachments specifically designed for Caterpillar tractors. In 1934, the company moved to Cedartown, Georgia, where it is presently located. It has remained in the construction equipment business and continues to offer its famed KG and other land-clearing blades. It is also still affiliated with Caterpillar.

FLECO blade
A FLECO land-clearing blade is seen on a Caterpillar D-8H tractor near Moneta, Virginia. RIGHT. A FLECO Root Rake is mounted on a Caterpillar D-7 tractor.

Matched to "Cat" track-type Tractors, the FLECO Root Rake is a useful tool for land clearing or reclamation.

Heil blade
A Heil cable-operated blade is seen on this Cletrac Model FDE tractor.

Heil blade
A Heil HB-60 hydraulic blade is attached to a Cletrac DD tractor. The blade measures 13 ft. wide.

THE ROME PLOW

The Rome Plow is a land-clearing blade and operator/tractor protection package offered by the Rome Plow Co. for Caterpillar D-5 through D-9 tractors. In the late 1950s, Rome offered its K/G land-clearing blades and rakes for Caterpillar tractors, and the name Rome Plow came into use for these attachments. K/G refers to surnames Kissner and Green of Lottie, Louisiana, inventors of the dozer blade with a knife-like cutting edge and a leading stinger bar to cut down large trees. The blade is generally mounted at a 30-degree angle to the right of the tractor.

James E. Kissner, along with his father John E. Kissner and father-in-law Edward Greene, started clearing land for their own use in the late 1940s. James Kissner related in a phone interview, "I could clear about two acres a day with our bulldozer. Then I hit a thicket of ash trees. Many were 50 feet tall and so thick you couldn't even walk through them. I went from clearing two acres a day to a quarter acre a day. With the bulldozer blade we had, you had to push a tree over, back up and push it out of the ground by the roots, and then push it into a pile. I figured there had to be a better way to do it."

The three men sat down and designed a blade that could cut through the ash thicket. The blade they wanted could move dense foliage and debris to one side and could also be used to push and grade dirt, so attachments did not have to be switched back and forth. "The three of us worked on the blade for three days in the summer of 1950. We built it under a tree behind the house where my wife was born. We found everything we needed to make it out of an old motor grader, and my dad and I took turns welding. Once we built it, we never changed it. From the first one we made, all we did was add that splitter on the end to cut bigger trees," said Kissner.

The first blade, called the K/G Shearing Blade, was mounted on a 1946 Caterpillar D-8 (2U) with a LeTourneau cable control, and it proved to be an immediate success.

Kissner remembered, "With the new blade, you didn't have to back up. You just kept going. It was kind of like mowing grass. We went from clearing ¼ acre a day to an acre an hour, even through the ash." As word got out about the blade they began making them for local contractors and developed a thriving business. "We had 7 or 8 people welding besides us, and we were working 10 to 12 hours a day, 7 days a week. Most were put on Caterpillars, but we also put them on Allis-Chalmers and Internationals. Then I began traveling around the country showing people how to install the blade and use it the right way. We had built about 350 blades when Carroll Mullen, president of the Rome Plow Co. called us about getting exclusive rights. Right after we signed with Rome, Caterpillar sent two vice presidents down here to talk to us about becoming an allied manufacturer, but it was too late," recalled Kissner.

After selling the rights to build their blade in 1957 to Rome, the Kissners continued buying and clearing land in Louisiana, and the Kissner family still owns three Caterpillar dozers with K/G blades.

The Rome Plow Co. continues to offer the blades in its latest product line. In addition to blades, Rome makes a wide variety of other construction and agricultural machinery including pull-scrapers, land levelers, rollers, harrows, ditchers and 4-wheel-drive tractors.

Rome Plows mounted mainly on Caterpillar D-7E, D-7F, and D-8H tractors were purchased in large numbers by the U.S. Army in the 1960s and 1970s. More than 1,500 were shipped to South Vietnam, where they were used to clear large areas of dense growth used by the enemy to hide, and the Rome Plow became synonymous with jungle-clearing equipment.

The Plow also proved to be an excellent tool for removing enemy bunkers and tunnels. In addition, all major roadways and supply routes had to have 100-yard clearings on each side to prevent ambushes and mine deployment. The first Army land-clearing teams were formed in 1967, and they began operating Rome Plows around Saigon. One of the first areas cleared was the Iron Triangle, a near impenetrable jungle where the Viet Cong established a stronghold. Using 45 Rome Plows and 500 conventional bulldozers, Army engineers and infantry cleared the area and destroyed the enemy's base camp, numerous tunnels, re-supply points and training camps. With the trees gone, the Viet Cong could not return and hide, as they had done previously.

Two years later, the 62nd Engineer Battalion became the first military unit devoted solely to land-clearing duty. Success of the battalion led to the formation of a number of other similar units. A land-clearing company (LCC) usually had 30 Rome Plows, and they were often run side-by-side to sweep as large an area as possible. An LCC could clear 180-200 acres of medium-density jungle in a day and the blades were sharpened at day's end. By the end of the war, Rome Plow units were scattered all over South Vietnam and more than 500,000 acres had been cleared. Often the operators worked close to enemy lines and were frequently fired upon. Additionally, temperatures could reach 130 degrees, and there were snakes, swarms of bees and other insects to contend with. Two out of three operators became casualties from enemy fire. The 62nd Battalion alone lost 27 operators and had more than 700 wounded. One operator received nine purple-heart medals. However, in spite of these odds, the rates of re-enlistment or voluntary extension of tours of duty were among the highest in the Army during this period.

In 1970, Rome Plows were used for a short period in Cambodia to uncover enemy camps and supply dumps along the Vietnamese border. Later that year, U.S. Army engineers started training South Vietnamese Army soldiers to run the Rome Plows, and they began taking over the land-clearing responsibilities. The last U.S. Army land-clearing unit left Vietnam in late 1971 as the war effort started to wind down.

In honor of this work, a Rome Plow on a Caterpillar D-7E tractor was placed on permanent display at the 62nd Engineer CBT Battalion Headquarters at Fort Hood, Texas in 2001. An inscription on the side of the cab reads: "For those who fought for it, freedom is something the protected will never know."

Rome K/G blade
A front view of the blade and canopy of the Rome Plow at Fort Hood, Texas. Rome Plows are also on display at Camp Shelby in Hattiesburg, Mississippi and at the Engineer's Museum at Fort Leonard Wood in Missouri. *Gene Garrison*

Rome K/G blade
A side view of Rome Plow No. 42 on a Caterpillar D-7E tractor, retired from the 62nd Engineer Battalion at Fort Hood, Texas. *Gene Garrison*

International Harvester blades

After buying the rights to the Bucyrus-Erie blade line in 1953, I-H continued offering the same blades for several years until it was able to design its own new line. These are the blades available for the TD-18A tractor in the 1954 I-H product line catalog.

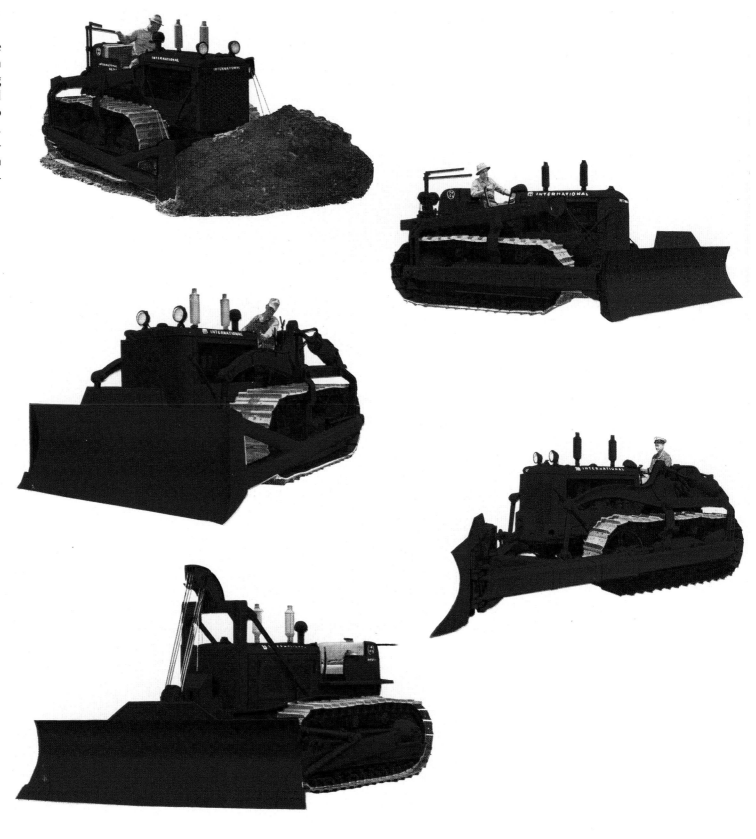

Isaacson blade
TOP LEFT. An Isaacson hydraulic blade is seen on a 1936 Caterpillar RD-7 tractor.

Continental blade
TOP RIGHT. A Continental hydraulic blade is mounted on an International TA-40 tractor on display at the Vintage Tracks Museum.

Isaacson blade
LOWER LEFT. An Isaacson DAS-18 blade is on an International Harvester TD-18 tractor.

LaPlant-Choate
A LaPlant-Choate cable blade is seen on a Caterpillar Fifty tractor.

LaPlant-Choate snowplow
In addition to earthmoving blades, LaPlant-Choate made snowplows including this hydraulically-operated blade on a 1930 Caterpillar Sixty tractor.

LaPlant-Choate blade
A LaPlant-Choate hydraulic blade is attached to this 1936 Caterpillar R-5 tractor in the Heidrick Agricultural Museum.

Rockland blade
A Caterpillar D-7M tractor with a Rockland brush rake is at work on a land clearing job in New Jersey. *David Werner*

Carco blades
Both cable and hydraulic blades were available for Allis-Chalmers and other crawler manufacturers under the Carco line. *Doug Frye*

Sidebooms

LEFT. An armada of at least eight Caterpillar 500-Series crawlers with sideboom cranes are at work on this large-diameter pipeline project in the Rockies. The machines include 572, 583, and 594 models with lifting capacities ranging from 90,000 to 200,000 lbs. *Caterpillar, Inc./ Jeff Huff*

Pulling rollers

A Caterpillar Sixty tractor pulls a sheepsfoot roller at the 1996 Easy Diggin' Show in Mt. Hope, New Jersey.

Pulling dump wagons

Before scrapers and off-road dump trucks were available, steel wheel and track wagons were used to haul rock and dirt in rough terrains. An Allis-Chalmers Model S is about to tow a tracked dump wagon at an HCEA Show in Seward, Nebraska.

CHAPTER TEN

OTHER ATTACHMENTS

Although the crawler was initially developed as an agricultural and logging machine, it was not long before its application to construction work was realized. The first construction attachments were implements that were pulled, the same ones pulled by animals and steam traction engines. These included graders, rollers, disks, dump wagons, and Fresno and rotary scrapers. Steam shovels, along with elevating graders and dump wagons pulled by tractors, were the primary tools for moving large quantities of earth and rock until the advent of the high-capacity scraper.

During the first two decades of the 20th century, the towed scraper evolved rapidly and gained popularity with contractors. Chain-driven bowls allowed larger capacities, but they required a separate operator in addition to the tractor driver. Scraper bowl capacities increased from 1 to 4 yards, and they were often used in trains of up to six units, which required several operators. Schmeiser, Western and Baker-Maney were the major early scraper manufacturers until the 1930s, when they were edged out by the cable-operated machines of Gar Wood, Bucyrus-Erie, Wooldridge and LeTourneau.

R.G. LeTourneau, the father of the modern scraper, began by "automating" existing scrapers with electric servo motors controlled by the tractor operator. He designed and built his first scraper in 1922 and made extensive use of the new arc-welding technology. LeTourneau continued testing and improving the electrically-controlled scrapers until 1928, when he launched the first cable-controlled scraper and companion power control unit on the rear of the tractor. That breakthrough greatly enhanced the value of the crawler tractor and the capacity of the scraper; by the mid-1930s, tractor-drawn scrapers were ubiquitous on earthmoving projects.

Rubber tires replaced the heavy steel wheels and capacities increased to 42 yards, a quantum leap from the scrapers of the 1920s. Multi-drum control units appeared in the early 1940s which permitted operation of two large capacity scrapers attached to one tractor. Although all are now hydraulically-controlled, scrapers today have basically the same design as LeTourneau's earliest machines. LeTourneau produced a host of other attachments including blades, rollers, rooters and rippers, dump wagons and a towed crane boom.

Other crawler attachments appearing during the late 1920s and 1930s included the sheepsfoot roller, pneumatic-tire roller, rooter, power-assisted elevating graders, push-graders (graders mounted to the front of a crawler), bucket loaders, and various types of booms such as sideboom pipelayers, center-boom half-swing, and non-swinging cranes and various types of winches. The Hyster Co. offered a unique set of universal excavator attachments for crawlers called Hystaways which were mounted to the back of the tractor. These included a shovel, backhoe, clamshell, dragline or lifting boom.

All of these early devices were either pulled and/or cable-controlled. However, as hydraulic technology improved, most of the cable functions on crawlers became hydraulically-operated including blades, loaders, cranes, scrapers and rippers. The Euclid BV high-capacity belt loader pulled by a large crawler tractor was a popular earthmoving machine of the 1940s and 1950s, and other specialized attachments appeared like air compressors and drills, pile drivers, augers, backhoes, log loaders, gravel-spreaders and cable-laying devices.

In addition to LeTourneau, the Trackson Co., Bucyrus-Erie, Drott, Maine Steel Products, Hyster Co., Tractomotive Corp., LaPlant-Choate, Baker Manufacturing, Gar Wood Industries, Heil, Superior, Hughes-Keenan, Isaacson Iron Works, Killefer Manufacturing, Wooldridge, W-K-M Co. and Athey Products were important suppliers of attachments other than or in addition to blades for crawlers. Some were affiliated with only one tractor manufacturer, but most offered attachments to fit all or most makes. Although all of these companies have either been absorbed or gone out of business, there are still a large number of crawler tractor attachment makers in business today.

One of the most popular dozer attachments currently is the 3-D geographic positioning system in which the grading is precisely adjusted to digitized specifications, eliminating the need for grade stakes and re-surveying.

Pulling scrapers
An International Harvester TD-24 tractor pulls a 27 ½ yard Bucyrus-Erie B-250 scraper while a second TD-24 pushes the rear and a third pulls a large LeTourneau scraper. *Gary Hansen*

Pulling rippers
A Caterpillar DD-9H combo poses with a large hydraulic single-tooth ripper. *David Maginnis*

Powering a pump
A Caterpillar D-7 powers a centrifugal pump to provide water for irrigation and drain standing water in low areas. *Don Heimburger*

80

For driving irrigation pumps with belt
or power take-off, these units assure

Pushing spreaders
A Jersey spreader is attached to a Caterpillar D-8 tractor for laying sub-base aggregate on a road-widening job near Salem, Virginia.

Pulling graders
Before integrally-built motor graders were designed, road grading was done by graders pulled by horses, wheel tractors and crawlers. A Caterpillar Model Ten pulls an Adams No. 3 grader.

Pushing graders
The Caterpillar Model Ten tractor fits neatly into this 1928 Caterpillar No. 10 Motor Patrol grader. Caterpillar bought the Russell Grader Manufacturing Co. the same year this grader was built, launching a line of equipment that it still dominates.

Pulling elevating graders
A Caterpillar Diesel Thirty Five tows a Caterpillar No. 42 elevating grader at the 2000 ACMOC Show in Chillicothe, Illinois.

Backhoe and loader
A No. 50 backhoe with swivel seat and No. 831 loader have been mounted on a Deere 440 tractor. *John Deere Construction Equipment Co./Jeff Huff*

Half-swing shovel
Half-swing shovels were popular in the late 1920s and 30s for light excavation duties such as digging basements and loading coal and aggregate. The Speeder Machine Co. offered this Model TS-40 on an early Caterpillar D-6 tractor. *Richard Yaremko*

Belt Loader
Euclid launched its track-mounted BV-series belt loaders in the mid-1940s, and they were used by every large earthmoving contractor during the 1950s and 60s. Designed to be pulled by the most powerful crawler tractors available, the BV belt loaders provided the lowest cost per yard for moving dirt during their time of production.

Utility Work

Another often overlooked use of crawlers is in utility work. Utility companies have used crawlers for right-of-way clearing, pole installation and cable-laying. As early as 1930, Utility Supply Co. offered cable reels and cable-laying plows for Caterpillar and other tractor makes. Davis Manufacturing was another builder of cable-laying attachments; it was taken over by Case in 1968. Case then offered its Model 475, an integrated cable-laying crawler equipped with a hydraulic plow on the rear and cable reel in front. American Tractor Equipment Co. made cable-laying attachments for most crawler makes for many years. Trackson, Utility Supply and Highway Trailer Co. sold crawler-mounted augers for installation of new power and telephone poles.

Utility Pole Auger/Installer

The Highway Trailer Co. of Edgerton, Wisconsin offered a Model 30-C auger and pole setter for Caterpillar's Model Thirty and other tractors during the 1920s and 1930s. *Jeff Huff*

Case Cable Layer

The Case Model 475 cable-laying crawler was offered from 1972 to 1980. It featured a large cable reel in front and a hydraulic plow blade on the rear. Powered by a 74-nhp diesel, it could lay up to 75 ft. of 2-in. cable per minute. *Case Corporation*

216

Mining and Petroleum

The mining industry is second after construction in the use of crawler tractors and accounts for most sales of the largest machines. It also utilizes nearly all of the wheel dozers. Most of the wheel dozers are used in surface mining for duties such as opening benches, bulldozing material toward excavators or conveyors, cleaning areas around power shovels and other excavators, helping move machinery, haul road development and maintenance, and mine land reclamation. However, some underground mines use crawler loaders and bulldozers for both surface and underground work. Eimco was the first manufacturer to develop an electric-powered loader for subsurface mines and tunnels, and later it offered a line of dozers and loaders for surface mining and construction work.

The petroleum industry uses crawlers with sideboom cranes, air compressors, and welders for pipeline and refinery construction, along with site preparation for drilling rigs and even for fighting oil and gas well fires. Although the pipeline and refinery work are construction applications, sideboom cranes are included in this section as they are non-excavation uses.

Caterpillar Pipe Layer
LEFT. After its purchase of the Trackson Co. in 1951, Caterpillar continued its line of sidebooms including this Model MDW8 Pipe Layer which features a hydraulically-controlled counterweight on a D-8 (13A) tractor from the early 1950s. *Caterpillar, Inc./Jeff Huff*

Trackson crane
Although mainly affiliated with Caterpillar, Trackson turret cranes were also placed on International TD-9 and TD-14 tractors as well as other makes. *Kevin Kohls*

Hughes-Keenan crane
BELOW. Hughes-Keenan offered cranes and other attachments for crawler and wheel tractors, including this Model MC-1R Roustabout crane on an Allis-Chalmers HD-7W tractor. *Jeff Huff*

Model MC-1R
Roustabout Crane
on HD-7W
Allis-Chalmers Tractor

SIDEBOOM CRANES

The first long-distance pipeline was completed in 1879 from Coryville to Williamsport, Pennsylvania, a distance of 110 miles. After that, local and regional pipelines sprung up all over Texas, Oklahoma, and other oil producing areas. Big boosts to pipelines occurred during World War II when the Big Inch (crude oil) and Little Inch (refined products) pipelines were constructed from Texas to the New York City area.

The concept of adding short booms and gin poles to crawlers developed during the 1920s as tractors became more reliable. The early sidebooms were attached to standard tractor models, but by the 1950s, crawlers were specially designed for sideboom service, including wide-gauge track frames, extra wide shoes, and beams mounted between track roller frames and tractors' main frames. Some models were also available with small backfiller blades.

The W-K-M Co. was a supplier of pipes, valves and other oil field equipment in Houston, Texas and started using crawler tractors with small booms to load and offload supplies. It soon began marketing sidebooms, winches and hoists as attachments. During the late 1920s, W-K-M became an affiliated supplier of sidebooms to Caterpillar, Cletrac, Monarch, and the United Tractor and Equipment Corp., a consortium of attachment manufacturers that allied with Allis-Chalmers in 1928.

The Trackson Co. became associated with Caterpillar in the early 1930s and offered booms for most of its tractor models. Caterpillar purchased Trackson in 1951 and started its own line of pipelayers. They were initially designated by an "M" followed by the tractor model number, such as MD-7 for a D-7 with sideboom. In the late 1950s, Caterpillar began its "500" series numbering system for pipelayers which is still in use; it currently offers four models with lifting capacities ranging from 40,000 to 230,000 lbs.

Allsteel Product Manufacturing Co. and Master Equipment Co. were also early sideboom makers with their products appearing in equipment catalogs from the late 1920s and 1930s. The Superior Equipment Co. aligned itself with International Harvester and offered sidebooms and other lifting equipment for IH's larger crawler models up to the 1970s.

Allis-Chalmers offered sidebooms from the Tractomotive Corp. in the late 1940s and 1950s and acquired Tractomotive

in 1959. Tractomotive was one of the first to offer hydraulically-controlled counterweights which could adjust for boom load and angle. Allis-Chalmers later offered sidebooms from CRC-Crose of Houston, Texas for its HD-21B crawler. Hughes-Keenan Co. of Ohio sold sideboom and swing cranes for most crawler makes during the 1940s and 1950s.

Midwestern Manufacturing Co. of Tulsa, Oklahoma began building sidebooms in 1946 for most makes of crawlers and was the first to offer a completely hydraulic-controlled pipelayer. It is still in the sideboom business and sells booms for both new and reconditioned Caterpillar tractors and smaller Komatsu models. Deere also offered several models of sideboom cranes for its crawlers during the 1960s and 1970s. Sideboom cranes are also used extensively in railroad construction, derailment and train wreck cleanup jobs. (See Chapter 11.)

Trackson Pipe Layer
The Trackson Co. was one of the early manufacturers of sideboom cranes for crawlers. In this 1938 scene, a Trackson Pipe Layer on a Caterpillar R-5 tractor lifts a valve for a new pipeline in a Wyoming oil field. *Jeff Huff*

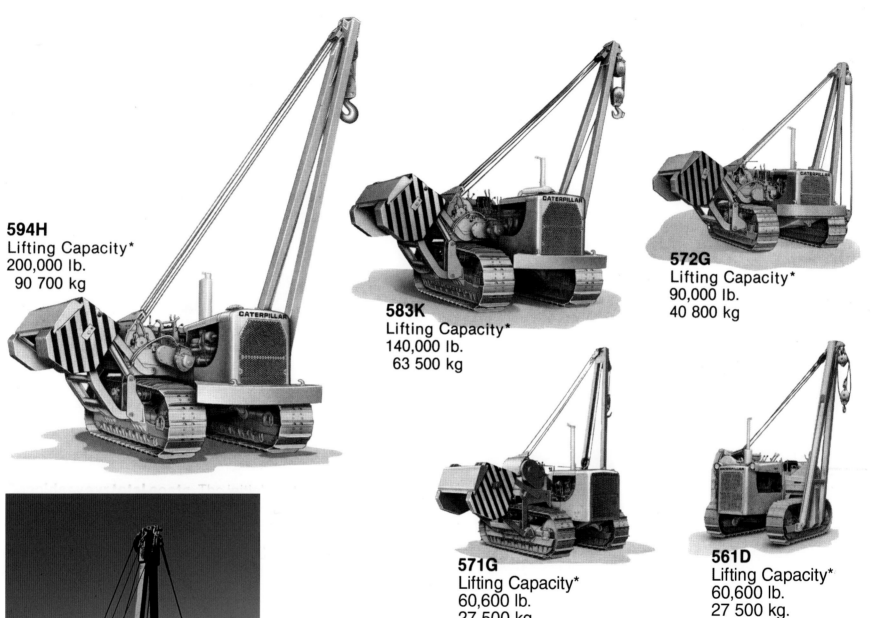

594H
Lifting Capacity*
200,000 lb.
 90 700 kg

583K
Lifting Capacity*
140,000 lb.
 63 500 kg

572G
Lifting Capacity*
90,000 lb.
40 800 kg

571G
Lifting Capacity*
60,600 lb.
27 500 kg.

561D
Lifting Capacity*
60,600 lb.
27 500 kg.

Caterpillar's mid-1970s Pipe Layer line
The five-model line included the 594H on a D-9H tractor, the 583K
on a D-8K, the 572G and 571G pipelayers on D-7G tractors, and
the 561D on a D-6D. *Vernon Simpson*

Trackson Pipe Layer
The smallest Trackson sideboom was the Model PD4
mounted on a Caterpillar D-4
tractor, in this case, a 1939 D-4
(7J) rated at 44 bhp.

CRC-Crose Pipeliner

After Allis-Chalmers acquired Tractomotive Corp. in 1959, it continued offering sideboom cranes for all of its larger tractor models from the HD-11 to the HD-21. In the late 1960s, A-C discontinued its own sideboom production and made the CRC-Crose Co. of Houston, Texas an allied supplier for the attachment. CRC-Crose offered only one model, the 21-B Pipeliner for the HD-21B tractor with a 20-ft. boom and a lifting capacity of 144,000 lbs. *Jeff Huff*

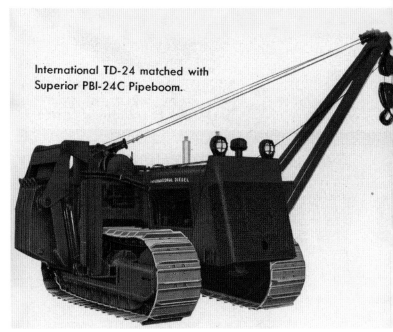

International TD-24 matched with Superior PBI-24C Pipeboom.

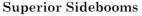

International TD-18A with Superior PBI-18A Pipeboom.

Superior Sidebooms

RIGHT. Superior Equipment Co. of Bucyrus, Ohio was the affiliated supplier of sideboom crane attachments for IHC during the late 1940s through the 1960s. Superior built cranes for the TD-9, -14, -15, -18, -20, -24 and -25 crawlers over this period, with lifting capacities ranging from 15,000 to 150,000 lbs. The IHC product line for 1954-55 shows Superior sideboom crane models available for its four largest crawler tractors: the TD-9, TD-14, TD-18 and TD-24. Boom lengths ranged from 13 ft. to 20 ft. and they could lift between 15,000 and 90,000 lbs. Superior also made ¾-swing cranes for the smaller crawler tractors, the T-6, TD-6, T-9, TD-9 and TD-14. *Doug Frye*

Farming applications

Crawler tractors have a wide range of applications for farming, including clockwise from upper left:

1. A D-2 pulls both a cornpicker and a hopper wagon
2. Three D-8 tractors pull a heavy-duty plow to reclaim barren land
3. A D-6 pulls a wheat combine
4. A D-2 pulls a two-bottom plow
5. A D-2 pulls a potato digger

Don Heimburger

Crawler tractors in agriculture

The crawler tractor evolved from the wheeled steam traction engine, so its earliest applications were in agriculture. Holt's first sale of its steam-powered crawler was to the Golden Meadows Development Corp. for plowing and disking marshland in Louisiana into farm land, and until the late 1920s, most crawlers were used in farming and logging.

Farms in the mid and far West were big by necessity and required large machines for planting and harvesting. The crawler was the ideal machine for this work, especially in wet, soft soils where steel-wheeled tractors performed poorly. This advantage lasted through the 1930s, when rubber-tired tractors with increased power took over much of the farm work.

By the late 1950s and early 1960s, most crawler manufacturers had written off farm business and concentrated on sales to the construction industry. However, during the late 1960s, the trend was reversed, and crawlers specially designed for agriculture appeared. This led to the rubber-tracked farm crawlers offered today by Case, Caterpillar and Deere.

Sickle bar
Caterpillar offered a sickle bar attachment for mowing hay and other feed crops such as this example mounted on a 1930 Model Ten tractor.

Crop and orchard spraying with a Caterpillar D-2 tractor.

Corn planter
A 76-in. gauge Cletrac Model E-76 pushes a two-row corn planter. The E-76 was the widest of the six track gauge configurations that were available for the row crop tractor.
Doug Frey

Logging

Another early use of crawler tractors was in logging (see Lombard in Chapter 7). During the first few years of the 20th century, Lombard steam crawlers demonstrated their utility in log hauling, and by the 1920s, crawlers had gained wide acceptance by the industry. Other forestry applications included building logging roads, tree felling, winching, brush clearing, and even powering portable saw mills. Forest fire fighting and prevention has been an important user of bulldozers, many of which are custom designed with special blades and protection devices.

Logging
A Caterpillar D-8 dozer pulls a Hyster logging arch to skid massive Douglas firs out of a Western forest.

Logging
A Willamette double-drum winch and rear-facing operator's seat are on this 1927 Caterpillar Thirty logging special tractor belonging to Hewitt Bros. Logging.

Working on the railroad

In this World War II-era scene, an International Harvester TD-18 dozer grades a steep cliff on the railroad right-of-way, while a TD-14 tractor equipped with an air compressor supplies power for the track maintenance crew to drive in spikes, join new rails and tamp ballast. A new diesel streamliner passes cautiously on the other track.

WORKIN' ON THE RAILROAD

All the Livelong Day with International Power

IT WILL BE a mighty peacetime song—"Workin' on the Railroad." Roadbeds, tracks, and equipment have taken a terrific pounding. A great reconstruction job must be done.

Look for International Industrial Power on that job. Look for International Tractors working all the livelong day along the right-of-way.

International works all the livelong day, powering off-track equipment—working with bulldozers, scrapers, compressors, generators, welding and cutting equipment, cranes, mowers and a variety of other types of machines.

Note that phrase—"*off-track* equipment."

And because they are *"off-track"* in contrast with *"rail-bound,"* International Tractors don't have to be hauled to a siding to let trains through. Schedules are kept. The job is done quicker. In addition to railroad construction and maintenance-of-way, International Crawler Tractors, Wheel Tractors and Power Units, with full-Diesel or carburetor-type engines, are assigned to scores of jobs in terminal, shop and yard.

International Power, toughened and improved by war, will be working on great peacetime jobs in many other industries, too, when the all-clear signal is given. International Power—rugged, dependable—is ready to help America and the world achieve new conquests on the frontiers of peace.

INTERNATIONAL HARVESTER COMPANY

180 North Michigan Avenue   Chicago 1, Illinois

INTERNATIONAL
HARVESTER

RE-SET YOUR SIGHTS FOR V-J DAY...Give to the blood bank... defend the food front...buy extra war bonds...fight inflation.

INTERNATIONAL HARVESTER
Power for Victory... Power for Peace

CHAPTER ELEVEN

CRAWLERS ON THE RAILROAD

Railroad rights-of-way often traverse extremely rugged terrain and lack accessibility from roads or even trails. Thus, railroads have relied on crawler tractors to do many of their chores. These include opening new mainlines, branches and sidings, building access roads, grading to maintain stable slopes and proper drainage, cleaning up after rock and mud slides, moving downed trees, clearing deep snow drifts, assisting in replacing track and ballast, and helping clean up after train wrecks and derailments. Railroads were quick to recognize the utility of crawlers and dozers and began purchasing them in the late 1920s. By the late 1930s, all Class I railroads had at least a few dozers in their maintenance-of-way departments; some had special flat cars with ramps to transport the machines to areas where they were needed.

Railroads have played an important part in the development and use of crawlers and dozers through the years. Early railroad industry publications show the marketing and use of crawlers on America's rail lines.

Once crawlers and dozers were available to market, they were shipped from the factory by railroad flat cars, and then used by the rail lines for everything from grading new right-of-ways to clearing timber near the tracks to spreading gravel. In a December, 1947 *Railway Purchases and Stores* magazine, an International Harvester ad reads: "Relocating a rail line calls for a lot of land clearing and earth work. International Diesel Crawlers, equipped with matched clearing dozers, are the machines for this work. On the job pic-

Tracks on Tracks
An International Harvester TD-14 tractor is equipped with a cable-operated wing blade and special track-walking treads to grade, spread ballast and improve drainage along railroad beds. *Don Heimburger*

A railroad contractor uses its Caterpillar D-9 crawlers with winterizing covers to pull rail cars from a wreck on the Norfolk & Western Railway west of Tolono, Illinois in the 1960s. *Collection of Don Heimburger*

tured, an International TD-9 was used to clear the land of stumps and roots along a new, 13 1/3-mile right-of-way, 90 to 160 feet wide."

A July, 1949 ad in the same magazine from Hughes-Keenan Corporation of Delaware, Ohio reads, "Reduce costs outdoors as well as in with roustabout cranes, the fast tractor-footed load-hustlers." The ad shows a crawler with a crane attached hauling a pipe. Another IH railway ad in 1947 shows a crawler with flanges on each side and special "walking" shoes moving down the tracks to improve the roadbed.

A Cletrac crawler equipped with a welder, bulldozer, Drott Bull Clam, compressor and snowplow are shown in a 1947 railway ad with the headline "Maintenance Handyman." A 1932 ad in *Railway Engineering & Maintenance of Way* shows a Caterpillar dozer pushing dirt on the side of the tracks as an early passenger train speeds by.

Of course, as railroads cut expenses in a major way in the 1960s, they resorted to outside contractors to clean up derailments. Contractors were hired to move heavy equipment, including husky dozers with side-booms, and to travel to a rail site quickly and re-rail cars and locomotives. This saved railroads from employing rail workers who were not needed unless a derailment occurred.

Throughout the years, crawlers and railroads have worked side by side, and it has been a mutually beneficial arrangement.

This massive Fiat-Allis HD-31 dozer takes a final ride by the Illinois Central Gulf from the Springfield, Illinois factory to its new owner. This photo was taken at Rutherford, Pennsylvania on March 20, 1978. *Bob's Photos*

Of course, railroads also haul construction equipment in their consists. Three Allis-Chalmers HD-5G loaders sit on an Illinois Terminal Railroad flat car in Fayetteville, North Carolina on October 11, 1952. *Bob's Photos*

TOP LEFT. Dozers clear a path on the Durango to Silverton branch of the Denver & Rio Grande Western Railroad in Colorado sometime in the 1940s or 1950s. The narrow gauge tracks are down there somewhere! *Collection of Don Heimburger, courtesy of Colorado Railroad Museum*

LEFT. A Caterpillar D-7 (3T) dozer rests on a pile of snow outside the Chama, New Mexico station of the narrow gauge Denver & Rio Grande Western after a large snow blanketed the station and nearby yard area. *John Norwood*

TOP RIGHT. This 1970s-era Caterpillar 977L loader with clamshell bucket waits on a lowboy trailer for its next assignment. It belongs to the R.J. Corman Derailment Service in Mississippi, and is part of a team of machines including side-boom tractors and dozers used for train wreck salvage and cleanup work.

LEFT. A derailment on the Wisconsin Central in 1989 at Colgate, Wisconsin brought out sideboom dozers to clear the wreck. *Russ Porter*

BOTTOM LEFT. Sidebooms move into position to re-rail a Soo Line diesel locomotive in 1984 near Slinger, Wisconsin. *Russ Porter*

BELOW. Railroad officials confer on the best way to solve a large derailment problem on the Milwaukee Road in the fall of 1977 at Wauwatosa, Wisconsin. *R. Ferge, collection of Russ Porter*

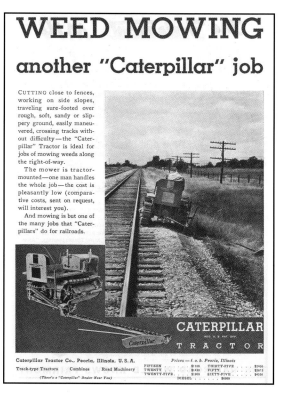

An Oliver-Cletrac crawler with rubber track pads and a welding package is being used on the Boston & Maine Railroad to build up uneven spaces between rail joints.

A Cletrac Model 25 with rubber track pads supplies power for a track crew to pull old spikes and hammer in new ones.

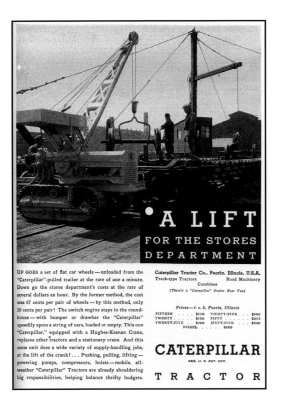

HIGHBALL
WITH OFF-TRACK WORK-POWER

An International UD-9 Diesel crawler with angled blade widens cuts and ditches along the main line of a southern railroad. One man, here, does the work of several gangs—and does it easily, cheaply, efficiently.

Semaphores are up! Tracks are clear while the maintenance work goes on—because reliable International diesel power operates off the rails.

An International TD-9 dozer grades the berm of a newly-laid section of track as a passenger train approaches.

CHAPTER TWELVE

CRAWLERS IN THE CIRCUS

In the 1930s circuses and carnivals traversed the country daily, assisted by hundreds of draft horses and mules. While circus management began to consider motor power as early as 1917 when a Killen-Strait tractor was demonstrated to Ringling Brothers Barnum & Bailey management, it wasn't until Ringling's labor problems in the late 1930s that Caterpillars from the production lines in Peoria and California began to see regular use on many American circuses. The romance and glory of the Caterpillar still lives and can be experienced and enjoyed daily at the Circus World Museum (CWM) in Baraboo, Wisconsin.

Circus Cat
A Caterpillar D-4 (7U) with street pads pulls a trailer full of tents and other equipment from a flat car as part of the work of moving the Royal American Circus from city to city. *Color rendering by Russ Porter*

Circus World Museum (CWM)

The CWM owns, or has on loan, eight Caterpillars that were used either on a circus or a carnival when those enterprises moved across the country by rail. The Ringling Bros. Barnum & Bailey ("The Greatest Show on Earth") used D-4s and D-7s, and at certain times would have as many as a dozen in use. RBB&B had one D-6 Caterpillar which was equipped with large rubber wheels and was referred to as "The Donut." This unit is part of a special display at the CWM supported by FABCO, Inc. of Milwaukee.

Three of the D-4s are used during the CWM's regular season from early May through Labor Day. These Caterpillars date from the late 1930s to the mid 1940s (Cat #3 - 1947; Cat #8 - 1936 and Cat #11 - 1948). They were used to move the historic circus wagons from the Circus World Museum collection onto and off the Great Circus Parade train in Baraboo and Milwaukee.

These circus crawlers were customized for circus use. The most significant modification was to the 60" gauge track which had to be equipped with rubber street pads. This innovation was necessary so that the cleats did not tear up the streets of the cities and towns visited by the circus. In addition the D-4s were fitted with a heavy duty push plate in front to protect the radiator, and a box and steps for the "pin men" who hitched and unhitched the wagons from the crawler.

When RBB&B used these machines they were often equipped with Hyster single- and double-cable winches which operated everything from stake pullers to derricks for loading canvas and lifting other heavy equipment. One D-4 with cleats was fitted with a blade. All the D-4s and D-7s with cleats were transported over the macadam streets on LaCrosse lowboy dollies.

The crawlers of the Circus World Museum and the Great Circus Parade are only part of the history preserved and presented for the public in Baraboo. The museum is owned by the State Historical Society of Wisconsin and operated by the Circus World Museum Foundation. For additional information, contact www.circusworldmuseum.com. *By John S. Lloyd and R.S. MacDougall*

Don Heimburger collection

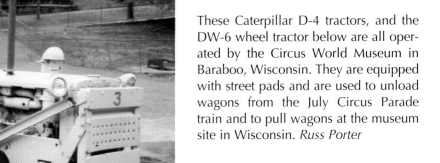

These Caterpillar D-4 tractors, and the DW-6 wheel tractor below are all operated by the Circus World Museum in Baraboo, Wisconsin. They are equipped with street pads and are used to unload wagons from the July Circus Parade train and to pull wagons at the museum site in Wisconsin. *Russ Porter*

A four-unit diesel Milwaukee Road circus train speeds through DuPlainville, Wisconsin with a Caterpillar D-6 dozer and a D-4 tractor on its way to the next show. *Russ Porter*

A Caterpillar D-4C crawler loads the Royal American Shows at West Allis, Wisconsin. *Russ Porter*

A Caterpillar D-6 rides a Coles circus flatcar on a steam-powered trip to Milwaukee. *Bruce Nelson*

CATERPILLAR TRACTORS
OWNED BY RINGLING BROTHERS AND BARNUM & BAILEY CIRCUS

RBB&B#	Year	Model	Serial Number	
A-5	1938	D-7	9G4470W	
A-4	1938	D-7	9G4580W	
B-1	1938	D-4	4G8895W	
A-2	1939	D-7	9G5576W	
A-3	1939	D-7	9G5583W	
B-2	1939	D-4	4G	
B-3	1939	D-4	7J235W	
B-4	1939	D-4	7J265W	
A-1	1941	D-7	7M2964	
		Trade-ins on new machines		
	1947	D-7	3T5331	
	1947	D-7	3T5332	
B-5	1946	D-4	5T3970W	
B-6	1948	D-4	7U2427	
B-7	1948	D-4	7U2854	
B-8	1950	D-4	7U8760	
B-9	1951	D-6	9U7630	Wheeled
B-10	1955	D-4	7U31488sp	

Royal American Shows D-4 Caterpillars owned by R. S. MacDougall

RBB&B#	Year	Model	Serial Number
C-5	1949	D-4	7U7662
C-4	1953	D-4	7U21745

Circus World Museum Caterpillar D-4 tractor hitches a ride on the Circus Train that ran to Milwaukee, Wisconsin in July of 1973. *Collection of Don Heimburger*

TOP RIGHT. Ringling Brothers on the road in this picture with a show line-up of their equipment including crawlers in Shreveport, Louisiana in 1947. *Robert MacDougall*

CENTER. In another Ringling Brothers scene, crawlers sit behind circus tents awaiting their call to load up everything again. *Robert MacDougall*

BOTTOM. Ringling Brothers Caterpillars A-3 (D-7) and B-6 (D-4) with padded treads move through the show grounds. *Steve Flint, collection of Robert Mac-Dougall*

Opposite Page
TOP LEFT. A D-7 Caterpillar Diesel spots seat wagon #17 in the Ringling Brothers circus big top tent in 1938 at Sarasota, Florida. *Circus World Museum*

TOP RIGHT. A D-7 crawler is pulled by a Ringling Brothers Barnum & Bailey Mack truck. Location and date is unkown. *Circus World Museum*

CENTER. The circus comes to town by rail! This May, 1939 scene shows a Caterpillar D-2 unloading flat cars in Washington, D.C. for a Ringling Brothers circus show. *Circus World Museum*

BOTTOM RIGHT. A Caterpillar D-4, equipped with a lift crane, loads circus equipment into a circus truck on May 1, 1951 at Sarasota for the Ringling Brothers Circus. *Circus World Museum*

BOTTOM LEFT. A Caterpillar D-7 loads and helps with general preparations for leaving Ringling's Sarasota, Florida winter quarters on May of 1948. *Circus World Museum*

CRAWLER TRACTOR MAKES AND MODELS

Model	Years Built	Horsepower (dbhp)	Weight (lbs.)	Engine / Notes
BALL TREAD Co. / YUBA Manufacturing Co. (1914 – 1930)				
12-20	1912 - 1915	12	7,600	4-cylinder
18-25	1913 - 1915	18	8,900	4-cylinder
12-20	1916 - 1921	12	6,750	4-cylinder
15-25	1920 - 1925	15	5,680	4-cylinder
20-35	1916 - 1925	20	10,000	4-cylinder
25-40	1921 - 1930	25	10,250	4-cylinder
35-60	1920 - 1930	35	18,000	
40-70	1919 - 1921	40	21,000	

Model	Years Built	bhp/ dbhp	Weight (lbs.)	Engine / Notes
BATES Machine & Tractor Co.				
Model B[1]	1914 – 1915	20 / 11		Erd 4-cyl., single rear track
Model C[1]	1916 – 1917	30 / 13		Erd 4-cyl., single rear track
Model 12-25[1]	1915 – 1917	25 / 12		Erd 4-cylinder
Model D[1]	1916 – 1919	20 / 12	4,400	Erd 4-cylinder
Model D	1920 – 1921	22 / 15[2]	4,600	Erd 4-cyl. kerosene
Model F	1920 – 1923	22.20 / 16.17	4,600	Midwest 4-cylinder
Model G	1921 – 1928	35 / 25	6,000	Midwest 4-cylinder
25	1924 – 1928	25 / 20		Beaver gasoline
30-40	1924 – 1926	40 / 30		
30	1924 – 1928	35 / 28	8,300	LeRoi 4-cylinder
35	1929 – 1937	52 / 43[2]	10,750	Waukesha 6-cylinder
40	1924 – 1929	approx. 40		Waukesha 4-cylinder
40 D	1937 only	approx. 40		Waukesha semi-diesel
45	1930 – 1937	66 / 45[2]	13,509	Waukesha 6 cylinder gas
50	1934 – 1937	55 / 45	13,500	Waukesha 4-cylinder
80	1929 – 1937	approx. 80	22,000	Waukesha 6-cylinder
80 Diesel	1929 – 1937	approx. 80	22,500	Waukesha semi-diesel

[1] Introduced by Joliet Oil Tractor Co. which was taken over by Bates in 1918, which was owned by Foote Bros., 1924-1935.
[2] Nebraska Tractor Testing Lab results.

Model / Series	Years built	bhp/dbhp (otherwise fwhp)	Weight (lbs)	Engine / Notes
CATERPILLAR Tractor Co. / CATERPILLAR, Inc. (1950 to 2002)				
D-2(4U/5U)	1947 - 1957	48 / 38	6,700 - 7,600	D311
D-3 (79U/82U)	1972 - 1979	62-65	13,600 -14,000	3204
D-3 LGP (6N/83U)	1973 - 1979	62-65	14,800 -15,800	3204
D-3B PS (23Y/27Y)	1979 - 1987	65	14,795	3204DI
D-3B LGP (24Y/28Y)	1979 - 1987	65	15,800	3204DI
D-3C	1987 - 1990	65	15,800	3204DI
D-3C Series II	1990 - 1993	70	15,500	3204DI
D-3C Series III	1993 - 2001	70	15,500 - 16,800	3046
D-3G XL, LGP	2002 -	70	16,193 - 17,126	3046
D-4(6U/7U)	1947 - 1959	55-63 / 39.4	10,200 - 13,300	D315
D-4(29A)	1958 only	63 / 50	13,500	Australia
D-4(30A)	1958 - 1959	63 / 50	13,900	Australia
D-4C	1959 - 1966	65 / 52	13,500 - 14,400	D330
D-4D /LGP	1967 - 1977	65 / 52	15,300 - 18,000	D330/3304
D-4E /LGP	1977 - 1991	75-80	19,874 - 22,240	3304
D-4H	1985 - 1991	95	22,600 - 26,800	3304
D-4H Series II	1992 - 1995	95	22,600 - 24,200	3204
D-4H XL/LGP Ser III	1993 - 1995	105	25,900 - 27,300	3304
D-4C Series II	1990 - 1993	80	16,019	3046

Model / Series	Years built	bhp/dbhp (otherwise fwhp)	Weight (lbs.)	Engine / Notes
D-4C Series III	1993 - 2000	80	16,019 - 17,032	3046
D-4G XL, LGP	2001-	80	17,126 - 17,952	3046
D-5(37J)	1966 - 1969	93	18,500	D315
D-5(50J/54J)	1969 - 1972	93	19,100	D333
D-5(62J/63J)	1969 - 1978	93-105	18,500 -19,100	D333
D-5(67J)	1968 - 1977	93	18,500	D333
D-5(81H)	1967 - 1968	93	18,200	D333
D-5(82/83/84H)	1967	93	18,200 - 19,200	D333
D-5(93J/94J)	1967 - 1977	93-105	24,480	D333
D-5(95J/96J)	1967 - 1971	93-105	25,000	D333
D-5(97J)	1970 - 1976	105	25,000	3306
D-5 LGP	1967 - 1977	105	27,800	3306
D-5 SA	1967 - 1977	105	21,300	3306
D-5B / LGP	1977 - 1985	105	25,400 - 32,400	3306
D-5H	1986 - 1991	120-130	28,800 - 33,800	3304
D-5H Series II	1992 - 1995	120	28,800 - 33,800	3304
D-5C	1991 - 1993	90	18,150 - 19,256	3046T
D-5C Series III	1993 - 2000	90	18,100 - 19,300	3046T
D-5G XL, LGP	2001 -	90	19,630 - 20,402	3046T
D-5M	1996 -	110	25,800 - 27,800	3116 DIT
D-5M LGP/XL	1996 -	110	27,000 - 28,880	3116 DIT
D-6(9A700)	1947 - 1959	80-93	15,875 - 23,800	Military
D-6(8U/9U)	1947 - 1959	80-93	22,500 - 23,800	D318
D-6B(37A/44A)	1959 - 1967	90-93	23,000 - 24,300	D333
D-6B(37H)	1965 - 1967	93	24,300	D333
D-6C /LGP	1963 - 1977	125-140	23,500	D333T
D-6D /LGP	1977 - 1998	140	30,900 - 38,300	3306T
D-6E	1992 - 1995	155	33,900	3306T
D-6H	1985 - 1991	165	39,700	3306T
D-6H Series II	1992 - 1995	165	39,900	3306T
D-6HXL/XR Ser. II	1994 - 1995	175	42,000	3306T
D-6H LGP	1985 - 1991	165	45,200	3306T
D-6H LGP Ser. II	1992 - 1995	180	45,400	3306T
D-6G	1996 - 2001	155	33,900	3306T
D-6M XL	1996 -	140	33,200	3116T
D-6M LGP	1996 -	140	36,400	3116T
D-6R	1996 -	165	39,700 - 40,400	3306T
D-6R XL/XR	1996 -	175	41,900 - 42,300	3306T
D-6R LGP	1996 -	185	45,200	3306T
D-6R XW	1996 -	185	43,800	3306T
D-7B(3T)	1944 - 1955	93-108	36,630	D8800
D-7C(17A)	1955 - 1959	128 / 102	36,100	D339
D-7D(17A)	1959 - 1961	140-160 / 112	36,600	D339T
D-7E	1961 - 1969	160 / 144	41,000 - 44,000	D339T
D-7F	1969 - 1975	180 / 144	41,400 - 44,300	3306T
D-7G /LGP	1975 - 1998	200	44,000 - 52,100	3306T
D-7H	1986 - 1991	200	44,600	3306T
D-7H /LGP Ser. II	1992 - 1995	215-230	55,000 - 59,800	3306T
D-7R	1996 - 2000	230	54,200	3306T
D-7R Ser II	2001 -	240	54,580	3176C
D-7R XR	1996 -	230	54,100 - 55,850	3306T
D-7R LGP	1996 -	240	58,800 - 59,300	3306T
D-8(2U)	1945 - 1953	132-160 / 131	36,610	D13000
D-8(13A)	1953 - 1955	85 / 150	39,000	D13000
D-8E(14A)	1954 - 1956	191 / 157.6	46,600	D342
D-8F(14A)	1956 - 1958	191 / 157.6	49,300	D342

Model / Series	Years built	bhp/dbhp (otherwise fwhp)	Weight (lbs.)	Engine / Notes
D-8F(9A1301)	1956 - 1958	191 / 157.6	49,300	D342 - Military
D-8D(15A)	1955 - 1956	191 / 157.6	43,500	D342
D-8G(15A)	1956 - 1958	191 / 157.6	48,500	D342
D-8H(35A)	1959 - 1960	225-235 / 173.7	53,655 - 57,200	D342T
D-8H(36A)	1958 - 1974	225-270 / 173.7	59,200	D342T
D-8H(46A)	1959 - 1974	225-270	57,700 - 60,500	D342T
D-8H(22A)	1958 - 1969	225-270	59,200	D342T
D-8H(52A)	1960 - 1969	225-270	57,700	D342T
D-8H(68A)	1960 - 1974	225-270	58,000	D342T
D-8K(66V)	1974 - 1982	300	68,700 - 69,300	D342T
D-8L /LGP	1982 - 1992	335	82,625	3408
D-8N	1987 - 1995	285	81,300	3406
D-8R	1996 - 2000	305	72,930 - 82,900	3406
D-8R LGP	1996 - 2000	305	74,360	3406
D-8R Series II	2001 -	305	83,500	3406E
D-9D(18A)	1955 - 1959	286 / 230	56,200	D353/D353T
D-9D(19A)	1955 - 1959	286-320 / 260	56,650	D353/D353T
D-9E(34A)	1959 - 1961	320	58,000	D353T
D-9E(49A/50A)	1959 - 1960	335	59,500	D353T
D-9G(66A)	1961 - 1974	385	77,300	D353TA
DD-9G(90J/91J)	1965 - 1974	770	176,900	Tandem D-9Gs
SxS D-9G(29N/30N)	1969 - 1974	770	188,600	Side-by-side D-9Gs
D-9H(90V)	1974 - 1980	410	91,000	D353TA
DD-9H(97V/98V)	1974 - 1977	820	178,800	Tandem D-9Hs
SxS D-9H(99V/12U)	1975 - 1977	820	183,900	Side-by-side D-9Hs
D-9L	1979 - 1986	460	114,653	3412DI
D-9N	1986 - 1996	370	103,500	3408
D-9R	1996 -	405-410	104,538 - 107,667	3408C/E
D-10(84W/76X	1977 - 1988	700	190,300	D348
D-10N	1987 - 1995	520	147,400	3412
D-10R	1996 -	580	144,169 - 145,500	3412E
D-11N	1986 - 1996	770	214,800 - 218,000	3508B
D-11R(8ZR)	1996 - 2000	770-850	225,500	3508B
D-11R	2001 -	850	230,100	3508BTA
D-11R CD	1996 - 2000	770-850	239,550	3508B
D-11R CD	2001 -	850	248,600	3508BTA

CLARK Equipment Co.

Model / Series	Years built	bhp/dbhp	Weight (lbs.)	Engine / Notes
CA-1 Airborne	1943 - 1945	28 / 20	3,350 / 4,350 w/blade	Waukesha 4-cylinder

CLEVELAND Tractor Co. (CLETRAC) and OLIVER Corp.
Early Letter Series

Model / Series	Years built	bhp/dbhp	Weight (lbs.)	Engine / Notes
R	1916 - 1917	18 / 10	2,500	Buda 4-cylinder
H	1917 - 1919	20 / 12	3,200	Weidley 4-cylinder
W (W-12)	1919 - 1932	20 / 12	3,418	Weidley or Cletrac 4-cylinder
F	1920 - 1922	16 / 9	2,000	Cletrac 4-cylinder.

Number Series

Model / Series	Years built	bhp/dbhp	Weight (lbs.)	Engine / Notes
15	1931 - 1933	26 / 22.1	5,800	Hercules 4-cylinder
20K	1925 - 1932	27 / 20	4,838	Cletrac 4-cylinder
20C	1933 - 1936	29 / 24.6	6,000	Hercules 4-cylinder
25	1932 - 1935	35.75 / 28.69	7,000	Hercules 6-cylinder
30A (A-30)	1926 - 1928	45 / 38	7,000	Wisconsin 6-cylinder
30B (B-30)	1929 - 1930	45 / 38	7,300	Wisconsin 6-cylinder
30G	1935 - 1936	38.5 / 33.4	7,950	Hercules 6-cylinder
35	1932 - 1936	49.43 / 44.2	10,400	Hercules 6-cylinder
35D	1934 - 1935	67.71/ 61.18	11,500	Hercules 6-cylinder diesel

Model	Years built	HP(bhp/dbhp)	Weight (lbs.)	Engine / Notes
40	1928 - 1931	55.5 / 40	11,628	Wisconsin 6-cylinder
40D	1935 - 1936	67.71/ 61.18	11,500	Hercules 6-cylinder diesel
40-30	1930 - 1931	45.6 /40.66	10,022	Hercules 6-cylinder
55-40	1931 - 1932	65.97/58.94	12,000	Wisconsin 6-cylinder
55	1932 - 1936	65.97/58.94	12,000	Wisconsin 6-cylinder
80-60	1930 - 1932	90.23/ 83.5	21,100	Wisconsin 6-cylinder
80	1932 only	90.23/ 83.5	21,900	Wisconsin 6-cylinder
80G	1932 - 1936	103 / 86.4	23,000	Hercules 6-cylinder
80D	1933 - 1936	103 / 92.3	24,000	Hercules 6-cylinder diesel
100	1927 - 1930	120 / 100	28,089	Wisconsin 6-cylinder
Letter Series (streamlined)				
AG	1936 - 1942	34.2 / 27.72	6,800	Hercules 4-cylinder
AG-6	1944 - 1957	38.8 / 30.6	7,411	Continental 6-cylinder
AD	1937 - 1959	38 / 30.5	8,012	Hercules 4-cylinder diesel
AD-2	1937 - 1940	38 / 30.5	7,471	Buda 4-cylinder diesel
BD (4 speed)	1936 - 1939	46 / 35	8,800	Hercules 6-cylinder diesel
BD (6 speed)	1939 - 1956	48.09 / 38.05	9,749	Hercules 6-cylinder diesel
BD-2	1937 - 1938	no information	Buda 6-cylinder diesel	
BG (4 speed)	1937 - 1939	44 / 35	8,350	Hercules 6-cylinder
BG (6 speed)	1939 - 1944	50 / 38	8,879	Hercules 6-cylinder
BGS / BGH	1944 - 1955	50 / 38	8,600-9,039	Hercules 6-cylinder
CG	1936 - 1942	55.39 / 48.4	11,500	Hercules 6-cylinder
DD (4 speed)	1936 - 1939	67.71 / 61.18	12,700	Hercules 6-cylinder diesel
DD (6 speed)	1939 - 1958	67.71 / 61.19	13,708	Hercules 6-cylinder diesel
DG (4 speed)	1936 - 1939	69 / 61.2	12,000	Hercules 6-cylinder
DG (6 speed)	1939 - 1956	69 / 61.2	12,917	Hercules 6-cylinder
E-31[1] (EN)	1934 - 1939	30.5 / 22.11	5,000	Hercules 4-cylinder
E-38[1] pre-stream.	1934 - 1936	30.5 / 22.11	5,050	Hercules 4-cylinder
E-38 streamlined	1936 - 1938	30.5 / 22.11	5,125	Hercules 4-cylinder
E-42[1]	1938 - 1942	30.5 / 22.11	5,225	Hercules 4-cylinder
E-62-68-76[1]	1934 - 1941	30.5 / 22.11	5,250	Hercules 4-cylinder
EHG-62-68-76[1]	1937 - 1941	30.5 / 22.11	5,600	Hercules 4-cylinder
ED2-38[1]	1937 - 1941	33 / 25	6,050	Buda 4-cylinder diesel
ED 38-42[1]	1938 - 1941	38 / 30.5	5,800	Hercules 4-cylinder diesel
ED2-42[1]	1937 - 1941	33 / 25	6,150	Buda 4-cylinder diesel
ED2-62-68-76[1]	1937 - 1940	33 / 25	6,125	Buda 4-cylinder diesel
EHD2-62-68-76[1]	1938 - 1941	33 / 25	6,350	Buda 4-cylinder diesel
FD (4 speed)	1936 - 1938	107.5 / 92.3	25,800	Hercules 6-cylinder diesel
FD (6 speed)	1938 - 1944	113.5 / 96.9	28,000	Hercules 6-cylinder diesel
FDLC	1941 - 1945	110 / 92.3	30,000	Cummins 6-cylinder diesel
FDE	1945 - 1952	130 / 110	30,025	Hercules 6-cylinder diesel
FG (4 speed)	1936 - 1938	110.93 / 94.29	24,500	Hercules 6-cylinder
FG (6 speed)	1938 - 1943	110.93 / 94.29	26,750	Hercules 6-cylinder
HG-31-42-60-68[1]	1939 - 1951	20.58-26.36/14.78-21.85	3,025-3,513	Hercules 4-cylinder
HGR	1945 - 1948	20.58 / 14.78	3,270	Hercules 4-cylinder
Military models				
MG-1	1941 - 1942	138 bhp	13,520	Hercules 6-cylinder
MG-2	1942 - 1943	150 bhp	13,800	Hercules 6-cylinder
MG-3	1942 only	150 bhp		Hercules 6-cylinder
OLIVER CLETRAC				
OC-3 31-42-60-68[1]	1951 - 1957	26.36 / 21.85	3,820	Hercules 4-cylinder

Model	Years Built	HP (belt / drawbar)	Weight (lbs.)	Engine / Notes
OC-3 kerosene	1951 - 1957	no information		Hercules 4-cylinder
OC-3-31 Cane	1952 - 1957	26.36 / 21.85	3,365	Hercules 4-cylinder
OC-4 G	1956 - 1958	26.36 / 21.85	4,255	Hercules 4-cylinder
OC-4-3G	1958 - 1965	30.2 / 24.06	4,345	Hercules 3-cylinder
OC-4-3D	1957 - 1965	30.45 / 24.75	4,390	Hercules 3-cylinder diesel
OC-6 D	1954 - 1960	43 / 34.74	5,750	Waukesha 6-cyl. diesel
OC-6 G	1954 - 1960	45 / 37	5,605	Waukesha 6-cylinder
OC-9 D	1959 - 1965	57.4 - 62	9,675	Hercules 4-cylinder diesel
OC-12 D	1954 - 1960	58.98 / 53.05	10,575	Hercules 6-cylinder diesel
OC-12 G	1954 - 1960	60.27 / 53.4	10,290	Hercules 6-cylinder
OC-15 D	1956 - 1961	104.64 / 94.17	17,335	Hercules 6-cylinder diesel
OC-18	1952 - 1960	161 / 133	33,300	Hercules 6-cylinder diesel

[1] Numbers indicate track gauges in inches

DEERE & Company

Model	Years Built	HP (belt / drawbar)	Weight (lbs.)	Engine / Notes
Lindeman BO-L[1]	1939 - 1947	18.53 / 14.03	4,420	Deere gasoline
MC	1948 - 1952	20.45 / 18.15	3,875	Replaced the BO
40C	1953 - 1955	24.9 / 22.4	4,000	Replaced the MC
420C	1956 - 1958	29.21 / 27.08	4,150- 4,700	Replaced the 40C
430C	1958 - 1960	29.21 / 27.08	4,700	Deere gas
440IC	1958 - 1960	29.72 / 24.12	5,850	Deere gas
440ICD	1958 - 1960	32.88 / 26.15	6,220	GM 2-53 Diesel
1010C	1960 - 1965	41.5ehp / 27.4-28.7	6,748-6,850	Deere gas and diesel
2010C	1960 - 1965	52ehp/ 35	8,762-8,864	Deere gas and diesel
350	1965 - 1970	42ehp/30	9,300	Deere gas and diesel
350B	1971 - 1986	42ehp	8,115-8,220	Deere 3-135
350C	1975 - 1986	42ehp	10,099	Deere 3-164
350D	1986 - 1988	48ehp	10,400	Deere 3-179D
400G	1988 - 1995	60ehp	11,820	Deere 4039D
400G LT	1990 - 1995	60ehp	12,200	Deere 4039D
450	1965 - 1970	57ehp/ 44	10,590-12,578	Deere gas and diesel
450B	1970 - 1976	65ehp	12,501	Deere 4-219
450C	1974 - 1983	65ehp	14,230	Deere 4-219T
450D	1983 - 1985	67ehp	14,640	Deere 4-219T
450E	1985 - 1988	70ehp	14,675-15,365	Deere 4-276D
450E LT	1985 - 1988	75ehp	15,350	Deere 4-276D
450G	1987 - 1995	70ehp	15,932-17,232	Deere 4-276D
450G IV	1996 - 1999	70ehp	15,840	Deere 4045T
450H	1999 -	70ehp	15,000	Deere 4045D
450H LT	1999 -	70ehp	15,500	Deere 4045D
450H LGP	1999 -	74ehp	16,500	Deere 4045T
550	1976 - 1983	72ehp	15,536	Deere 4-276T
550A	1983 - 1985	78ehp	15,580	Deere 4-276T
550B	1985 - 1988	78ehp	15,501	Deere 4-276T
550G	1988 - 1995	80ehp	16,641-18,330	Deere 4-276T
550G IV	1996 - 1999	80ehp	17,600	Deere 4045T
550H LT	1999 -	80ehp	16,800	Deere 4045T
550H LGP	1999 -	84ehp	17,500	Deere 4045T
650G	1987 - 1995	90ehp	18,510-19,122	Deere 4-276T
650G IV	1996 - 1999	90ehp	18,480	Deere 4045T
650H LT	1999 -	90ehp	18,500	Deere 4045T
650H LGP	1999 -	90ehp	19,100	Deere 4045T
650H XLT	1999 -	90ehp	18,600	Deere 4045T
700H (LGP/LT/XLT)	2000 -	115nhp	25,800-27,900	Deere 6068T

Model	Years Built	HP (belt / drawbar)	Weight (lbs.)	Engine / Notes
750 /LGP/WT	1976 - 1986	110ehp	29,239-34,000	Deere 6-414T
750B /LGP/WT	1985 - 1995	120ehp	29,550-35,000	Deere 6-414T
750C	1996 - 1999	148ghp	33,660	Deere 6068T
750C WT	1996 - 1999	148ghp	33,250	Deere 6068T
750C LGP	1996 - 1999	148ghp	36,494	Deere 6068T
750C Series II (LGP/LT/WT)	2000 -	140nhp	33,736-36,576	Deere 6068T
850 /LGP	1978 - 1985	145ehp	36,124-44,000	Deere 6-619T
850B /LGP	1985 - 1995	165ehp	36,730-45,000	Deere 6-466A
850C	1996 - 1999	192ghp	40,155	Deere 6081A
850C WT	1996 - 1999	185ghp	40,238	Deere 6081A
850C LGP	1996 - 1999	185ghp	42,702	Deere 6081A
850C Series II (LT/LGP/WT/WXLT)	2000 -	185nhp	42,418-44,582	Deere 6081A
950J(LT/LGP)	2003 -	247nhp	54,245-56,372	Liebherr D-926 TI
1050C	2001 -	324nhp	73,985-77,245	Liebherr D-9406

[1] Lindeman Power Equipment Co. converted John Deere Model BO and other Deere wheel tractors to crawlers; the B for Model, O for Orchard, the intended use.

EIMCO Corp. "Tractor-Dozer"

Model	Years Built	HP(fwh)	Weight (lbs.)	Engine / Notes
103	1959 - 1962	100-120	21,600	GM 4-53 or Cummins 4-cyl.
103B	1962 - 1964	150	24,500	GM 4-71
103C	1964 - 1969?	159	28,000	GM-4-71 or Cummins 6-cyl.
105	1954 - 1956	100-20[1]	29,955	Cummins 4-cyl. or GM 4-53
105B	1956 - 1961	143	32,000	Cummins 4-cyl. or GM 4-71
106	1959 - 1962	205	39,500	GM 6V-71
106B	1962 - 1964	218	41,800	GM 6V-71
106C	1964 - 1969?	218-232	41,800	GM 6V-71 or Cummins V8R-240
165	1962 - 1963	175	31,000	GM 6V-53 or Cummins V6R-180
165B	1963 - 1964	175	34,000	GM 6V-53 or Cummins V6R-180
165C	1964 - 1969	175	38,300	GM 6V-53 or Cummins V6R-180

[1] Tested at Nebraska Tractor Testing Lab in 1958 at 72.29 dbhp; no belt hp reported.

EUCLID / TEREX

Model	Years built	HP (Gross / Flywheel)	Weight (lbs.)	Engine / Notes
TC-12	1954 - 1956	388 / 365[1]	64,000	Twin GM 6-71s
TC-12-1	1956 - 1958	436 / 413[1]	67,000	Twin GM 6-71s
TC-12-2	1958 - 1964	454 / 425[1]	71,250	Twin GM 6-71s
TC-12-3	1964 - 1966	454 / 425[1]	71,250	Twin GM 6-71s
82-80 BA	1966 - 1967	454 / 425[1]	71,250	Twin GM 6-71Ns
82-80 DA	1967 - 1974	476 / 440[1]	73,000	Twin GM 6-71Ns
C-6	1955 - 1957	218 / 207	34,000	GM 6-71
C-6-1	1958 - 1959	218 / 207	34,000	GM 6-71
C-6-2	1959 - 1961	227 / 213	42,000	GM 6-71
C-6-3	1961 - 1963	227 / 213	42,000	GM 6-71
C-6-4	1963 - 1965	238 / 224	43,100	GM 6-71
C-6-5	1965 - 1966	240 / 225	43,100	GM 6-71
82-30 EA	1966 - 1967	239 / 225	45,700	GM 6-71N
82-30 FA	1967 - 1973	239 / 225	45,700	GM 6-71N

82-30 FT	1967 - 1973	239 / 225^2	45,700	GM 6-71T
82-30 FAM	1967 - 1972	239 / 225	45,700	GM 6-71N
82-30 B	1973 - 1982	277 / 245^2	60,232	GM 8V-71T
82-40 AA	1966 - 1967	290 / 275	59,280	GM 8V-71N
82-40 BA	1967 - 1968	290 / 275	59,280	GM 8V-71N
82-40 CA	1968 - 1969	290 / 275	59,280	GM 8V-71N
82-40 DA	1969 - 1973	290 / 275	59,980	GM 8V-71N
82-40 DAT	1969 - 1973	308 / 290^2	61,850	GM 8V-71T
82-50	1973 - 1982	415 / 370^2	83,242	GM 12V-71T
82-20	1973 - 1975	208 / 180^2	42,685	GM 6-71T
82-20 B	1976 - 1982	232 / 205^2	42,710	GM 6-71T
D-400C	1981 - 1984	100 / 90	23,700	Hanomag
D-600D	1981 - 1984	160 / 144	35,300	Hanomag D-962K
D-700D	1981 - 1984	218 / 201	44,000	Hanomag D-963A1
D-750	1982 - 1984	277 / 260^2	61,872	GM 8V-71T
D-800	1982 - 1986	/ 350^2	86,037	GM 12V-71T

[1] Two engines, totals for both.
[2] Turbocharged.

INTERNATIONAL HARVESTER Co.

Model	Years Built	HP (belt/drawbar)	Weight (lbs.)	Engine / Notes
TracTracTor Series				
10-20	1925 - 1931[1]	24.8 / 19.6	6,250	1,504 units built
T-20	1932 - 1939	26.6 / 23.3	7,010	15,198 units built
T-35	1937 - 1939	44.4 / 36.6	10,600	5,585 units of T-/ TD-35 blt.
TD-35	1937 - 1939	42.2 / 37.1	11,245	4-cylinder diesel
TA-40	1932 - 1939	51 / 44	12,000	1,666 units built
TD-40	1933 - 1939	53.5 / 48	12,750	first IH diesel (D-40)
TK-40	1932 - 1939	49 / 42	12,000	kerosene
Styled Series and later models				
T-4	1959 - 1964	34 / 26.3	5,349	C-123
T-5	1959 - 1964	40 / 30.9	5,967	C-135
TD-5	1959 - 1964	37 / 29.61	6,122	BD-144
T-6	1940 - 1956	36 / 30	7,130	U-6
TD-6	1940 - 1956	31-40 / 28-34	7,210	UD-6
T-6(Series 61)	1956 - 1959	50 / 41.5	8,375	U-264
TD-6(Series 61)	1956 - 1959	50 ehp/ 42.3	8,470	D-281
T-6(Series 62)	1959 - 1970	50 ehp	8,500	
TD-6(Series 62)	1959 - 1970	52 ehp	8,597	D-282
T-7C[2]	1969 - 1974	54-60 ehp	12,360	C-175/ C-200
TD-7C	1969 - 1974	54-60 ehp	12,510	D-206
TD-7E	1974 - 1982	65 ehp	14,047	D-239 4-cylinder
TD-8C	1969 - 1974	67-73 ehp	15,400	D-239
TD-8E	1973 - 1982	78 ehp	17,479	DT-239 4-cyl. turbo.
T-9	1940 - 1956	41 / 32	9,700-10,955	U-9
TD-9	1940 - 1949	44 / 39	9,900-11,650	UD-9
TD-9A	1950 - 1956	51.5 / 40.5	10,819	UD-9A
TD-9(Series 91)	1956 - 1959	66 / 55	11,925	UD-350
TD-9(Series 92)	1959 - 1962	66 / 56	11,800	DT-282
TD-9B	1962 - 1973	75 ehp	12,765	D-282, power shift
TD-9B	1962 - 1973	66 ehp	12,540	DT-282, direct drive

TD-12	1981 - 1982	110 bhp	28,900	D-466
T-14	1939 - 1949	62 / 52	16,000	U-14
TD-14	1939 - 1949	72 / 57	16,400	UD-14
TD-14A	1949 - 1955	76 / 65	16,825	UD-14A
TD-14(Series 141)	1955 - 1956	83 / 61	25,345	D-460
TD-14(Series 142)	1956 - 1958	95 / 78.5	21,095	D-460
TD-15(Series 150)	1958 - 1961	105 ehp / 77	21,950	D-554, replaced TD-14
TD-15(Series 151)	1961 - 1962	115 ehp / 85	22,150-22,845	D-554
TD-15B	1963 - 1973	115-120 ehp / 96	22,350	DT-361/DT-407
TD-15C	1972 - 1982	140 ehp / 110	23,217	DT-466B
TD-18	1939 - 1948	97 / 80.5	23,360	UD-18
TD-18A	1949 - 1955	125 / 89.3	25,600	UD-18A
TD-18(Series 181)	1955 - 1958	124 ehp	26,340	D-691
TD-18(Series 182)	1955 - 1958	128 ehp / 105.8	28,900	D-691
TD-20(Series 200)	1958 - 1960	134 / 111	29,300	D-691, replaced TD-18
TD-20(Series 201)	1961 - 1962	140 ehp/ 113	29,690	DT-691
TD-20B	1963 - 1970	150 ehp	30,300	DT-691/DT-429
TD-20C	1971 - 1975	170 ehp	34,341	DVT-573B
TD-20E	1975 - 1982	210 ehp	46,600-48,955	DVT-800
TD-24	1947 - 1954	180 nhp/ 167 / 140	38,350	UD-24
TD-24(Series 241)	1955 - 1959	190 nhp / 161	41,520	UD-1091 gear drive
TD-24(Series 241)	1957 - 1959	202 nhp / 175	42,215	UD-1091 torque conv.
TD-25(Series 250)	1959 - 1962	220 ehp / 184.7 db	44,850	DT-817
TD-25B	1962 - 1972	230 ehp	59,400	DT-817B
TD-25C	1968 - 1979	285 ehp	68,000	DT-817C
TD-25E	1979 - 1982	310 ehp	69,870	DTI-817C
TD-30	1962 - 1967	320 ehp	61,000	DTI-817 power shift
TD-30	1962 - 1967	280 ehp	60,000	DT-817 direct drive
T-340	1959 - 1965	35 / 31	5,532	C-135
TD-340	1959 - 1965	36 / 32	5,821	D-166
500 Gas	1966 - 1970	47 ehp / 31.3 db	9,250	C-146
500 Diesel	1966 - 1970	47 ehp / 31.3 db	9,500	D-155
500C	1969 - 1974	44 ehp / 30 db	9,500	D-155
500E	1975 - 1979	44 ehp / 30 db	10,700	D-155

[1] Only a few tractors were built for testing from 1925 to 1927; actual production began in 1928.
[2] Although offered in sales literature, no records indicate that the T-7C went into production.

U.S. TRACTOR Co., Warren, Ohio (Became American Tractor Corp. in 1950) (all nhp)

Model 10-A	1946 - 1950	31.2	3,425	Continental gas
Model 10-B	1946 - 1950	31.2	3,425	kerosene
Model 10-C	1946 - 1950	31.2	3,425	diesel

WHEEL DOZER MAKES AND MODELS

Model	Years Built	HP (fwhp unless noted)	Weight (lbs.)	Engine / Notes
ALLIS-CHALMERS Manufacturing Co. (See Appendix A in Volume I)				
CATERPILLAR Tractor Co. /CATERPILLAR, Inc.				
DW-10/10S[1]	1951 - 1955	115	31,250	D318
DW-20/20S[1]	1952 - 1956	225	45,500	D337
668/668S	1956 - 1958	300	43,750	D337F
814[3]	1970 - 1980	170	40,100	D333
814B[3]	1981 - 1998	210	46,137	3306
814F	1999 -	220-240	40,944-47,877	3306 DITA/3176C
824[3]	1963 - 1965	275	60,080	D343
824B	1966 - 1981	300	61,500	D343
824C	1982 - 1998	310	66,975	3406
824G Series II	1999 -	339	63,325	3406E ATAAC
834[3]	1963 - 1974[4]	360	76,000	D343
834B	1982 - 1998	450	102,195	3408
834G	1999 -	481	103,849	3456
844	1998 -	620	162,410	3412E HEUI
854G	1998 -	800	212,230	3508B EUI
830M[3]	1962 - 1965	335	52,000	D343, military
830MB[3]	1966 - 1970?	357	52,900	D343, military

[1] cable control blade only
[2] cable or hydraulic control blade offered
[3] hydraulic control blade only
[4] not produced between 1974 and 1981

Model	Years Built	HP	Weight (lbs.)	Engine / Notes
CF & I, INC.				
Multi-Wheel 70	1970 - 1978	670 fwhp - total	140,000	twin 335-hp diesels
EUCLID / GM EUCLID DIVISION / TEREX		HP (ghp)		
1FPM	1949	190		GM 6-71
3FPM	1951	300		Cummins NHRS
4FPM	1952	300		Cummins NHRS
1TPM	1953	300	48,000	Cummins NHRS, military
5FPM-G	1954	235		Cummins NHS, military
1UPM	1954			military
6FPM	1954	218 /207 fwhp		GM 6-71
9FPM	1955	218 /207 fwhp		GM 6-71
10FPM	1959	227		GM 6-71
7UPM	1961	109 /105 fwhp		GM 3-71
9UPM	1962	152 /144 fwhp		GM 4-71
11UPM	1957	127 /119 fwhp		GM 4-71
10FPM	1959	227		GM 6-71
6TPM-G	1960	280		GM 8-71, military
Terex PX-81	1969	500	119,650	GM 12V-71T
FWD-WAGNER, INC. / WAGNER TRACTOR, INC.		HP (ghp)		
IND-14	1957 -	150 ghp		
IND-18	1957 -	210		
WI-14	1964 -	220		
WI-17	1964 -	250		
WI-24	1964 -	320		
WI-30	1965 -	700 (total)	100,000	Twin Cummins Diesels
420	1968 -	128	20,000	GM 4-53
WD-30	1970 -	700	120,000	Twin Cummins Diesels

Model	Years Built	HP (fwhp)	Weight (lbs.)	Engine / Notes
HOUGH DIVISION - INTERNATIONAL HARVESTER CO.				
D-500 articulated	1961 - 1974	600 ghp	128,000	Cummins VT-12-700-CI
	1961 - 1974	635 ghp	128,000	GM 16V-71
D-400 articulated	1964 - 1968	400	105,000	Cummins VT-12-525-CI
	1964 - 1968	400	105,000	GM 12V-71
D-120 rigid frame	1961 - 1962	300	56,800	IH DT-817/ Cum. NRT6-BI
D-120B rigid frame	1962 - 1964	300/290	58,000	IH/Cum. above/GM 8V-71
D-120C articulated	1964 - 1969	280	68,000	Cummins NT-310
	1964 - 1969	284	68,000	GM 8V-71
D-120C articulated	1970 - 1974	285	66,900	IH D-817B
	1970 - 1974	275	66,900	Cummins NT-855C
D-100 rigid frame	1961 - 1967	220	40,000	IH D-817
D-100B articulated	1964 - 1967	220	40,000	Cummins NH-220-CI
	1964 - 1967	218	40,000	GM 6V-71
D-90C articulated	1964 - 1968	165	44,000	IH DT-573
	1964 - 1968	162	44,000	Cummins V6R-180
	1964 - 1968	164	44,000	GM 6V-53
H-400C (coal dozer)	1975 - 1982	580	140,000	Cummins VT-1701C
	1975 - 1982	500	140,000	GM 12V-71T
LAPLANT-CHOATE MANUFACTURING CO.				
TD-300 Motor-Dozer	1948 - 1950	225 fwhp	47,000	Buda diesel
MARION POWER SHOVEL CO.				
V-220	1974	1,500 ghp	300,000	electric with GM diesel gen.
MELROE CO.				
M870	1978 - 1982	670 ghp (2 engines)	140,000	Caterpillar/GM/Cummins
M880	1978 - 1982	850 ghp (2 engines)	224,000	Caterpillar/GM/Cummins
MICHIGAN - CLARK EQUIPMENT CO. / V.M.E. AMERICAS (ghp, unless noted)				
180	1955 - 1957	165	27,000	Waukesha 135-DKBS
180	1958 - 1964	162-170	40,000	GM 6V-53 or Cum. C-464C
180 Series III	1965 - 1969	170	40,000	GM 6V-53 or Cum. C-175CI
280	1957 - 1962	262-310	60,000-61,700	Cum. NT-310CI/ GM 8V-71
280 Series III	1963 - 1967	290-335	66,000	Cum. NTO-310CI/ GM 8V-71N
280 articulated	1967 - 1981	318-335	69,700	GM 8V-71N/ Cum. NT-855C
280B	1982 - 1984	335	69,900	
280C	1984 - 1994	302 fwhp	65,650	Cummins NTA 855-C355
290M	1962 - ?	350 fwhp	54,190	Military model, Cummins NT-380
380	1957 - 1960	375	94,000	Cum. NTRO 6B1/ GM 8V-71
380 Series II	1961 - 1968	430 - 450 fwhp	98,000	GM 12V-71N/Cum. NVH-12CI
380 articulated	1969 - 1979	450 - 473 fwhp	108,800	Cummins V-1710-C
380B	1979 - 1988	500 - 572 fwhp	118,000	Cummins VT-1710-C635
W380	1989 - 1994	572 fwhp	123,300	Cummins VTA 28C
480	1958 - 1966	600/635	105,000-145,000	Cum.VT-1710/GM 16V-71/ Cummins VT-12-635CI
M-R-S MANUFACTURING CO.		fwhp/ghp		
I-80T	1965 -	141/167		IHC DT-436
I-90	1961 -	175/200		Cummins C-175-CI
I-92	1970 -	215/265		GM 6V-71N
I-100	1964 -	143/167	24,000	GM 4-71
I-100	1964 -	186/225	24,000	Cummins V6-200
I-100	1970 -	295/335		Cummins NRT6-BI
I-105	1964 -	215/265		GM 6V-71N

I-105	1970 -	422/475	45,660	GM 12V-71N
I-110	1963 -	260/300		IHC UDVT-573
I-110	1970 -	450/525		GM 8V-71N
I-115	1978 -	550/600		Cummins
I-120	1978 -	/675		Cummins
125	1951 - 1955	109/125	25,000	IHC or Cummins
150	1952 - 1959	137/158	25,350	IHC UD-18A or Cummins
190	1955 - 1958	250/288	33,290	Cummins NHBIS-600
190	1959 -	/375		Cummins NRT6-BI
190B	1961 -	325/380		Cummins VT8-380
200	1955 -	295/335	38,500	Cummins NRT6-BI
200	1964 -	335/400	39,500	GM 8V-71 /Cum.NRT6-BI
250	1955 -	525/500	33,700	Cummins
250	1965 -	595/635	44,850	Cummins

PEERLESS MANUFACTURING CO.

V-Con V250	1970 - 1973	1000 ghp (total)	250,000	electric with GM diesel gen.

PETTIBONE-MULLIKEN CORP.

RTD-90	Late 1960s-early 70s	636 fwhp (2 engines)	91,000	GM 8V-71N

RAYGO-WAGNER, INC.

		(ghp)		
Grizzly 100	1971 -	320	67,000	Cummins NTA-855C-335
Grizzly 150	1971 -	456	123,000	GM 12V-71N
CHD-17 Chip-Dozer	1977 -	335	47,240	Cummins NT-855C-335
CHD-24 Chip-Dozer	1978 -	400	66,400	Cummins NTA-855C-400
CHD-30 Chip-Dozer	1978 -	700	120,000	Cummins VTA-1710C-700
CHD-40/60 Coal Dozer	1978 -	700	120,000	Cummins VTA-1701C-700
CHD-15/28 Coal Dozer	1978 -	335	54,100	Cummins NT-855C-335
CD-500 Coal-Dozer	1981 - 1985	335	54,100	Cummins NT-855C-335
CD-800 Coal-Dozer	1979 -	380	66,400	Cummins NTA-855C-380
CD-1200 Coal Dozer	1978 -	700	120,000	Cummins VTA-1710C-700

R.G. LeTOURNEAU, INC. / LeTOURNEAU-WESTINGHOUSE CO. (ghp)

Model A	1947 - 1950	500-750	100,000	only a few built
Model B	1947 - 1954	300	50,000	Buda Super Diesel
Model C	1947 - 1948	160-180	28,600	Buda 6DC-844 dsl.
Model Super C	1949 - 1972	165-218 fwhp	36,000	Buda 6DA-844/Cummins HRB600/ GM 6-7
Model Twin C	1956 - 1958	420-total	80,000	Twin GM 6-71s
Model Super D	1947 - 1955	122	28,170	GM 4-71
Model D	1956 - 1960	143	26,100	GM 4-71

R.G. LeTOURNEAU, INC.[1] (ghp)

K-50	1960	420 (1 engine)	90,000	3-wheel tractor
K-53	1960 - 1964	420 (1 engine)	90,000	3-wheel tractor
K-54	1960 - 1965	420 (1 engine)	90,500	4-wheel articulated tractor
K-100	1959	600 (1 engine)	106,300	4-wheel articulated tractor
K-103	1961 - 1965	840 (2 engines)	132,000	3-wheel tractor
K-104	1962	840 (2 engines)	142,000	4-wheel articulated tractor
K-205	1962	1,260 (3 engines)	280,000	5-wheel tractor
T-300A	1965	320 (1 engine)	72,000	articulated
T-450A	1968 - 1969	475 (1 engine)	82,000	articulated
T-450B	1970	530 (1 engine)	83,750	articulated
T-600A	1968 - 1969	635 (1 engine)	135,000	articulated
T-600B	1970	635 (1 engine)	136,440	articulated
D-450B	1969	475 (1 engine)	105,000	articulated
D-300C	1965	320 (1 engine)	52,000	articulated
SL-20 (dozer-loader)	1966	840 (2 engines)		4-wheel articulated

[1] All with DC electric wheel drive from GM or Cummins generator engines.

MARATHON-LeTOURNEAU (MARATHON MANUFACTURING CO.)[1] (ghp)

D-800 LeTro-Dozer	1978 - 1985	860 or 900	214,400	articulated
D-800 LeTro-Dozer (Coal)	1981 - 1985	860 or 900	193,000	articulated
D-800 LeTro-Dozer (Reclamation)	1981 - 1985	860 or 900	194,400	articulated

[1] All with GM 16V-92T or Cummins KT2300-C engines.

LeTOURNEAU TECHNOLOGIES (ROWAN COMPANIES, INC.)[2]

D-950	2004 -	1,050 ghp	230,000	articulated

[2] Available with Detroit Diesel 16V-Series 2000 or Cummins QST-30 engines

BULLDOZER BLADE MANUFACTURERS

A.C. Anderson, Inc., Wildwood, New Jersey

Anderson manufactured the "Impdozer," a one- or two-cylinder hydraulic blade attachment for Cletrac tractor models AD, AG, ADH, AGH and HG.

Allis-Chalmers Manufacturing Co., Milwaukee, Wisconsin

(See company profile in Volume I.) After purchasing LaPlant-Choate in 1952 and Baker in 1955, A-C was able to offer its own line of hydraulic and cable-operated blades and other crawler tractor accessories. Blade widths ranged from 6 ft. 8 in. for the HD-6 straight (9 ft. for the angledozer) to 12 ft. 7 in. for the HD-21 (15 ft. for the angledozer). A-C also offered a 15-ft.- wide straight blade for coal handling. Three new blades were offered with the HD-41 in 1970: a full-U measuring 17 ft. wide and 6 ft. high, a semi-U measuring 20 ft. by 7 ft., and a cushion blade that was 11 ft. 4 in. wide and 5 ft. high.

American Tractor Equipment Co. (ATECO), Oakland, California

ATECO began manufacturing hydraulic blades for various crawler tractor makes including Cletrac, using a patent developed by the McMillan Brothers of San Francisco, California in 1929. ATECO also built hydraulic rippers for International Harvester and other crawler manufacturers.

Amundson Implement Co., Norcross, Minnesota

Amundson built special oversized U-shaped blades for coal and other lightweight material handling for A-C models HD-11, HD-16 and HD-21 tractors.

Arrow Manufacturing Co., Denver, Colorado

Arrow built hydraulic dozer blades for Allis-Chalmers and other makes of tractors in the late 1940s and 50s.

Athey Products Corp., Chicago, Illinois
(now Wake Forest, North Carolina)

The company was established in 1922 as the Athey Truss Wheel Co. Athey made hydraulic blades for the Cat model Thirty Five and Fifty tractors during the 1930s.

Austin-Western Road Machinery Co., Chicago, Illinois

The company was established in 1902 with the purchase of the Austin Manufacturing Co. by the Western Wheeled Scraper Co. It became the Austin-Western Road Machinery Co. in 1934, was bought by the BLH Corp. in 1951 and by Clark Equipment Co. in 1971. Although best known for its pulled and motorized graders, A-W made blades for Cletrac Model 35 and other tractors in the 1930s. See also Western Wheeled Scraper Co.

Baker Manufacturing Co., Springfield, Illinois

(See company profile In Chapter Nine.) Baker built the first "backfiller" blade in 1918 and offered one of the first commercial bulldozer blades in 1924. The company patented the "Gradebuilder" and "Backfiller" line of blades and manufactured both hydraulic and cable blades, mainly for Monarch and Allis-Chalmers tractors. The hydraulic blades for the early A-C tractors had unique vertical lifting cylinders that formed an arch over the center of the tractor while the cable blade attachment for the HD-14 had a arch gantry. Baker introduced the HD-9X and HD-15X dozers in 1953 which used narrow (8 ft. wide) blades attached to the tractor main frame without side push-beams.

Balderson, Inc., Wamego, Kansas

Founded in 1949 by Willard Balderson, the company built dozer blades, tree and rock clearing blades and rakes and loader buckets primarily for Caterpillar tractors. Balderson was famous for fabricating the 48-ft. wide blade for the Caterpillar twin D-9 "Double Dude" surface mine reclamation dozers in the late 1960s.

BeGe Manufacturing Co., Gilroy, California

BeGe Manufacturing began in the early 1930s offering agricultural implements primarily for central California farmers. Best known as a builder of pull-scrapers and land levelers, the company was acquired by Oliver in 1953 to add construction equipment compatible with its wheel and crawler tractors. After the acquisition, BeGe developed hydraulic dozer blades for the mid-sized Oliver OC-series crawlers.

Blair Manufacturing Co., Chicago, Illinois

Blair built hydraulic blades and ½-yd. loaders for Monarch and early Allis-Chalmers tractors. Blair was a member of the United Tractor and Equipment Corp., a group of tractor attachment makers during the late 1920s and 1930s.

Blaw-Knox Co., Pittsburgh, Pennsylvania

A venerable name in construction equipment, Blaw-Knox built hydraulic blades in the 1930s through an affiliation with American Tractor Equipment Co. The blades were built mainly for Caterpillar tractors.

Bodinson Manufacturing Co., San Francisco, California

Bodinson was a California dredge and tractor implement manufacturer that made hydraulic blades for Monarch, Allis-Chalmers and other makes of tractors in the 1930s. The blades were sold under the name "Bodie" dozers.

Buckeye Traction Ditcher Co., Findlay, Ohio

The Buckeye Traction Ditcher Co. was established in 1906, purchased by Gar Wood Industries in 1945, and became a division of Sargent Industries in 1971. Buckeye, and later Gar Wood, made hydraulic- and cable-operated blades mainly for Allis-Chalmers tractors. (See Gar Wood Industries.)

Bucyrus-Erie Co., South Milwaukee, Wisconsin

Bucyrus-Erie was established in 1927 with the merger of the two steam shovel building companies. The merged company built hydraulic blades for International Harvester T- and TD-6, 9, 14, 18 tractors and cable blades for TD-18 and TD-24 tractors between 1938 and 1953. Bucyrus-Erie tractor attachments were sold exclusively by IH dealers. The B-E straight bulldozer blades and its "Bullgrader" angledozer blades were very popular with contractors in the 1940s and 1950s.

Bunch Backfiller Co., Pomona, California

Bunch manufactured backfilling blades for tractors in the late 1920s and 30s.

Carco (Pacific Car and Foundry Co.), Renton, Washington

Carco offered the first cable winch unit in 1932 and built hydraulic and cable blades and winches for Allis-Chalmers and other makes of tractors in the 1930s, 1940s, and 1950s.

Case Corporation, Racine, Wisconsin

(See company profile in Volume I.) Case began building hydraulic dozer blades and loader buckets in 1957 for the crawler tractor line it acquired from American Tractor Co. American Tractor made blades and loader attachments for its Terratrac crawler line from 1950 to 1957.

Caterpillar, Inc., Peoria, Illinois

(See company profile in Chapter One.) Caterpillar built only tractors and graders until 1946, when it began offering cable operated blades for D-6, D-7 and D-8 tractors, identified as 6S, 7S and 8S blades. Caterpillar also offered angle-dozer blades (7A for the D-7 and 8A for the D-8). The company built both front and rear-mounted cable control units (No.24 was a front-mounted, single-drum unit for its D-6, D-7and D-8 tractors; the No.25 was a rear-mounted, double-drum unit for the same three models. Cat began manufacturing hydraulic blades in 1948, dropping their previous supplier, LaPlant-Choate. Hydraulic blades were first offered for the D-2 (2S) and D4 (4S) models but, by the late 1950s, were offered on all models. Caterpillar's early blade widths ranged from 6 ft. 8 in. (D-2) to 11 ft. 3 in. for the D-8 and 13 ft. 4 in. for the D-8 angledozer. By the late 1950s, the D-8 blade was up to 12 ft. 1 in. (14 ft. 10 in. for the angledozer). The largest blade made by Caterpillar is 22 ft. wide for the D11T.

Clark Equipment Co., Benton Harbor, Michigan

(See company profile in Chapter Eight) Clark Equipment Co. gained its first experience building blades when it won a contract to manufacture the CA-1 Airborne Dozer during World War II. After acquiring Michigan Power Shovel Co. in 1953, Clark began building wheel loaders and dozers. Clark built blades and loader buckets for its Michigan line of wheel tractors which were introduced in 1957.

Continental Manufacturing Co., East Chicago, Illinois

Continental offered hydraulic strait and angledozer blades primarily for International Harvester TracTracTors in the 1930s and early 1940s, when Continental became part of Gar Wood Industries.

Crook Company, Los Angeles, California

Crook built cable-operated bulldozer blades during the 1930s.

CRS-Crose, Houston, TX

CRS-Crose offered blades and pipelayer sidebooms for Allis-Chalmers tractors in the late 1960s and early 1970s.

Dakota Manufacturing Co., Fargo, North Dakota

Dakota built hydraulic blades for small- and medium-sized tractors during the 1940s and 1950s.

Davis Manufacturing Co., Davis, California

Davis built "Hydrig" brand blades for Cletrac models 30 and 55 tractors, which featured a unique cam-and-pushrod hydraulic system to raise and lower the blade. The company mainly built blades for the U.S. Forest Service in the late 1920s and early 1930s.

Deere & Company, Moline, Illinois

(See company profile in Chapter Three) Deere introduced the Model 61 blade for its Model 40 and MC tractors in 1952 and opened a Construction Equipment Division in 1955. After that, Deere produced a full line of hydraulic blades and loader buckets for its crawler tractors.

Drott Manufacturing Corp., Milwaukee, Wisconsin

Drott made hydraulic bulldozer and angledozer blades for International Harvester along with its better known line of hydraulic loader attachments. Drott introduced the "Bull Clam," a combination dozer blade and clamshell bucket which it later called the 4-in-1 bucket. When the front half of the bucket was raised, the rear half served as a bulldozer blade. When hydraulically lowered, it could grab loose material and be raised for loading like a front-end loader. Drott established a joint marketing agreement with International in 1950; however, by the mid-1950s, IHC began building its own blades and other tractor attachments. Drott became part of the Case Corporation in 1968.

Eimco Corp., Salt Lake City, Utah

(See company profile in Chapter 4) In addition to underground mining machinery, Eimco built a variety of blades and loader buckets for all of its crawler tractor models offered during the 1950s and 60s. These included straight, angledozer, and U blades, as well as push blocks, and brush rakes.

Emsco Derrick and Equipment Co., Los Angeles, California

Emsco offered cable-operated bulldozer and angledozer blades in the late 1930s.

Esco Corp., Portland, Oregon

Founded in 1913 as the Electric Steel Foundry Co., Esco has produced and continues to offer a variety of buckets for shovels, backhoes and draglines, along with specialty buckets and blades for crawler tractors.

Essex Engine & Machine Corp., Belleville, New Jersey

Essex made the hand-cranked "Hall" blade for the Cletrac Model 15 and other tractors in the 1920s and hydraulic "Essex" blades for Cletrac models 20, 30 and 40 tractors in the 1930s.

Euclid Road Machinery Co., Euclid (Cleveland), Ohio

(See company profile in Chapter Five.) Euclid made hydraulic dozer blades during the 1920s and 1930s for most of the popular makes of crawler tractors. Ironically, when Euclid entered the crawler business in 1954, it had to subcontract blades and lifting equipment to Gar Wood Industries. After GM's Euclid Division purchased Gar Wood in 1963, Euclid and its successor Terex produced their own blades.

Florida Land Clearing Equipment Co. (FLECO), Jacksonville, Florida

FLECO was a manufacturer of rock rakes, tree pushers and other land-clearing blades and rakes, including the "Stumper," a device resembling a push-block with teeth that mounted on the C-frame of the bulldozer. The company also offered the "V-Tree Cutter," a V-shaped blade with a sharp, serrated lower cutting edge. This blade was available for Caterpillar tractor models D-4, D-5, D-6, D-7, and D-8. FLECO is still in business, offering brush rakes and buckets for most makes of crawler tractors.

Foote Brothers Gear and Machine Co., Chicago, Illinois

Foote Brothers manufactured hydraulic blades for Bates tractors, which it acquired in 1929.

Frank G. Hough Co., Libertyville, Illinois

Hough built hydraulic blades that could be exchanged for buckets on both its Payloader wheel tractors and International Harvester crawlers during the late 1940s and early 1950s. Hough became part of International Harvester in 1952 and built blades for the Paydozer wheel dozer line during the 1960s and 70s.

F.W. McCoy Co., Denver, Colorado

McCoy offered the "Rock Rake" for Cat D-7 and D-8 tractors in the late 1940s and 1950s.

Gar Wood Industries, Inc., Detroit, Michigan and Findlay, Ohio

(See company profile in Chapter Nine.) During the 1940s, Gar Wood became a major manufacturer of construction equipment including dozer blades, scrapers, rippers, spreaders, and even cranes and shovels. The company was an allied supplier for Allis-Chalmers during the 1940s and early 50s, supplying "Bulldozer," "TipDozer" and "Dozecaster" cable blades for the HD-14, 15, 19, and 20 tractors and hydraulic blades for the HD-5, 7, 9, 10, 15 and 20 tractors. Gar Wood supplied hydraulic and cable blades for Euclid's C-6 and TC-12 tractors, and its attachments were also used on most other makes of tractors, though not in large numbers. Gar Wood acquired Buckeye Traction Ditcher and Continental Steel in the 1940s, both of which offered dozer blades.

H.F. Davis Tractor Co., Holyoke, Massachusetts

Davis, the Cletrac dealer for Massachusetts, built "Walsh" brand hand-operated blades exclusively for Cletrac (Models 20, 30 and 40) during the late 1920s and 1930s. They also made a line of snow plow blades for these and later Cletrac models into the 1950s.

Hi-Way Service Corp., Milwaukee, Wisconsin

Established in the mid-1920s, Hi-Way Service offered hand-operated and hydraulic bulldozer, backfiller, and snow plow blades and other attachments under its Wausau brand name. Hi-Way was an affiliated supplier to Caterpillar, providing attachments for all of its 1920s and early 1930s tractor models from the Ten to the Sixty.

Hussey Engineering & Equipment Co., Oyster Bay, New York

Hussey made hand-operated and hydraulic bulldozer and backfiller blades for Cletrac Model 20 and 30 tractors.

Hyster Company, Portland, Oregon; now Danville, Illinois and Greenville, North Carolina

Hyster was established in 1929 as the Willamette Ersted Co. to build winches for the logging industry. The name Hyster came from "Hoist'er", the word called out to begin a lift, and it was officially adopted in 1934. The company built push and drag blades in the 1930s and continued supplying winches to Caterpillar tractors through the 1950s.

International Harvester Co., Melrose Park, Illinois

(See company profile in Chapter Six.) International Harvester relied on Bucyrus-Erie, Isaacson, Heil, Continental and other attachment manufacturers to supply blades for its tractor line and began a joint marketing venture with Drott Manufacturing Corp. in 1950 for front-end loaders. After acquiring the rights to Bucyrus-Erie and Heil tractor attachments the mid-1950s, International began offering its own cable and hydraulically operated blades.

Isaacson Iron Works, Seattle, Washington

Issacson was organized in 1907 and became a popular blade manufacturer during the 1930s and 1940s. The company built "Circle I Brand" Trac-Dozer cable and hydraulic blades primarily for International Harvester tractors. Isaacson offered both front- and rear-mounted power control units for its blades. It also sold a line of "Klearing-Dozer" brush rake blades.

J.D. Adams Manufacturing Co., Indianapolis, IN

Founded in 1885, Adams was best known for its line of road graders. Adams became part of the LeTourneau-Westinghouse Co. in 1954. Adams built cable blades for International Harvester and other tractors that looked similar to LeTourneau's overhead cable rigs.

Kay-Brunner Steel Products Co., Los Angeles, California

Kay-Brunner made hydraulic blades during the 1930s and 1940s and was the first manufacturer to offer the single-lever hydraulic tilt blade.

Killefer Manufacturing Co., Los Angeles, California

The Killefer Manufacturing Co. was founded by John Killefer in the early 1900s. It started out building leveling devices for irrigated farms in southern California. Killefer introduced the concept of substituting a small bucket for a dozer blade to excavate dirt in the early 1920s and also offered hand-cranked and hydraulic dozer blades. The company was purchased by Deere in the 1950s.

LaPlant-Choate Manufacturing Co., Inc., Cedar Rapids, Iowa

(See company profile in Chapter Nine.) LaPlant-Choate introduced the "Trailbuilder" hydraulic blade in 1935 and followed it with angledozers and cable-operated blades mainly for Caterpillar D-2 through D-8 tractors. The wide overhead frame and large front sheave for the cable blade gave it the appearance of a turret crane. Other blades or blade attachments offered by L-C were a Treedozer (hydraulic), V-shaped Brush Cutter (hydraulic), Root Cutter (hydraulic), Brush Rake (cable or hydraulic), Stinger Blade (cable or hydraulic), Stump Splitter (cable or hydraulic), and a rake attachment for both cable and hydraulic dozer blades. L-C established a joint sales and service arrangement with Caterpillar in the late 1930s and was a major supplier of blades for military dozers during World War II. Caterpillar terminated the arrangement in 1948 and began offering its own line of blades.

LeTourneau-Westinghouse Co., Peoria, Illinois

(See Chapter Eight) As Marathon-LeTourneau and now as part of the Rowan Companies, LeTourneau offers blades for its large diesel-electric wheel dozers.

LeTourneau, Inc., Longview, Texas

As Marathon-LeTourneau and now as part of the Rowan Companies, LeTourneau, Inc. offers blades for its diesel-electric wheel dozers. (See Chapter 8.)

Lindeman Power Equipment Co., Yakima, Washington

(See company profile in Chapter Three) Lindeman started in 1925 as a tractor implement maker and expanded to producing crawler conversions for John Deere tractors in 1939. The company offered hydraulic blades for its Model BO-L converted crawler tractor until its acquisition by Deere in 1947.

Maine Iron Works (later Maine Steel, Inc.), South Portland, Maine

Maine Iron Works manufactured a line of snowplows including angle blades, V-blades and wings along with earthmoving blades under the "Sargent" brand name. Maine also built a cable-operated "overshot" front loader attachment for Cletrac and other tractors.

Masters Equipment Co., Los Angeles, California

Masters, an affiliated attachment supplier to Caterpillar, offered a line of cable-controlled blades during the early 1930s.

McMillan Brothers Co., San Francisco, California

McMillan Brothers, a San Francisco excavating contractor, began experimenting with various blade attachments to crawler tractors in the early 1920s. McMillan originated the idea of welding teeth onto dozer blades in the late 1920s. The company built cable- and chain-controlled blade attachments for Holt and Caterpillar tractors for all model sizes up to the Sixty. McMillan sold its blade patents to Ateco in 1929.

Mead-Morrison Manufacturing Co., Boston, Massachusetts

Mead-Morrison offered snowplows and backfiller blades for its own line of crawler tractors (see Chapter Seven) as well as for other makes of tractors during the late 1920s and early 1930s.

Mixermobile Manufacturers Co., Portland, Oregon

Established in the mid-1930's by the Wagner brothers, the company began offering the "Duo-Way Scoop Dozer" in 1948. This was a three-wheeled front loader with a hydraulic blade for backfilling mounted on the rear. Wagner also made the "Scraper-Dozer," a wheeled tractor with a scraper and a dozer blade on the rear for leveling each scraper load as it was dumped. The company later offered the DM-10 "Dozermobile" wheel dozer; larger articulated wheel dozers were offered in the 1960s and 70s by FWD-Wagner, Inc. FWD-Wagner and later RayGo purchased the Wagner dozer line.

M.P. McCaffrey Inc., Los Angeles, California

McCaffrey built hand-crank operated blades for small tractors during the 1930s and an early cable-operated front loader in 1939.

Mississippi Road Service (M-R-S), Flora, Mississippi

M-R-S made blades for its numerous wheel tractor models during the 1950s, 1960s and 1970s for both commercial sales and military contracts.

Niess and Company, Minneapolis, Minnesota

Niess manufactured gear-operated "Bully" blades in the 1930's for the Cletrac Model 30 and 40 tractors.

Omsteel Industries, Ltd., Omaha, Nebraska

Omsteel made front-mounted dozer blades for Caterpillar motor graders during the 1950s and 1960s.

Pomeroy Tractor & Implement Co., Pomeroy, Washington

The Caterpillar dealer for southeastern Washington state from the 1930s through the 1950s, Pomeroy built light-duty blades and other implements for Cat crawler tractors under the "Starr" brand.

Preco, Inc., Los Angeles, California

Preco produced blades with ripper teeth and teeth for converting straight blades to rippers and rock rakes.

R.G. LeTourneau, Inc., Stockton, California, and Peoria, Illinois

(See company profile in Chapters Eight and Nine.) R.G. LeTourneau built the first powered (electric) cable-lifted blade in 1928 for an earthmoving job at Oroville, California. Two years later the company produced the first side-mounted cable-control unit (CCU) with a small gantry on the radiator. The CCU was chain-driven by the tractor's engine, and it paved the way for cable-lifted blades and myriad other tractor-operated attachments. LeTourneau designed the first angledozer in 1933 and began supplying blades to Allis-Chalmers in 1932 for its L-series tractors. Also in 1932, LeTourneau designed a rear-mounted blade for pulling loads of dirt, known as the Tractor Mounted Scraper.

By 1935, it was selling cable blades for all Caterpillar tractor models and most models from A-C, Cletrac, and other manufacturers – over 120 blade models in all. LeTourneau offered three standard configurations of the blade gantry: Type A, radiator mounted, Type B with front and rear gantries and an overhead cable channel, and Type C, a mid-tractor V-shaped gantry. The company also developed the Tiltdozer, a hybrid of the straight dozer and angledozer blades. LeTourneau and Caterpillar had a joint marketing agreement between 1933 and 1945 that allowed LeTourneau equipment and attachments to be sold and serviced by Caterpillar dealers.

Rockit Corp., Calumet, Michigan

A newcomer to the blade business, Rockit introduced its first dozer blade in 2000. Its Power Blade line features hydraulically-operated extendable blade wings for small and mid-size crawler tractors. The joy-stick controlled Power Blade can change from a grading blade to a U-blade and tilt from side to side. Two models are offered: one which expands from 8 ft. 7 in. to 10 ft. 2 in., and the other from 9 ft. 7 in. to 11 ft. 2 in.

Rockland Manufacturing Co., Bedford, Pennsylvania

This company began in the early 1950s with its first product, the Rockland RF-1 clearing rake. The RF-3 appeared in the early 1960s featuring adjustable and reversible steel alloy teeth, allowing the operator to change tooth spacing for different job conditions. Rockland also offered a variety of other blades including U-blades for coal and other light material handling and front-end loader buckets. The company still offers a line of specialty dozer blades, brush rakes and loader buckets.

Rome Plow Co., Cedartown, Georgia

(See company profile in Chapter Nine.) Rome Plow began building its K/G land-clearing blades for Caterpillar tractors in the 1950s and still manufactures the K/G blade line. During the Vietnam War, a Caterpillar D-7E with a Model K/G blade and a reinforced operator's cage came to be known as a Rome Plow and was an Army term for any jungle-clearing equipment.

Russell Grader Manufacturing Co., Minneapolis, Minnesota

Russell Grader built horse-drawn "Bull Dozer" blades in the 1910s for filling ditches and gullies. The device consisted of a metal blade attached to a set of wheels with rigging for two horses to push the blade. Russell became part of Caterpillar Tractor Co. in 1928.

Servis Equipment Co., Dallas, Texas

Servis offered hydraulically-operated blades for International Harvester and other makes of farm and industrial wheel tractors.

Southwest Welding and Manufacturing Co., Alhambra (Los Angeles), California

Southwest made cable-operated blades for Allis-Chalmers' HD-10, HD-14, and HD-19 tractors in the 1940s.

Superior Equipment Co., Bucyrus, OH

An affiliated supplier of attachments for International Harvester, Superior offered backfiller blades along with its line of sidebooms and swing cranes for most IH crawler models.

Teale & Co., Omaha, Nebraska

Teale produced the Duncan Dozer hydraulic blade line during the 1940s for small and medium-sized crawler tractors. The smallest blade fit the Caterpillar D-2, International T-6 and TD-6, and Cletrac Model A machines and weighed 1,650 lbs. A larger model weighing 2,200 lbs. was made for Caterpillar D-4, International T-9 and TD-9, Allis-Chalmers HD-5, and Cletrac B and D model tractors. Dozer blades for other makes and models were available by special order.

The Heil Co., Milwaukee, Wisconsin, and Hillside, New Jersey

Heil was established in 1901, and is still in the construction business, though it no longer makes blades. Heil built the hydraulically-operated Trailbuilder and angledozer blades for International Harvester TD-6, 9, and 14 tractors and cable blades for larger IH tractors including TD-18 and 24. Heil also offered hydraulic blades for Cletrac tractors including Models BD, BG, DD and DG, and for most of the Oliver-Cletrac OC-series crawlers including both hydraulic and cable-operated blades for its largest dozer, the OC-18.

The Miami Trailer-Scraper Co., Troy, Ohio

Miami offered cable-operated blades and hand-operated backfiller blades for Cletrac Models 20 and 30 during the late 1920s and early 1930s.

Trackson Co., Milwaukee, Wisconsin

Trackson was established in 1922 and began building tractor equipment including cable-operated blades for Caterpillar in 1936. Though best known for its line of cable and hydraulic excavator attachments known as Traxcavators, the company built other tractor attachments such as blades, swing cranes and sideboom pipelayers. Caterpillar purchased Trackson in 1951 and began offering its own line of crawler loaders.

Tractomotive Corp., Deerfield, Illinois

Founded by Vander M. Doebus, an ex-Allis-Chalmers engineer in 1945, Tractomotive built hydraulic blades for the military from the mid to late 1940s and developed an all-hydraulic front loader attachment for the A-C HD-5 tractor in 1946, designated as the model HD-5G. Two dozer attachments were also offered for the HD-5G: one with a 6 ft 3.5-in. wide blade and another with an 8-ft. width. In 1950, Tractomotive introduced a 4-yd. loader bucket attachment for the HD19G, a capacity record for its time. Allis-Chalmers acquired Tractomotive in 1959.

Ulrich Manufacturing Co., Roanoke, Illinois

Ulrich offered the Varidozer blade and other attachments for Caterpillar tractors during the 1950s and 1960s. The Varidozer could be changed hydraulically to any angle of tilt in the three dimensions within the normal range of movement of the blade. The center of the blade was vertically split to form a forward or reverse "V" blade.

Wallace Machine Co., Portland area, Oregon

Wallace was one of a number of small machine shops in the Pacific Northwest that specialized in logging equipment for crawler tractors. In business from the late 1940s through the 1950s, Wallace built rather unique hydraulic dozer blades with the lift cylinders mounted parallel to the tracks.

Ware Machine Works Inc., Ware, Massachusetts

Founded by John Pilch in 1942, Ware built loader buckets, backhoes and other attachments for crawler and wheel tractors. Most of the Oliver crawler loaders came with Ware buckets.

Western Wheeled Scraper Co., Aurora, Illinois

Western offered what may have been the first factory-built, horse-drawn bulldozer attachment in 1915. The device consisted of a 4-ft. metal blade mounted to the front of a 7½-ft. wooden tongue with a pair of wheels and a driver's seat. Two or even four horses or mules were hitched to the tongue. The blade could be tilted upwards by a rope connected to a lever next to the driver. The axle could be turned at an angle with the tongue to control the direction of the pushing and minimize sluing of the wheels. A counterweight was also available to stabilize the wheels. Western merged with Austin Manufacturing Co. in 1902 to become the Austin-Western Road Machinery Co.

William Bros Boiler and Manufacturing Co., Minneapolis, Minnesota

Although best known for rollers and compactors, Bros built Power Plus hydraulic blades for the Caterpillar D-6 and other models during the 1940s and 1950s.

Wooldridge Manufacturing Co., Sunnyvale and Alhambra (Los Angeles) California

Founded by Mack Wooldridge and Harold Gusman in 1938, the company grew rapidly into a major supplier of earthmoving equipment. Mack Wooldridge was a Cletrac dealer in the Bay area of California. He began building hydraulic blades for his Cletrac tractors (Models 20 and 30) in 1927; by 1930, he added a blade for the Cletrac 40 and was selling more than 200 blades a year. Wooldridge also offered one-, two-, three- and four-drum cable control units for blades and tractor-pulled scrapers. Wooldridge was acquired by the Curtiss-Wright Corp. in 1958.

INDEX